Before the Door of God

Before the Door of God

An Anthology of Devotional Poetry

EDITED BY Jay Hopler &
Kimberly Johnson

Yale

UNIVERSITY PRESS

New Haven and London

Yale University Press books may be purchased in quantity for educational, business, or
promotional use. For information, please e-mail sales.press@yale.edu (U.S. office) or
sales@yaleup.co.uk (U.K. office).

Designed by Sonia Shannon.
Set in Fournier type by Integrated Publishing Solutions, Grand Rapids, Michigan.
Printed in the United States of America.

Library of Congress Cataloging-in-Publication Data
Before the door of God : an anthology of devotional poetry / edited by Jay Hopler
and Kimberly Johnson.
pages cm
Includes bibliographical references and index.
ISBN 978-0-300-17520-2 (alk. paper)
1. Devotional poetry. 2. Religious poetry. I. Hopler, Jay, 1970– editor of compilation.
II. Johnson, Kimberly, 1971– editor of compilation.
PN6110.R4B425 2013
808.81'9382—dc23   2013012747

A catalogue record for this book is available from the British Library.

This paper meets the requirements of ANSI/NISO Z39.48–1992 (Permanence of Paper).

10 9 8 7 6 5 4 3 2 1

Contents

PART TWO

EARLY CHRISTIAN LYRICS THROUGH THE FIFTEENTH CENTURY

PART THREE

PSALM TRANSLATIONS OF THE ENGLISH
RENAISSANCE: THE BIBLE AS ART

PART FOUR

THE FLOURISHING OF THE DEVOTIONAL LYRIC IN THE POST-REFORMATION ERA

PART FIVE

THE POETIC SUBLIME: THE EIGHTEENTH AND NINETEENTH CENTURIES

PART EIGHT

THE TWENTY-FIRST-CENTURY DEVOTIONAL LYRIC

Editors' Preface

Before the Door of God: An Anthology of Devotional Poetry tells the story of devotional lyric poetry in English by tracing its development from its origins in the ancient world to its current post-postmodern incarnations. In so doing, it demonstrates not only that the devotional lyric remains in vigorous practice in contemporary poetry—indeed, that it is grounding much twenty-first-century Anglophone poetry and refocusing it on those concerns which have animated the art for centuries—but also that it arises from a long historical tradition that extends to the very origins of Western culture. This anthology brings together some of the finest poems of the Western literary tradition and does so with the hope of generating a conversation—not just among scholars, artists, and academics, but among readers generally—about the relationships among literature, history, and the idea of the spiritual.

In identifying the poems here collected as devotional lyric poems, we are distinguishing our field of survey from that of religious poetry, a category so large as to be completely unmanageable as the organizing principle of a poetry collection that aspires to cohesion and concision, especially if the term "religious" is broadened even slightly to include the ideas of the spiritual and the mystic. After all, if one were to bring together even a small fraction of all the religious/spiritual/mystical poems of merit written over the past three millennia, the product would be a multivolume encyclopedia of unimaginable, and ultimately unusable, proportions. In an effort to narrow the scope of the collection, therefore, we have chosen to interpret the term "devotion" as being *almost* synonymous with the term "colloquy." The vast majority of the poems in *Before the Door of God* are addresses to the unknown, conversations (albeit one-sided) with the divine, in whatever way these authors have interpreted that term. These criteria explain why Yeats's poem "A Prayer on Going into My House" appears in this volume—a beautiful piece, though one of his lesser-known poems, to be sure—but his justifiably famous "The Second Coming" is absent. For all of its lyrical and rhetorical brilliance, "The Second Coming" is a mystically inflected meditation on the Apocalypse, as opposed to a direct, personal, and immediate engagement with the divine. It is a poem about devotion; it is not a devotional poem.

And because the pieces we have included in *Before the Door of God* are in fact poems, works of art and not literal representations of faith, the devotional gesture as we have defined it and as it is here represented is usually not explicitly, consistently, or uncomplicatedly doctrinal. These poems confront two of humankind's most powerful actuations: the drive to create and the drive to know a creator; the result of this confrontation—of these pieces encountered in the aggregate—is a new context in which it is possible to examine how the cultural commonplaces of the theological tradition can sometimes enrich a poem's potential meaning. It would be difficult, for example, to fix John Donne's theology based on his poems because his poems are not religious tracts, and while John Berryman's poetic sequence "Eleven Addresses to the Lord" declares in its very title its intentions, his poem "Dream Song 28: Snow Line" relies on resonances and associations to suggest its devotional narrative. In a different, less thematically focused context, "Snow Line" would likely be read as a bitter, confessional bleat, the poem's lost-sheep speaker taking the thinly veiled place of the author in order to comment on humanity's increasing hopelessness and despondency. In the context of so many other poems that are making use of language familiar from spiritual discourse, however, a more complicated reading of the poem becomes apparent: the sheep who has climbed too high and become lost where the air is thin and the sustenance sparse is the soul, its desire for reunion with the Shepherd ("the strange one with so few legs") and the Shepherd's agent (the sheepdog, "the barker") a desire not only for rescue, but for salvation.

The vast majority of the poems included in this volume are written from an identifiably Christian perspective. This should not be interpreted as an editorial bias, or as an attempt to make the volume somehow denominational; rather, it is a reflection of the historical and cultural conditions that gave rise to devotional poetry in English. The Anglophone cultures from which come the majority of the poets included in this anthology have been, and continue to be, predominantly Christian. But the English-speaking world is becoming more—and more rapidly—culturally diverse, and as it does so, its poetry likewise reflects a wider spectrum of devotional perspectives, as later sections of this anthology demonstrate.

One final point concerning our selection criteria: even with our parameters significantly narrowed, so much excellent devotional lyric poetry has been written over the past three thousand years that this volume could easily have been larger. Indeed, had we had the luxury of assembling this anthology in a perfect world where the only considerations were aesthetic ones, we would have made it so.

Every book is a team effort, and we could not have completed this volume without the timely encouragement of our families, friends, and colleagues. *Before the Door of God: An Anthology of Devotional Poetry* would not have been possible without the financial support of the University of South Florida and the College of Humanities at Brigham Young University. For guidance and enthusiasm, we would like to thank Jennifer Banks, Christina Tucker, Heather Gold, Suzanne Tibor, Piyali Bhattacharya, Noreen O'Connor-Abel, and everyone at Yale University Press. Moreover, a project such as this one, because of its long historical reach, necessarily crosses several fields of expertise, and we are grateful that we could supplement our knowledge of a number of historical periods with the help of Kevis Goodman, Keith Johnson, Nicholas Mason, Kristin Matthews, and Brett McInelly. To Donald M. Friedman, Sidney Gottlieb, Linda Gregerson, Jonathan F. S. Post, and Anton Vander Zee we offer our sincerest thanks for their close readings of the manuscript and their insightful comments and critiques. And we are grateful to Katherine Lassetter and Brice A. Petersen, who helped to keep our editorial interventions reader-friendly. Our debt to the many scholars who have delved into dark archives and shuffled dusty manuscripts, who have attempted to make sense of a history that resists sense-making, and who have worked to explain the relationship between literature and the cultural force of faith is, we hope, implicit in our suggestions for further reading. Finally, we are grateful to the poets whose breathtaking poems have made this project seem very little like labor, and very much like praise.

JAY HOPLER

"A Heauenly Poesie"
The Devotional Lyric

Who sayes that fictions onely and false hair
Become a verse? Is there in truth no beautie?
Is all good structure in a winding stair?
May no lines passe, except they do their dutie
    Not to a true, but painted chair?

Is it no verse, except enchanted groves
And sudden arbours shadow course-spunne lines?
Must purling streams refresh a lovers loves?
Must all be vail'd, while he that reades, divines,
    Catching the sense at two removes?

Shepherds are honest people; let them sing:
Riddle who list, for me, and pull for Prime:
I envie no mans nightingale or spring;
Nor let them punish me with losse of ryme,
    Who plainly say, *My God, My King*.

GEORGE HERBERT WROTE THESE lines in the early seventeenth century, and titled his poem "Jordan." As the title suggests, Herbert's poem calls for a kind of baptism of poetry, a sanctification of attention that would replace both the carnal pleasures of romance and the idolatrous ornamentation of artifice with a simple declaration of divine majesty. Herbert's poem rejects "fictions" for a style of writing that privileges plain-spoken truths, claiming that truth itself offers beauty and does not need the veils of poetic invention in order to engage an audience. Herbert's poem turns on the view, extending back to Plato's *Republic*, that there is a fundamental enmity between art and truth; Herbert's subject—the praise of God he makes explicit in the poem's last line—specifies that truth as a spiritual condition. In Herbert's poem it is spiritual truth that opposes the artificial utterances of verse, the holiness of plainness set against the embroidered idol of poetry.

But of course, Herbert's own poem undermines this purported argument. "Jordan" is, after all, a poem, and an ostentatiously *poetic* poem at that: its rhyme scheme contributes its own counterclaims to the poem's rhetorical claims, consistently sustaining the complex pattern of repeated sounds even as the penultimate line defies those who would condemn Herbert's "losse of ryme." Its syntax is as wrought as any winding stair. Its questions are couched in the "two removes" of metaphor, as when he describes straight-talking poets as honest "Shepherds," invoking the animating fiction of the pastoral tradition. In short, "Jordan" wears its elaborate poetic strategies on its sleeve, belying the poem's own insistence that poetry makes for a poor medium of praise. Indeed, it is the carefully constructed artificiality of the poem that allows readers to be so surprised, and so moved, by its concluding gesture, its turn to "plainly say, *My God, My King.*" That plain speech resonates, in part, because it stands in such marked contrast to the lines that have preceded it, lines that present a veritable enchanted grove of poetic language. So it is that the spiritual argument of "Jordan" is communicated to us *because* of the poem's artifice, not in spite of it; Herbert deliberately uses the devices his poem seems to criticize in order to set off more effectively his declaration of faith.

"Jordan" slyly inverts its criticism about poetry's fitness for expressions of faith in part because Herbert knows well that a long tradition of devotional poetry makes the case for him. Half a century before Herbert composed his volume of religious poems *The Temple*, which was published in 1633, Sir Philip Sidney had offered up his *Defence of Poesie* against contemporary critics of the genre. To answer the skeptics' objections that poetry was immoral and dishonest in its elevation of the imaginary and fantastical, Sidney identifies a dignified, even sanctified, lineage for the art. He points out that "Among the *Romanes* a Poet was called *Vates*, which is as much as a diuiner, foreseer, or Prophet," and explains that the act of writing poems was so admired by the ancients that it was termed "*Vaticinium*, and *Vaticinari*" ("prophecy, and prophesying"); likewise, he reminds his reader, the ancient Greek oracles delivered their prophecies in verse. Sidney goes on to reinforce these ancient "pagan" perspectives with evidence from the biblical tradition, in order to claim that this art is no trifle but rather "a heauenly poesie": "And may not I presume a little farther, to shewe the reasonablenesse of this word *Vatis,* and say that the holy *Davids* Psalms are a diuine *Poeme?* If I do, I shal not do it without the testimony of great learned men both auncient and moderne. But even the name of Psalmes wil speak for me, which being interpreted, is nothing but Songs."[1] Sidney's *Defence* articulates the ways in which poetry has always been deeply bound up with spirituality, and explicitly identifies the composition of poetry as a task that has been traditionally understood as engaging the divine.

As Sidney's brief survey of ancient views of poetry makes clear, poetic *inspiration* (a term that connotes the breathing in of spirit to the creative mind) has historically played a central role in religious worship. Many of the poems that remain to us from the ancient world are devotional, including hymns, petitions, and songs of praise from a variety of ancient cultures. Indeed, *lyric* poetry arose anciently in the context of musical performance; the name of the genre announces its association with the lyre, the instrument that provided musical accompaniment. Performances of poetic supplications to gods were featured in the religious rituals of ancient Greece, Rome, and Israel, as well as Egypt and other early Mediterranean cultures. The musical structures helped to make these supplications memorable, repeatable, and pleasurable, which ensured their transmission in oral cultures. In its earliest manifestations, the lyric functions in many respects as a hymn, and while these two poetic modes distinguish themselves from one another as history progresses, the lyric ever retains vestiges of its early ritual usage. Given that its ancient use was in a spiritual context, it is perhaps not surprising that the lyric shares many of the same preoccupations as religious devotion. But even if we leave aside its ancient origins in devotional practice, the lyric as a literary genre is remarkably well-suited to devotion.

What do we mean when we refer to a piece of writing as *lyric?* As it has evolved over the centuries, lyric poetry is a mode of writing that imitates the movements of a single mind as it negotiates a set of concerns. The single mind whose movements are recorded by the lyric poem is sometimes called the *lyric subject,* or the *lyric I,* though that pronoun may not appear explicitly in the poem. This is the figure who speaks the poem, and though this *I* may bear resemblance to a particular historical person (perhaps even to the poem's author), it is nevertheless a distinct and individuated figure, a poetic principle rather than a biographical self. The lyric might be most helpfully understood as "the fictional representation of a nonfictional utterance."[2] (As contemporary poet Billy Collins once quipped, "The person who speaks my poems is not me. For one thing, my speaker drinks tea, and I drink coffee.") The poem can be thought of as

---

1. *The Defence of Poesie* (London: William Ponsonby, 1595), B3v–B4r.
2. Jonathan Culler, "Changes in the Study of the Lyric," in *Lyric Poetry: Beyond New Criticism*, ed. Chaviva Hošek and Patricia Parker (Ithaca: Cornell University Press, 1985), 39.

lineamenting the speaker, in a very real sense given that the poem's *lines* give a shape to the speaker. The utterance of a lyric poem presents itself as arising in response to a particular occasion—not necessarily a specific event, but rather a sense of some conceptual predicament, impediment, or problem which generates the response of speech. This motivating condition is sometimes called the *lyric occasion,* and one of the functions of the lyric poem is to gain some new understanding by which to harmonize or reconcile that occasion. And though a lyric poem may have a narrative that unfolds over its course, the first drama it relates is the coming into being of that speaking voice, and the need for that voice to speak out of and respond to its occasion. In other words, the lyric's existence is its first story. As American poet Wallace Stevens wrote, "The poem is the cry of its occasion, / Part of the res itself and not about it."[3]

In the lyric tradition, the most basic problems or occasions to which a poem responds, overtly or implicitly, are death and the isolation of selfhood. To be human is to die, inevitably. But poetic speech endures with a kind of immortality. Among other effects, it preserves the human voice far beyond the scale of human life. We read a poem by Horace two thousand years after his death, and that voice is vivid and undiminished by time. Second, in part because of the structural musicality of lyric poetry— its emphasis on recurrences of rhyme and cadence, line- and stanza-form, sonic and visual arrangements—the voice that is preserved over centuries comes to the reader's corporeal as well as intellectual awareness, resurrected anew, as it were, through each new reader's ears and eyes and breath and heartbeats. American poet Robert Hass describes this phenomenon as a kind of possession, in which "a poet actually reaches in and takes over your body while you're reading and experiencing his poem."[4] Likewise, to be human is to live with the knowledge that we are each disconnected from one another, bound up in our own limited and subjective experience, unable to truly know even those we love most, and unable to be known. Nineteenth-century poet Gerard Manley Hopkins called this insurmountable subjectivism our "self-taste." But lyric poetry, because it records from the *I*-perspective the process of a mind working through ideas, allows readers the sense of leaping over the divide between one mind and another, experiencing in sympathy what another has experienced. The lyric's *I*-perspective allows the reader to participate vicariously in the speaker's point of view, which reduces the strangeness between self and other, and produces a kind of understanding or empathy. Immortality and compassion are not just the fundamental preoccupations embedded into lyric poetry; they are also the animating concerns of religion.

As the lyric *I* begins to differentiate itself as a speaking figure, it often accom-

---

3. "An Ordinary Evening in New Haven," 73–74, in *The Auroras of Autumn* (New York: Alfred A. Knopf, 1950). Stevens's term *res* here is a Latin word, roughly signifying *thing* or *reality*.

4. *Poetry in Person: 25 Years of Conversation with America's Poets,* ed. Alexander Neubauer (New York: Knopf, 2010), 21.

plishes that task by positing itself (again, usually implicitly) against a suite of other entities: *I* am not that tree, *I* am not that rock, *I* am not Shakespeare, *I* am not *You*. Just as there is an *I* implied in the speech of a poem, so too is there an implied *You*. Sometimes that *You* is identified and even named: "Batter my heart, three person'd God," begins one of John Donne's Holy Sonnets; "What *immortal hand* or *eye,* / Could frame thy fearful *symmetry?*" William Blake asks his "Tyger, Tyger." Sometimes the *You* blurs into the reader-position, as in Emily Dickinson's halting query, "I'm Nobody! Who are you? / Are you—Nobody—too?" Sometimes the *You* persists merely as the idea of a recipient, the poem's address to whom seems to be private speech that the reader has overheard, as when Sir Thomas Wyatt ruminates on his romantic frustrations: "They flee from me that sometime did me seek," he reflects, and though the poem does not specify to whom he relates his tale, we are aware of being in the presence of its confiding. The poem's awareness of its addressee at times generates a direct declamation, an apostrophe, as in the opening lines of Percy Bysshe Shelley's "To a Skylark": "Hail to thee, blithe spirit!" Whether the poem acknowledges its imagined auditor so dramatically or not, the idea of the addressee helps to provide an alternate position against which the lyric *I* can differentiate its unique selfhood.

As crucial as is the lyric task of differentiating the speaker's self is its dramatization of the process of negotiating some problem or processing some perception. Again, lyric poems enact the drama of a mind *figuring something out*. This generic trait makes lyric poetry a particularly responsive tool for investigating the unknown: because the lyric turns upon the drama of discovery, it lends itself well to the consideration of mystery. And in Western culture, from the time of ancient cultures whose philosophies and literatures influenced the development of our own, the preeminent figure for the Unknowable is God. Whether one conceives of a god figure literally or metaphorically, the perceptual inaccessibility of the divine ensures that it endures in our cultural awareness as the fundamental principle of mystery and unknowability. With their shared interest in plumbing mystery and defining the self in the context of such uncertainty, poetry and religion stand as two sympathetic and often overlapping responses to the same existential curiosities. Little wonder, then, that the long history of the poetic tradition has found itself entwined with religious observance and spiritual questioning. If the lyric as a genre represents the thoughts and feelings of a single mind in the process of engaging difficult questions, many of those difficult questions in the Western tradition have coalesced around metaphysical and/or theological subjects. Theology has provided a natural center of gravity for lyric exploration, and as long as there have been lyric poems, there have been devotional lyrics.

The devotional lyric should be understood as finally distinct in its evolution, however, from the hymnic tradition. Though the lyric's early uses included serving as ritual hymns, over time the lyric took on divergent generic characteristics. As we have come to understand these poetic forms, the devotional speech of hymns tends to be corporate, to speak for a community of worshippers (think of the emphatic plural of Martin Luther's sixteenth-century hymn "A Mighty Fortress Is Our God"), whereas the lyric is defined by its performance of a single speaker. The hymn may incline toward narrative, summarizing the might and deeds of the deity, as in the biblical song of praise attributed to Moses at Exodus 15.1–19. The genre also tends to rely on exhortation and imperatives to make its points, as in the familiar English translation of Francis of Assisi's thirteenth-century hymn: "All creatures of our God and King, / Lift up your voice and with us sing: / Hallelujah! Hallelujah!" The hortatory tone and the public, communal focus of the hymn are contrasted, again, by the lyric, which is characterized by negotiating rather than by such imperative certainty, by processual engagement rather than conclusive summaries. We experience it as overheard rather than proclaimed, emphasizing the effect of interiority rather than public and communal celebration or supplication. Still, the shared genealogy between hymnic and lyric traditions is at times detectable in the searchingly personal expressions of a hymn.

The lyric's conceit of privacy combines with its exploratory and processual impulses to create an extraordinary devotional art. The devotional lyric proves a supple and flexible medium for representing the varieties of spiritual encounter, from hosannah to lamentation to accusation to bewilderment to defiance to denial, as well as the dynamic interplay between these various, even contradictory, stances. Indeed, the devotional lyric is fraught with paradox: it achieves a transhistorical sense of readerly communion and compassion by inscribing a version of deeply private experience; it valorizes the human by interrogating the divine; it answers the desire for a devotional object not by granting miraculous access to the divine but by presenting itself as an object worthy of our attention and patience. It is a call without a response, a versicle with no expectation of an antiphon, and in the absence of reply we focus instead on the act of the offering. In the devotional lyric, as George Herbert well knew, it is the offering of art that does "plainly say." What it says is the cry of each one of us: *I am here.*

KIMBERLY JOHNSON

FURTHER READING

Blasing, Mutlu Konuk. *Lyric Poetry: The Pain and the Pleasure of Words.* Princeton: Princeton University Press, 2007.

Culler, Jonathan. "Changes in the Study of Lyric." In *Lyric Poetry: Beyond New Criticism,* ed. Chaviva Hošek and Patricia Parker, 38–54. Ithaca: Cornell University Press, 1985.

Dubrow, Heather. *The Challenges of Orpheus: Lyric Poetry and Early Modern England.* Baltimore: Johns Hopkins University Press, 2008.

Grossman, Allen. *The Sighted Singer: Two Works on Poetry for Readers and Writers.* Baltimore: Johns Hopkins University Press, 1992.

Stewart, Susan. *Poetry and the Fate of the Senses.* Chicago: University of Chicago Press, 2002.

A Note on the Texts

WHEREVER POSSIBLE, WE HAVE chosen to print each text in its original form—including archaic spellings, punctuation, capitalization and italics, and orthography—in order to preserve as much as possible its integrity as a historical artifact. Because spelling in English became standardized only in the eighteenth century, variances in spelling abound in older texts. These variances include the interchangeability of *u* and *v*, which were graphic variants of a single letter ("loue" and "vs"), the use of *i* for *j* ("Iordan"), the use of *y* as a vowel with a short *i* sound ("artycle" and "lookyng"), the frequent presence of the final silent *e* ("crosse"), and the use of *c* for *t* in *-tion* endings ("redempcyon"). Because printing conventions themselves likewise were in flux, readers should be aware that variances in typesetting persist through the seventeenth century, including idiomatic capitalization and italics.

We have endeavored to intervene in the texts as little as possible, but where sense is not readily available to modern readers, we have included marginal glosses. Longer phrases and phrases that appear in languages other than English are clarified in footnotes.

Unattributed translations are the work of Kimberly Johnson.

Before the Door of God

I

The Ancient Origins of the
Devotional Lyric

THE POETIC TRADITION IN Western culture traces its roots to the Mediterranean civilizations of the ancient world, and from the first, the devotional impulse has found expression in poetry. Among the oldest poems known to us are the Homeric Hymns, ancient poems in praise of Greek deities, which were written down after a long period of oral transmission. Ancient hymns were intended to be chanted or sung, by one singer or by a chorus of singers, and utilized the formal structures of poetry—including rhythm, sonic effects, and formal parallelism—to achieve both musicality and memorability. Roman hymns, which developed under the influence of Greek poetry, adopted Greek measures and modes even as they adopted and Romanized Greek deities.

The standard organization of these ancient hymns consisted of an invocation, a section in which the god is praised, and a petition. The invocation invites the deity to listen to the hymn, to give ear to its praises and pleas. In the laudatory section, the petition seeks to win the god's favor by glorifying the god's might and actions; this section often runs toward epic, as the hymn may include a long and flattering account of the god's history, making special mention of past instances in which the god displayed a willingness to help mortals. Finally, the petitioner requests some favor or assistance from the deity, a request that often comes on behalf of the civic community, as when the writer of the Homeric Hymn to Demeter concludes with a request that the goddess grant abundance and plenty to men. Though this structure persists throughout ancient hymnody, the poems themselves gave voice to a spectrum of emotional positions from praise to complaint to a persuasion approaching bribery (the Homeric Hymn to Apollo promises that if the god grants the petitioner's request, he will write poems that bear the god's reputation to all cities).

Devotional poems of the Hebrew Bible trace a slightly different ancestry, related to hymn-like celebrations of the gods from Egypt and Mesopotamia, but like the hymns of ancient Greece and Rome, they seem to have been made use of in ritual contexts, and were sung and played in temple ceremonies. The Book of Psalms was translated into Koine Greek as part of the Septuagint, a translation of the Hebrew canon undertaken in large part by Alexandrian Jews beginning in the third century B.C.E., which indicates the degree to which ancient Greek and Hebrew cultures overlapped. As Christianity developed in the region, it appropriated texts and philosophies from each of these major ancient cultures; indeed, Christianity's indebtedness to Greek, Roman, and Hebraic texts and traditions helped ensure the preservation of the literary and philosophical texts of antiquity even after these cultures had passed the period of their ascendancy.

This rich hymnic tradition interacted in exciting ways with the ancient genre of lyric poetry, which expressed or approximated personal emotions in musical structures. Most hymns of the ancient world are corporate expressions, offering petitions on behalf of a community, and their stance is largely honorific toward the deity and imperative toward humanity in exhorting all to praise; further, by spending much time summarizing the deeds of the deity, hymns prioritize the narrative they tell to celebrate the deeds and qualities of the god, rather than prioritizing the private negotiation of some concern as lyric generally does. In contrast to the hymnic tradition, lyrics are grappling rather than laudatory, processual rather than summative, personal rather than corporate. Still, many ancient poems reflect the close proximity of lyric and hymnic modes, and the works selected here demonstrate how easily the hymnic mode blurs into lyric conventions, as their ancient authors move between praise and complaint, cajoling and vaunting, ever seeking to define not only the deity being addressed but the position of the speaking self.

FURTHER READING

Alter, Robert. *The Art of Biblical Poetry*. New York: Basic Books, 1987.

————. *The Book of Psalms: A Translation with Commentary*. New York: Norton, 2007.

Bloch, Ariel, and Chana Bloch. "In the Garden of Delights" [Introduction]. *The Song of Songs: A New Translation with an Introduction and Commentary*. New York: Random House, 1995.

Flinker, Noam. *The Song of Songs in English Renaissance Literature: Kisses of Their Mouths*. Rochester, N.Y.: Brewer, 2000.

Furley, William D., and Jan Maarten Bremer. *Greek Hymns*. 2 volumes. Tübingen: Mohr Siebeck, 2001.

Martin, Gladys. "The Roman Hymn." *Classical Journal*, 34, no. 2 (1938): 86–97.

Noakes, Susan. "Gracious Words: Luke's Jesus and the Reading of Sacred Poetry at the Beginning of the Christian Era." *The Ethnography of Reading*, ed. Jonathan Boyarin. Berkeley: University of California Press, 1993.

Wood, Renate. "Poetry and the Self: Reflections of the Self in Early Greek Lyrics." *Poets Teaching Poets: Self and the World*, ed. Gregory Orr and Ellen Bryant Voigt. Ann Arbor: University of Michigan Press, 1996.

The Book of Psalms / תְּהִלִּים
(c. SEVENTH CENTURY B.C.E.)

THE BOOK OF PSALMS CONTAINS one hundred and fifty poems of varied styles, subjects, and moods. They represent the work of multiple authors over centuries of Hebrew history; though the bulk were probably composed in the seventh and sixth centuries B.C.E., some of the poems in this great devotional anthology may date from as early as the tenth century B.C.E., while others may have been written as late as the fifth century B.C.E., shortly before the collection was composited. The Hebrew title for the book is *tehilim*, or praises, but not all the poems engage in precisely that activity— they plead, complain, and wrestle, and it is this complexity that has allowed them to resonate through so many historical periods and spiritual traditions. The notion that the poems were written, altogether or in part, by ancient King David lacks a historical foundation; that ascription is based on the David story in 1 and 2 Samuel, where the young David is represented as a poet and musician. As biblical scholar Robert Alter explains, the phrase "a Psalm of David," which is affixed to the beginning of many psalms, signifies not just possession but also "'for,' 'in the manner of,' 'suitable to,' and so forth." The translation here comes from the 1611 King James Bible (also known as the Authorized Version), perhaps the most widely familiar, and certainly the most widely influential, rendering of biblical text into English. Other psalm translations appear in Part 3 of this anthology.

Psalm 6

לַמְנַצֵּחַ בִּנְגִינוֹת עַל־הַשְּׁמִינִית מִזְמוֹר לְדָוִד:
יְהֹוָה אַל־בְּאַפְּךָ תוֹכִיחֵנִי וְאַל־בַּחֲמָתְךָ תְיַסְּרֵנִי:
חׇנֵּנִי יְהֹוָה כִּי אֻמְלַל אָנִי רְפָאֵנִי יְהֹוָה כִּי נִבְהֲלוּ עֲצָמָי:
וְנַפְשִׁי נִבְהֲלָה מְאֹד [כ= וְאַתְּ] [ק= וְאַתָּה] יְהֹוָה עַד־מָתָי:
שׁוּבָה יְהֹוָה חַלְּצָה נַפְשִׁי הוֹשִׁיעֵנִי לְמַעַן חַסְדֶּךָ:
כִּי אֵין בַּמָּוֶת זִכְרֶךָ בִּשְׁאוֹל מִי יוֹדֶה־לָּךְ:
יָגַעְתִּי בְּאַנְחָתִי אַשְׂחֶה בְכׇל־לַיְלָה מִטָּתִי בְּדִמְעָתִי עַרְשִׂי אַמְסֶה:
עָשְׁשָׁה מִכַּעַס עֵינִי עָתְקָה בְּכׇל־צוֹרְרָי:
סוּרוּ מִמֶּנִּי כׇּל־פֹּעֲלֵי אָוֶן כִּי שָׁמַע יְהֹוָה קוֹל בִּכְיִי:
שָׁמַע יְהֹוָה תְּחִנָּתִי יְהֹוָה תְּפִלָּתִי יִקָּח:
יֵבֹשׁוּ וְיִבָּהֲלוּ מְאֹד כׇּל־אֹיְבָי יָשֻׁבוּ יֵבֹשׁוּ רָגַע:

To the chiefe musician on Neginoth vpon Sheminith,[1] A Psalme of Dauid.

O Lord, rebuke me not in thine anger, neither chasten me in thy hot displeasure.
Have mercy vpon me, O Lord, for I am weake:
O Lord, heale mee, for my bones are vexed.
My soule is also sore vexed: but thou, O Lord, how long?
Returne, O Lord, deliuer my soule: oh saue mee for thy mercies sake.
For in death there is no remembrance of thee: in the graue who shall giue thee
    thankes?
I am weary with my groning; all the night make I my bed to swim:
I water my couch with my teares.
Mine eie is consumed because of griefe;
it waxeth olde because of all mine enemies.
Depart from me, all yee workers of iniquitie:
for the Lord hath heard the voice of my weeping.
The Lord hath heard my supplication; the Lord will receive my prayer.
Let all mine enemies be ashamed and sore vexed:
let them returne and be ashamed suddainly.

---

1. The headnote indicates instructions for the psalm's performance: it is to be a song with musical accompaniment in octaves (*Sheminith*), and it is addressed to the leader of that portion of temple musicians who played on stringed instruments (or *Neginoth*).

Psalm 8

לַמְנַצֵּחַ עַל־הַגִּתִּית מִזְמוֹר לְדָוִד:
יְהוָה אֲדֹנֵינוּ מָה אַדִּיר שִׁמְךָ בְּכָל־הָאָרֶץ אֲשֶׁר תְּנָה הוֹדְךָ עַל־הַשָּׁמָיִם:
מִפִּי עוֹלְלִים וְיֹנְקִים יִסַּדְתָּ עֹז לְמַעַן צוֹרְרֶיךָ לְהַשְׁבִּית אוֹיֵב וּמִתְנַקֵּם:
כִּי־אֶרְאֶה שָׁמֶיךָ מַעֲשֵׂה אֶצְבְּעֹתֶיךָ יָרֵחַ וְכוֹכָבִים אֲשֶׁר כּוֹנָנְתָּה:
מָה־אֱנוֹשׁ כִּי־תִזְכְּרֶנּוּ וּבֶן־אָדָם כִּי תִפְקְדֶנּוּ:
וַתְּחַסְּרֵהוּ מְּעַט מֵאֱלֹהִים וְכָבוֹד וְהָדָר תְּעַטְּרֵהוּ:
תַּמְשִׁילֵהוּ בְּמַעֲשֵׂי יָדֶיךָ כֹּל שַׁתָּה תַחַת־רַגְלָיו:
צֹנֶה וַאֲלָפִים כֻּלָּם וְגַם בַּהֲמוֹת שָׂדָי:
צִפּוֹר שָׁמַיִם וּדְגֵי הַיָּם עֹבֵר אָרְחוֹת יַמִּים:
יְהוָה אֲדֹנֵינוּ מָה־אַדִּיר שִׁמְךָ בְּכָל־הָאָרֶץ:

To the chiefe Musicion vpon Gittith,[2] a Psalme of Dauid.

O Lord our Lord, how excellent is thy name in all the earth!
who hast set thy glory aboue the heauens.
Out of the mouth of babes and sucklings
hast thou ordained strength, because of thine enemies,
that thou mightest still the enemie and the auenger.
When I consider thy heauens, the worke of thy fingers,
the moone and the starres which thou hast ordained;
What is man, that thou art mindfull of him?
and the sonne of man, that thou visitest him?
For thou hast made him a little lower then the Angels;
and hast crowned him with glory and honour.
Thou madest him to haue dominion ouer the works of thy hands;
thou hast put all things vnder his feete.
All sheepe and oxen, yea and the beasts of the field.
The foule of the aire, and the fish of the sea,
and whatsoeuer passeth through the paths of the seas.
O Lord our Lord, how excellent is thy name in all the earth!

---

2. Hebrew: *Wine-press*, which may indicate a tune of that name, or alternatively, may identify the psalm as meditating on the theme of justice (see Isaiah 63.3).

Psalm 23

מִזְמוֹר לְדָוִד
יְהֹוָה רֹעִי לֹא אֶחְסָר:
בִּנְאוֹת דֶּשֶׁא יַרְבִּיצֵנִי
עַל־מֵי מְנֻחוֹת יְנַהֲלֵנִי:
נַפְשִׁי יְשׁוֹבֵב
יַנְחֵנִי בְמַעְגְּלֵי־צֶדֶק לְמַעַן שְׁמוֹ:
גַּם כִּי־אֵלֵךְ בְּגֵיא צַלְמָוֶת לֹא־אִירָא רָע כִּי־אַתָּה עִמָּדִי שִׁבְטְךָ וּמִשְׁעַנְתֶּךָ הֵמָּה יְנַחֲמֻנִי:
תַּעֲרֹךְ לְפָנַי שֻׁלְחָן נֶגֶד צֹרְרָי
דִּשַּׁנְתָּ בַשֶּׁמֶן רֹאשִׁי כּוֹסִי רְוָיָה:
אַךְ טוֹב וָחֶסֶד יִרְדְּפוּנִי כָּל־יְמֵי חַיָּי
וְשַׁבְתִּי בְּבֵית־יְהֹוָה לְאֹרֶךְ יָמִים

A Psalme of Dauid.

The Lord is my shepheard, I shall not want.
He maketh me to lie downe in greene pastures:
he leadeth mee beside the still waters.
He restoreth my soule:
he leadeth me in the pathes of righteousnes, for his names sake.
Yea though I walke through the valley of the shadowe of death,
I will feare no euill:
for thou art with me,
thy rod and thy staffe, they comfort me.
Thou preparest a table before me, in the presence of mine enemies:
thou anointest my head with oyle, my cuppe runneth ouer.
Surely goodnes and mercie shall followe me all the daies of my life:
and I will dwell in the house of the Lord for euer.

Psalm 42

לַמְנַצֵּחַ מַשְׂכִּיל לִבְנֵי־קֹרַח:
כְּאַיָּל תַּעֲרֹג עַל־אֲפִיקֵי־מָיִם
כֵּן נַפְשִׁי תַעֲרֹג אֵלֶיךָ אֱלֹהִים:
צָמְאָה נַפְשִׁי לֵאלֹהִים לְאֵל חָי
מָתַי אָבוֹא וְאֵרָאֶה פְּנֵי אֱלֹהִים:
הָיְתָה־לִּי דִמְעָתִי לֶחֶם יוֹמָם וָלָיְלָה בֶּאֱמֹר
אֵלַי כָּל־הַיּוֹם אַיֵּה אֱלֹהֶיךָ:
אֵלֶּה אֶזְכְּרָה וְאֶשְׁפְּכָה עָלַי נַפְשִׁי

כִּי אֶעֱבֹר בַּסָּךְ אֶדַּדֵּם עַד־בֵּית אֱלֹהִים
בְּקוֹל־רִנָּה וְתוֹדָה הָמוֹן חוֹגֵג:
מַה־תִּשְׁתּוֹחֲחִי נַפְשִׁי וַתֶּהֱמִי עָלָי הוֹחִילִי
לֵאלֹהִים כִּי־עוֹד אוֹדֶנּוּ יְשׁוּעוֹת פָּנָיו:
אֱלֹהַי עָלַי נַפְשִׁי תִשְׁתּוֹחָח עַל־כֵּן אֶזְכָּרְךָ
מֵאֶרֶץ יַרְדֵּן וְחֶרְמוֹנִים מֵהַר מִצְעָר:
תְּהוֹם־אֶל־תְּהוֹם קוֹרֵא לְקוֹל צִנּוֹרֶיךָ
כָּל־מִשְׁבָּרֶיךָ וְגַלֶּיךָ עָלַי עָבָרוּ:
יוֹמָם יְצַוֶּה יְהוָה חַסְדּוֹ וּבַלַּיְלָה שִׁירֹה עִמִּי
תְּפִלָּה לְאֵל חַיָּי:
אוֹמְרָה לְאֵל סַלְעִי לָמָה שְׁכַחְתָּנִי
לָמָּה־קֹדֵר אֵלֵךְ בְּלַחַץ אוֹיֵב:
בְּרֶצַח בְּעַצְמוֹתַי חֵרְפוּנִי צוֹרְרָי
בְּאָמְרָם אֵלַי כָּל־הַיּוֹם אַיֵּה אֱלֹהֶיךָ:
מַה־תִּשְׁתּוֹחֲחִי נַפְשִׁי וּמַה־תֶּהֱמִי עָלָי
הוֹחִילִי לֵאלֹהִים
כִּי־עוֹד אוֹדֶנּוּ יְשׁוּעֹת פָּנַי וֵאלֹהָי:

To the chiefe Musician, Maschil, for the sonnes of Korah.[3]

As the Hart panteth after the water brookes, so panteth my soule after thee, O God.
My soule thirsteth for God, for the liuing God:
when shall I come and appeare before God?
My teares haue bene my meate day and night;
while they continually say vnto me, Where is thy God?
When I remember these things, I powre° out my soule in mee;   *pour*
for I had gone with the multitude, I went with them to the house of God;
with the voyce of ioy and praise, with a multitude that kept holy day.
Why art thou cast downe, O my soule, and why art thou disquieted in me?
hope thou in God, for I shall yet praise him for the helpe of his countenance.
O my God, my soule is cast downe within me:
therefore will I remember thee from the land of Iordane,
and of the Hermonites, from the hill Missar.[4]
Deepe calleth vnto deepe at the noyse of thy water-spouts:
all thy waues and thy billowes are gone ouer me.
Yet the Lord will command his louing kindnes in the day time,

---

3. *Maschil* signals that it is a song of instruction, intended for didactic purposes.

4. Mount Hermon, situated in the northeast of Palestine, is a series of ridges near the source of the Jordan River. The Missar seems to refer to a small land feature now unknown, though the word *mitzar* in Hebrew signifies something little.

and in the night his song shalbe with me,
and my prayer vnto the God of my life.
I will say vnto God, My rocke, why hast thou forgotten me?
why goe I mourning, because of the oppression of the enemy?
As with a sword in my bones, mine enemies reproch mee:
while they say dayly vnto me, Where is thy God?
Why art thou cast downe, O my soule? and why art thou disquieted within me?
hope thou in God, for I shall yet praise him,
who is the health of my countenance, and my God.

Psalm 98

שִׁירוּ לַיהוָה שִׁיר חָדָשׁ כִּי־נִפְלָאוֹת עָשָׂה
הוֹשִׁיעָה־לּוֹ יְמִינוֹ וּזְרוֹעַ קָדְשׁוֹ:
הוֹדִיעַ יְהוָה יְשׁוּעָתוֹ לְעֵינֵי הַגּוֹיִם גִּלָּה צִדְקָתוֹ:
זָכַר חַסְדּוֹ | וֶאֱמוּנָתוֹ לְבֵית יִשְׂרָאֵל רָאוּ כָל אַפְסֵי אָרֶץ אֵת יְשׁוּעַת אֱלֹהֵינוּ:
הָרִיעוּ לַיהוָה כָּל־הָאָרֶץ פִּצְחוּ וְרַנְּנוּ וְזַמֵּרוּ:
זַמְּרוּ לַיהוָה בְּכִנּוֹר בְּכִנּוֹר וְקוֹל זִמְרָה:
בַּחֲצֹצְרוֹת וְקוֹל שׁוֹפָר הָרִיעוּ לִפְנֵי הַמֶּלֶךְ יְהוָה:
יִרְעַם הַיָּם וּמְלֹאוֹ תֵּבֵל וְיֹשְׁבֵי בָהּ:
נְהָרוֹת יִמְחֲאוּ כָף יַחַד הָרִים יְרַנֵּנוּ:
לִפְנֵי־יְהוָה כִּי בָא לִשְׁפֹּט הָאָרֶץ
יִשְׁפֹּט־תֵּבֵל בְּצֶדֶק וְעַמִּים בְּמֵישָׁרִים:

A Psalme.

O sing vnto the Lord a New song, for hee hath done marueilous things:
his right hand, and his holy arme hath gotten him the victorie.
The Lord hath made knowen his saluation:
his righteousnesse hath hee openly shewed in the sight of the heathen.
Hee hath remembred his mercie and his trueth toward the house of Israel:
all the ends of the earth haue seene the saluation of our God.
Make a ioyfull noise vnto the Lord, all the earth:
make a lowd noise, and reioyce, and sing praise.
Sing vnto the Lord with the harpe: with the harpe, and the voice of a Psalme.
With trumpets and sound of cornet: make a ioyfull noise before the Lord, the King.
Let the sea roare, and the fulnesse thereof: the world, and they that dwell therein.
Let the floods clap their handes: let the hilles be ioyfull together
before the Lord, for he commeth to iudge the earth:
with righteousnesse shall hee iudge the world, and the people with equitie.

Sappho

(c. 625–c. 570 B.C.E.)

SAPPHO'S "HYMN TO APHRODITE" is the ancient Greek poet's sole extant poem; the bulk of her work survives only in fragments. Little is known of her biography, but she was certainly renowned for her art during her lifetime, as she is mentioned by a number of contemporary sources as one of the ancient world's greatest lyric poets. An epigram ascribed to Plato describes her as the "Tenth Muse," augmenting the number of nine mythological sister-goddesses who were thought to inspire the arts. Sappho seems to have spent most of her life on the Greek island of Lesbos, though she may have been exiled to Sicily during a period of political turmoil on Lesbos. The English rendering here appears in British polymath Henry Thornton Wharton's (1846–1895) influential volume *Sappho: Memoir, Text and Selected Renderings with a Literal Translation* (1885), the first translation of Sappho's poem to acknowledge her use of the feminine pronoun for her beloved.

Fragment 1

Ποικιλόθρον᾽, ἀθάνατ᾽ Ἀφρόδιτα,
παῖ Δίος, δολόπλοκε, λίσσομαί σε
μή μ᾽ ἄσαισι μήτ᾽ ὀνίαισι δάμνα,
    πότνια, θῦμον·

ἀλλὰ τυῖδ᾽ ἔλθ᾽, αἴποτα κἀτέρωτα
τᾶς ἔμας αὔδως ἀΐοισα πήλυι
ἔκλυες, πάτρος δὲ δόμον λίποισα
    χρύσιον ἦλθες

ἄρμ᾽ ὑποζεύξαισα· κάλοι δέ σ᾽ ἆγον
ὦκεες στροῦθοι περὶ γᾶς μελαίνας
πύκνα δινεῦντες πτέρ᾽ ἀπ᾽ ὠράνω αἴθε-
    ρας διὰ μέσσω.

αἶψα δ᾽ ἐξίκοντο· τὺ δ᾽, ὦ μάκαιρα,
μειδιάσαισ᾽ ἀθανάτῳ προσώπῳ,
ἤρε᾽, ὅττι δηῦτε πέπονθα κὤττι
    δηῦτε κάλημι,

κώττι μοι μάλιστα θέλω γένεσθαι
μαινόλᾳ θύμῳ· τίνα δηὖτε Πείθω
μαῖς ἄγην ἐς σὰν φιλότατα, τίς σ’, ὦ
        Ψάπφ’, ἀδικήει;

καὶ γὰρ αἰ φεύγει, ταχέως διώξει,
αἰ δὲ δῶρα μὴ δέκετ’ ἀλλὰ δώσει,
αἰ δὲ μὴ φίλει, ταχέως φιλήσει
        κωὐκ ἐθέλοισα.

ἔλθε μοι καὶ νῦν, χαλεπᾶν δὲ λῦσον
ἐκ μεριμνᾶν, ὄσσα δέ μοι τελέσσαι
θῦμος ἰμέρρει, τέλεσον· σὺ δ’ αὔτα
        σύμμαχος ἔσσο.

Immortal Aphrodite of the broidered throne,
daughter of Zeus, weaver of wiles, I pray thee
break not my spirit with anguish
        and distress, O Queen.

But come hither, if ever before
thou didst hear my voice afar
and listen, and leaving thy father's
        golden house camest

with chariot yoked, and fair fleet sparrows
drew thee, flapping fast
their wings around the dark earth,
        from heaven through mid sky.

Quickly arrived they; and thou, Blessed One,
smiling with immortal countenance,
didst ask What now is befallen me,
        and Why now I call,

and What I in my mad heart
most desire to see. *What Beauty now
wouldst thou draw to love thee?*
        Who wrongs thee, Sappho?

*For even if she flies she shall soon follow,
and if she rejects gifts shall yet give,
and if she loves not shall soon love,
        however loth.*

Come, I pray thee, now too, and release me
from cruel cares; and all that my heart desires
to accomplish, accomplish thou,
    and be thyself my ally.

The Book of Jeremiah / יִרְמְיָהוּ
(EARLY SIXTH CENTURY B.C.E.)

THE BOOK OF JEREMIAH IS ONE of the major prophetic books of the Hebrew
Bible. It has been conjectured that Jeremiah lived during the reigns of Josiah and other
monarchs of the southern kingdom of Judah. His writings seem to correspond to, and
to respond to, the seizing (in around 586 B.C.E.) of Jerusalem and destruction of Solo-
mon's Temple by Nebuchadnezzar and the forces of Babylon, the narrative of which is
offered in 2 Kings 21–25 and 2 Chronicles 33–36. In addition to the prophetic writings
in the Book of Jeremiah, Jeremiah is traditionally credited with authoring the Book of
Lamentations, and the historical records of 1 Kings and 2 Kings. As with the selections
from the Book of Psalms, the translation here comes from the 1611 King James Bible.

Chapter 10.19–24

אוֹי לִי֙ עַל־שִׁבְרִ֔י נַחְלָ֖ה מַכָּתִ֑י וַאֲנִ֣י אָמַ֔רְתִּי אַ֛ךְ זֶ֥ה חֳלִ֖י וְאֶשָּׂאֶֽנּוּ׃
אׇהֳלִ֣י שֻׁדָּ֔ד וְכׇל־מֵיתָרַ֖י נִתָּ֑קוּ בָּנַ֤י יְצָאֻ֙נִי֙ וְאֵינָ֔ם אֵין־נֹטֶ֥ה עוֹד֙ אׇהֳלִ֔י וּמֵקִ֖ים יְרִיעוֹתָֽי׃
כִּ֤י נִבְעֲרוּ֙ הָ֣רֹעִ֔ים וְאֶת־יְהֹוָ֖ה לֹ֣א דָרָ֑שׁוּ עַל־כֵּן֙ לֹ֣א הִשְׂכִּ֔ילוּ וְכׇל־מַרְעִיתָ֖ם נָפֽוֹצָה׃
ק֣וֹל שְׁמוּעָ֔ה הִנֵּ֖ה בָאָ֑ה וְרַ֥עַשׁ גָּד֖וֹל מֵאֶ֣רֶץ צָפ֑וֹן לָשׂ֞וּם אֶת־עָרֵ֤י יְהוּדָה֙ שְׁמָמָ֔ה מְע֖וֹן תַּנִּֽים׃
יָדַ֣עְתִּי יְהֹוָ֔ה כִּ֛י לֹ֥א לָאָדָ֖ם דַּרְכּ֑וֹ לֹֽא־לְאִ֣ישׁ הֹלֵ֔ךְ וְהָכִ֖ין אֶֽת־צַעֲדֽוֹ׃
יַסְּרֵ֥נִי יְהֹוָ֖ה אַךְ־בְּמִשְׁפָּ֑ט אַל־בְּאַפְּךָ֖ פֶּן־תַּמְעִטֵֽנִי׃

Woe is mee for my hurt, my wound is grieuous: but I sayd, Truely this is a griefe, and
    I must beare it.

My Tabernacle is spoyled, and all my cordes are broken: my children are gone foorth
    of me, and they are not: there is none to stretch foorth my tent any more, and to set
    vp my curtaines.

For the Pastours are become brutish, and haue not sought the Lord: therefore they
    shall not prosper, and all their flockes shall be scattered.

Behold, the noise of the bruit is come, and a great commotion out of the North countrey, to make the cities of Iudah desolate, and a denne of dragons.

O Lord, I know that the way of man is not in himselfe: it is not in man that walketh, to direct his steps.

O Lord, correct mee, but with iudgement, not in thine anger, lest thou bring me to nothing.

The Book of Job / אִיּוֹב

(C. SIXTH–FOURTH CENTURIES B.C.E.)

ONE OF THE LITERARY BOOKS of the Hebrew Bible, this text relates the story of a man called Job, who, after being tried and afflicted by a supernatural figure described as "the adversary," discusses the nature of God's justice with three friends. After they debate the meaning of suffering for some time, God speaks from a whirlwind, chastening the men for speaking in their ignorance and affirming his sovereignty and control over human existence. The motif of the righteous sufferer is an ancient one, predating the composition of Job and appearing in texts throughout the Mediterranean. In this passage, Job is the speaker. The English text provided here is from the 1611 King James Bible.

Chapter 10

נָקְטָה נַפְשִׁי בְּחַיָּי אֶעֶזְבָה עָלַי שִׂיחִי אֲדַבְּרָה בְּמַר נַפְשִׁי:
אֹמַר אֶל אֱלוֹהַּ אַל תַּרְשִׁיעֵנִי הוֹדִיעֵנִי עַל מַה תְּרִיבֵנִי:
הֲטוֹב לְךָ כִּי תַעֲשֹׁק כִּי תִמְאַס יְגִיעַ כַּפֶּיךָ וְעַל עֲצַת רְשָׁעִים הוֹפָעְתָּ:
הַעֵינֵי בָשָׂר לָךְ אִם כִּרְאוֹת אֱנוֹשׁ תִּרְאֶה:
הֲכִימֵי אֱנוֹשׁ יָמֶיךָ אִם שְׁנוֹתֶיךָ כִּימֵי גָבֶר:
כִּי תְבַקֵּשׁ לַעֲוֹנִי וּלְחַטָּאתִי תִדְרוֹשׁ:
עַל דַּעְתְּךָ כִּי לֹא אֶרְשָׁע וְאֵין מִיָּדְךָ מַצִּיל:
יָדֶיךָ עִצְּבוּנִי וַיַּעֲשׂוּנִי יַחַד סָבִיב וַתְּבַלְּעֵנִי:
זְכָר נָא כִּי כַחֹמֶר עֲשִׂיתָנִי וְאֶל עָפָר תְּשִׁיבֵנִי:
הֲלֹא כֶחָלָב תַּתִּיכֵנִי וְכַגְּבִנָּה תַּקְפִּיאֵנִי:
עוֹר וּבָשָׂר תַּלְבִּישֵׁנִי וּבַעֲצָמוֹת וְגִידִים תְּשֹׂכְכֵנִי:
חַיִּים וָחֶסֶד עָשִׂיתָ עִמָּדִי וּפְקֻדָּתְךָ שָׁמְרָה רוּחִי:
וְאֵלֶּה צָפַנְתָּ בִלְבָבֶךָ יָדַעְתִּי כִּי זֹאת עִמָּךְ:

אִם חָטָאתִי וּשְׁמַרְתָּנִי וּמֵעֲוֺנִי לֹא תְנַקֵּנִי:

אִם רָשַׁעְתִּי אַלְלַי לִי וְצָדַקְתִּי לֹא אֶשָּׂא רֹאשִׁי שְׂבַע קָלוֹן וּרְאֵה עָנְיִי:

וְיִגְאֶה כַּשַּׁחַל תְּצוּדֵנִי וְתָשֹׁב תִּתְפַּלָּא בִי:

תְּחַדֵּשׁ עֵדֶיךָ נֶגְדִּי וְתֶרֶב כַּעַשְׂךָ עִמָּדִי חֲלִיפוֹת וְצָבָא עִמִּי:

וְלָמָּה מֵרֶחֶם הֹצֵאתָנִי אֶגְוַע וְעַיִן לֹא תִרְאֵנִי:

כַּאֲשֶׁר לֹא הָיִיתִי אֶהְיֶה מִבֶּטֶן לַקֶּבֶר אוּבָל:

הֲלֹא מְעַט יָמַי וַחֲדָל וְשִׁית מִמֶּנִּי וְאַבְלִיגָה מְּעָט:

בְּטֶרֶם אֵלֵךְ וְלֹא אָשׁוּב אֶל אֶרֶץ חֹשֶׁךְ וְצַלְמָוֶת:

אֶרֶץ עֵפָתָה כְּמוֹ אֹפֶל צַלְמָוֶת וְלֹא סְדָרִים וַתֹּפַע כְּמוֹ אֹפֶל:

My soule is weary of my life, I will leaue my complaint vpon my selfe; I will speake in the bitternesse of my soule.

I will say vnto God, Doe not condemne mee; shewe me wherefore thou contendest with me.

Is it good vnto thee, that thou shouldest oppresse? that thou shouldest despise the worke of thine hands? and shine vpon the counsell of the wicked?

Hast thou eyes of flesh? or seest thou as man seeth?

Are thy dayes as the dayes of man? are thy yeeres as mans dayes,

That thou enquirest after mine iniquitie, and searchest after my sinne?

Thou knowest that I am not wicked, and there is none that can deliuer out of thine hand.

Thine hands haue made me and fashioned me together round about yet thou doest destroy me.

Remember, I beseech thee, that thou hast made me as the clay, and wilt thou bring me into dust againe?

Hast thou not powred me out as milke, and cruddled° me like cheese?   *curdled*

Thou hast cloathed me with skin and flesh, and hast fenced me with bones and sinewes.

Thou hast granted me life and fauour, and thy visitation hath preserued my spirit.

And these things hast thou hid in thine heart; I know that this is with thee.

If I sinne, then thou markest me, and thou wilt not acquite me from mine iniquitie.

If I be wicked, woe vnto me; and if I be righteous, yet will I not lift vp my head: I am full of confusion, therefore see thou mine affliction:

For it increaseth: thou huntest me as a fierce Lion: and againe thou shewest thy selfe marueilous vpon me.

Thou renuest thy witnesses against me, and increasest thine indignation vpon me; Changes and warre are against me.

Wherfore then hast thou brought me forth out of the wombe? Oh that I had giuen vp the ghost, and no eye had seene me!

I should haue bene as though I had not bene, I should haue bene caried from the wombe to the graue.

Are not my dayes few? cease then, and let me alone that I may take comfort a litle,

Before I goe whence I shall not returne, euen to the land of darknes and the shadow of death,

A land of darknes, as darknes it selfe, and of the shadow of death, without any order, and where the light is as darkenes.

Anacreon

(c. 582–485 b.c.e.)

FROM TEOS, IN ASIA MINOR, Anacreon became known for his poetry while he was still a youth. He was invited to become the court poet of Polycrates, the tyrant of the Aegean island Samos, and later joined the Athenian court of Hipparchus. He retired to the place of his birth, and lived out his days there. He wrote lyrics, elegies, and iambic poetry, though his work survives mostly in fragments. This poem petitions Dionysos, the god of wine and ecstatic ritual, who was adopted by the Romans as Bacchus.

ὦναξ, ᾧ δαμάλης Ἔρως
καὶ Νύμφαι κυανώπιδες
πορφυρέη τ' Ἀφροδίτη
συμπαίζουσιν· ἐπιστρέφεαι δ'
ὑψηλῶν κορυφὰς ὀρέων,
γουνοῦμαί σε· σὺ δ' εὐμενής
ἔλθ' ἡμῖν, κεχαρισμένης δ'
εὐχολῆς ἐπακούειν.

Κλεοβούλῳ δ' ἀγαθὸς γένευ
σύμβουλος, τὸν ἐμόν γ' ἔρωτ',
ὦ Δεύνυσε, δέχεσθαι.

O Lord, with whom the conqueror Eros
And the dark-eyed Nymphs
And radiant Aphrodite
Frolic, O you who frequent
The lofty mountain peaks,
I beg you: come graciously
To me, take pleasure
In my prayer and hear it!
To Kleoboulos give
This good counsel, O Dionysos:
To return my love.

The Book of Jonah / יוֹנָה

(c. FIFTH–FOURTH CENTURIES B.C.E.)

A TEXT IN THE HEBREW BIBLE, the Book of Jonah tells the tale of a Hebrew prophet named Jonah who is sent by God to prophesy the destruction of Nineveh, seat of the ancient Assyrian empire, but tries to escape his divine commission by fleeing on a ship. At sea, the ship is taken by a storm, and the sailors throw Jonah overboard to appease the wrath of God. He is swallowed by a great sea creature, and after three repentant days in the creature's belly, he is vomited out upon land. The book was probably composed in the period following the Babylonian captivity of Judah; the Prayer of Jonah, which appears below, may be a later interpolation. As with other biblical selections, the English text comes from the 1611 King James Bible.

Chapter 2: Jonah's Prayer

וַיֹּאמֶר קָרָאתִי מִצָּרָה לִי אֶל יְהֹוָה וַיַּעֲנֵנִי מִבֶּטֶן שְׁאוֹל שִׁוַּעְתִּי שָׁמַעְתָּ קוֹלִי:
וַתַּשְׁלִיכֵנִי מְצוּלָה בִּלְבַב יַמִּים וְנָהָר יְסֹבְבֵנִי כָּל מִשְׁבָּרֶיךָ וְגַלֶּיךָ עָלַי עָבָרוּ:
וַאֲנִי אָמַרְתִּי נִגְרַשְׁתִּי מִנֶּגֶד עֵינֶיךָ אַךְ אוֹסִיף לְהַבִּיט אֶל הֵיכַל קָדְשֶׁךָ:

אֲפָפוּנִי מַיִם עַד נֶפֶשׁ תְּהוֹם יְסֹבְבֵנִי סוּף חָבוּשׁ לְרֹאשִׁי:
לְקִצְבֵי הָרִים יָרַדְתִּי הָאָרֶץ בְּרִחֶיהָ בַעֲדִי לְעוֹלָם וַתַּעַל מִשַּׁחַת חַיַּי יְהוָה אֱלֹהָי:
בְּהִתְעַטֵּף עָלַי נַפְשִׁי אֶת יְהוָה זָכָרְתִּי וַתָּבוֹא אֵלֶיךָ תְּפִלָּתִי אֶל הֵיכַל קָדְשֶׁךָ:
מְשַׁמְּרִים הַבְלֵי שָׁוְא חַסְדָּם יַעֲזֹבוּ:
וַאֲנִי בְּקוֹל תּוֹדָה אֶזְבְּחָה לָּךְ אֲשֶׁר נָדַרְתִּי אֲשַׁלֵּמָה יְשׁוּעָתָה לַיהוָה:

I cried by reason of mine affliction vnto the Lord, and hee heard mee; out of the belly of hell cried I, and thou heardest my voyce.

For thou hadst cast mee into the deepe, in the middest of the Seas, and the floods compassed me about: all thy billowes & thy waues passed ouer me.

Then I said, I am cast out of thy sight; yet I will looke againe toward thy holy Temple.

The waters compassed mee about euen to the soule; the depth closed mee round about; the weedes were wrapt about my head.

I went downe to the bottomes of the mountaines: the earth with her barres was about me for euer: yet hast thou brought vp my life from corruption, O Lord my God.

When my soule fainted within mee, I remembred the Lord, and my prayer came in vnto thee, into thine holy Temple.

They that obserue lying vanities, forsake their owne mercy.

But I wil sacrifice vnto thee with the voice of thanksgiuing, I will pay that that I haue vowed: saluation is of the Lord.

Homeric Hymn to Ares

(c. THIRD CENTURY B.C.E.)

THE HOMERIC HYMNS ARE A collection of thirty-three Greek poems of unknown authorship, dating mostly from the seventh and sixth centuries B.C.E., though this hymn to the war god Ares seems to have been composed much later. The term "Homeric" indicates not that they were written by the author of the *Iliad* and *Odyssey*, but rather that they employ the dactylic hexameter of Homer's ancient epics. The poems range in length from 3 to over 500 lines, the longer poems relating epic narratives. The short invocations, like this brief prayer to Ares, served as preludes to festival epic recitations. The English version here is the work of Canadian poet and translator Daryl Hine (b. 1936), whose *Homeric Hymns* first appeared in 1972.

Εἲς Ἄρεα

Ἄρες ὑπερμενέτα, βρισάρματε, χρυσεοπήληξ,
ὀβριμόθυμε, φέρασπι, πολισσόε, χαλκοκορυστά,
καρτερόχειρ, ἀμόγητε, δορισθενές, ἕρκος Ὀλύμπου,
Νίκης εὐπολέμοιο πάτερ, συναρωγὲ Θέμιστος,
ἀντιβίοισι τύραννε, δικαιοτάτων ἀγὲ φωτῶν,
ἠνορέης σκηπτοῦχε, πυραυγέα κύκλον ἑλίσσων
αἰθέρος ἑπταπόροις ἐνὶ τείρεσιν, ἔνθα σε πῶλοι
ζαφλεγέες τριτάτης ὑπὲρ ἄντυγος αἰὲν ἔχουσι:
κλῦθι, βροτῶν ἐπίκουρε, δοτὴρ εὐθαρσέος ἥβης,
πρηὺ καταστίλβων σέλας ὑψόθεν ἐς βιότητα
ἡμετέρην καὶ κάρτος ἀρήιον, ὥς κε δυναίμην
σεύασθαι κακότητα πικρὴν ἀπ᾽ ἐμοῖο καρήνου,
καὶ ψυχῆς ἀπατηλὸν ὑπογνάμψαι φρεσὶν ὁρμήν,
θυμοῦ αὖ μένος ὀξὺ κατισχέμεν, ὅς μ᾽ ἐρέθησι
φυλόπιδος κρυερῆς ἐπιβαινέμεν: ἀλλὰ σὺ θάρσος
δός, μάκαρ, εἰρήνης τε μένειν ἐν ἀπήμοσι θεσμοῖς
δυσμενέων προφυγόντα μόθον Κῆράς τε βιαίους.

To Ares

Ares—exceedingly puissant, oppressor of chariots, golden
Helmeted, savior of garrisons, powerful-spirited, strong-armed
Shield-bearer clad in bronze armor, unwearied Olympian bulwark,
Strength of the javelin, father of Victory, happy in battle,
Ally of Justice and tyrant of enemies, leader of just men,
Sceptered commander of masculine virtue, revolving your fire-bright
Orb through the midst of the sevenfold path of the planets in aether
Where, incandescent, your coursers maintain you above the third orbit[5]—
Listen, defender of humans and giver of flourishing youth, let

---

5. The planet Mars was considered the "third star," or third of seven planets in a wandering course, by ancient Greeks, and occupied the third orbit above the earthly sphere.

Shine a propitious ray from above on the course of our lifetime,
Grant us your martial strength, to the end that I may be enabled
Once and for all to remove wretched cowardice far from my person,
Also to conquer within me the treacherous urge of my spirit;
Help me as well to control the sharp passionate temper provoking
Me to embark upon blood-chilling mayhem, and give me the courage,
Blest, to remain in the comfortable legal prescriptions of peacetime,
Thereby avoiding the conflict of foes and a violent ending.

The Song of Songs / שִׁיר הַשִּׁירִים
(c. THIRD CENTURY B.C.E.?)

THE SONG OF SONGS, WHICH is also known as the Song of Solomon or Canticles, is a suite of ancient near-Eastern erotic poems whose inclusion in the biblical canon has prompted millennia of interpretive debate. Across religious exegetical traditions, the book has been understood allegorically; the Jewish Midrash reads the Song as a figure for the love of God for the people of Israel, a love whose profound intimacy caused the ancient rabbis to describe the text as "the Holy of Holies," a literary version of the most sacred sanctum of the temple. The Song was regarded by Christian theologians either as a typological depiction of the relationship between Christ and the Church or as an allegory of the soul's relationship to Christ and God. The dating of the book's composition is uncertain, but scholars have identified in the Song some influence of Greek language and poetic conventions, which argues that it was composed when the Israelites were under Hellenistic rule; in any case, it seems to have been written some time after the historical Solomon's reign in the tenth century B.C.E. Again, the English text provided here is from the 1611 King James Bible.

Chapter 2

אֲנִי חֲבַצֶּלֶת הַשָּׁרוֹן שׁוֹשַׁנַּת הָעֲמָקִים׃
כְּשׁוֹשַׁנָּה בֵּין הַחוֹחִים כֵּן רַעְיָתִי בֵּין הַבָּנוֹת׃
כְּתַפּוּחַ בַּעֲצֵי הַיַּעַר כֵּן דּוֹדִי בֵּין הַבָּנִים בְּצִלּוֹ
חִמַּדְתִּי וְיָשַׁבְתִּי וּפִרְיוֹ מָתוֹק לְחִכִּי׃
הֱבִיאַנִי אֶל בֵּית הַיַּיִן וְדִגְלוֹ עָלַי אַהֲבָה׃
סַמְּכוּנִי בָּאֲשִׁישׁוֹת רַפְּדוּנִי בַּתַּפּוּחִים כִּי

חוֹלַת אַהֲבָה אָנִי:
שְׂמֹאלוֹ תַּחַת לְרֹאשִׁי וִימִינוֹ תְּחַבְּקֵנִי:
הִשְׁבַּעְתִּי אֶתְכֶם בְּנוֹת יְרוּשָׁלַ‍ִם בִּצְבָאוֹת
אוֹ בְּאַיְלוֹת הַשָּׂדֶה אִם תָּעִירוּ
וְאִם תְּעוֹרְרוּ אֶת הָאַהֲבָה עַד שֶׁתֶּחְפָּץ:
קוֹל דּוֹדִי הִנֵּה זֶה בָּא מְדַלֵּג עַל הֶהָרִים
מְקַפֵּץ עַל הַגְּבָעוֹת:
דּוֹמֶה דוֹדִי לִצְבִי אוֹ לְעֹפֶר הָאַיָּלִים הִנֵּה זֶה
עוֹמֵד אַחַר כָּתְלֵנוּ מַשְׁגִּיחַ מִן הַחַלֹּנוֹת מֵצִיץ מִן הַחֲרַכִּים:
עָנָה דוֹדִי וְאָמַר לִי קוּמִי לָךְ רַעְיָתִי יָפָתִי וּלְכִי לָךְ:
כִּי הִנֵּה הַסְּתָו עָבָר הַגֶּשֶׁם חָלַף הָלַךְ לוֹ:
הַנִּצָּנִים נִרְאוּ בָאָרֶץ עֵת הַזָּמִיר הִגִּיעַ וְקוֹל
הַתּוֹר נִשְׁמַע בְּאַרְצֵנוּ:
הַתְּאֵנָה חָנְטָה פַגֶּיהָ וְהַגְּפָנִים סְמָדַר נָתְנוּ
רֵיחַ קוּמִי לָךְ רַעְיָתִי יָפָתִי וּלְכִי לָךְ:
יוֹנָתִי בְּחַגְוֵי הַסֶּלַע בְּסֵתֶר הַמַּדְרֵגָה הַרְאִינִי
אֶת מַרְאַיִךְ הַשְׁמִיעִנִי אֶת קוֹלֵךְ כִּי קוֹלֵךְ עָרֵב וּמַרְאֵיךְ נָאוֶה:
אֶחֱזוּ לָנוּ שׁוּעָלִים שֻׁעָלִים קְטַנִּים מְחַבְּלִים
כְּרָמִים וּכְרָמֵינוּ סְמָדַר:
דּוֹדִי לִי וַאֲנִי לוֹ הָרֹעֶה בַּשּׁוֹשַׁנִּים:
עַד שֶׁיָּפוּחַ הַיּוֹם וְנָסוּ הַצְּלָלִים סֹב דְּמֵה לְךָ
דוֹדִי לִצְבִי אוֹ לְעֹפֶר הָאַיָּלִים עַל הָרֵי בָתֶר:

I Am the rose of Sharon, and the lillie of the valleys.

As the lillie among thornes, so is my loue among the daughters.

As the apple tree among the trees of the wood, so is my beloued among the sonnes.
I sate downe vnder his shadow with great delight, and his fruit was sweete to my
   taste.

Hee brought me to the banketting° house, and his banner ouer   *banquetting*
   mee, was loue.

Stay me with flagons, comfort me with apples, for I am sicke of loue.

His left hand is vnder my head, and his right hand doeth imbrace me.

I charge you, O ye daughters of Ierusalem, by the Roes
and by the hindes° of the field, that ye stirre not vp,   *deer*
   nor awake my loue, till she please.

The voice of my beloued! behold! hee commeth leaping vpon the mountaines,
   skipping vpon the hils.

My beloued is like a Roe, or a yong Hart: behold, he standeth behind our wall, he
  looketh foorth at the windowe, shewing himselfe through the lattesse.

My beloued spake, and said vnto me, Rise vp, my Loue, my faire one, and come
  away.

For loe, the winter is past, the raine is ouer, and gone.

The flowers appeare on the earth, the time of the singing of birds is come, and the
  voice of the turtle° is heard in our land.   *dove*

The fig tree putteth foorth her greene figs, and the vines with the tender grape giue a
  good smell. Arise, my loue, my faire one, and come away.

O my doue! that art in the clefts of the rocke, in the secret places of the staires: let me
  see thy countenance, let me heare thy voice, for sweet is thy voice, and thy counte-
  nance is comely.

Take vs the foxes, the litle foxes, that spoile the vines: for our vines haue tender
  grapes.

My beloued is mine, and I am his: he feedeth among the lillies.

Untill the day breake, and the shadowes flee away: turne my beloued and be thou like
  a Roe, or a yong Hart, vpon the mountaines of Bether.[6]

Chapter 4

הִנָּךְ יָפָה רַעְיָתִי הִנָּךְ יָפָה עֵינַיִךְ יוֹנִים מִבַּעַד
לְצַמָּתֵךְ שַׂעְרֵךְ כְּעֵדֶר הָעִזִּים שֶׁגָּלְשׁוּ מֵהַר גִּלְעָד:
שִׁנַּיִךְ כְּעֵדֶר הַקְּצוּבוֹת שֶׁעָלוּ מִן הָרַחְצָה
שֶׁכֻּלָּם מַתְאִימוֹת וְשַׁכֻּלָה אֵין בָּהֶם:
כְּחוּט הַשָּׁנִי שִׂפְתוֹתַיִךְ וּמִדְבָּרֵךְ נָאוֶה כְּפֶלַח
הָרִמּוֹן רַקָּתֵךְ מִבַּעַד לְצַמָּתֵךְ:
כְּמִגְדַּל דָּוִיד צַוָּארֵךְ בָּנוּי לְתַלְפִּיּוֹת אֶלֶף
הַמָּגֵן תָּלוּי עָלָיו כֹּל שִׁלְטֵי הַגִּבֹּרִים:
שְׁנֵי שָׁדַיִךְ כִּשְׁנֵי עֳפָרִים תְּאוֹמֵי צְבִיָּה
הָרֹעִים בַּשּׁוֹשַׁנִּים:
עַד שֶׁיָּפוּחַ הַיּוֹם וְנָסוּ הַצְּלָלִים אֵלֶךְ לִי אֶל
הַר הַמּוֹר וְאֶל גִּבְעַת הַלְּבוֹנָה:

---

6. Possibly Bithron, a hilly region east of the Jordan River; sometimes translated figuratively as either
  "the mountains of separation" or "the mountains of spices."

כֻּלָּךְ יָפָה רַעְיָתִי וּמוּם אֵין בָּךְ:
אִתִּי מִלְּבָנוֹן כַּלָּה אִתִּי מִלְּבָנוֹן תָּבוֹאִי תָּשׁוּרִי
מֵרֹאשׁ אֲמָנָה מֵרֹאשׁ שְׂנִיר וְחֶרְמוֹן מִמְּעֹנוֹת
אֲרָיוֹת מֵהַרְרֵי נְמֵרִים:
לִבַּבְתִּנִי אֲחֹתִי כַלָּה לִבַּבְתִּנִי בְּאַחַת
(בְּאַחַד כתיב)
מֵעֵינַיִךְ בְּאַחַד עֲנָק מִצַּוְּרֹנָיִךְ:
מַה יָּפוּ דֹדַיִךְ אֲחֹתִי כַלָּה מַה טֹּבוּ דֹדַיִךְ מִיַּיִן
וְרֵיחַ שְׁמָנַיִךְ מִכָּל בְּשָׂמִים:
נֹפֶת תִּטֹּפְנָה שִׂפְתוֹתַיִךְ כַּלָּה דְּבַשׁ וְחָלָב
תַּחַת לְשׁוֹנֵךְ וְרֵיחַ שַׂלְמֹתַיִךְ כְּרֵיחַ לְבָנוֹן:
גַּן נָעוּל אֲחֹתִי כַלָּה גַּל נָעוּל מַעְיָן חָתוּם:
שְׁלָחַיִךְ פַּרְדֵּס רִמּוֹנִים עִם פְּרִי מְגָדִים
כְּפָרִים עִם נְרָדִים:
נֵרְדְּ וְכַרְכֹּם קָנֶה וְקִנָּמוֹן עִם כָּל עֲצֵי
לְבוֹנָה מֹר וַאֲהָלוֹת עִם כָּל רָאשֵׁי בְשָׂמִים:
מַעְיַן גַּנִּים בְּאֵר מַיִם חַיִּים וְנֹזְלִים מִן לְבָנוֹן:
עוּרִי צָפוֹן וּבוֹאִי תֵימָן הָפִיחִי גַנִּי יִזְּלוּ
בְשָׂמָיו יָבֹא דוֹדִי לְגַנּוֹ וְיֹאכַל פְּרִי מְגָדָיו:

Behold, thou art faire, my loue, behold thou art faire, thou hast doues eyes within thy lockes: thy haire is as a flocke of goats, that appeare from mount Gilead.[7]

Thy teeth are like a flocke of sheepe that are euen shorne, which came vp from the washing: whereof euery one beare twinnes, and none is barren among them.

Thy lips are like a threed of scarlet, and thy speach is comely: thy temples are like a piece of a pomegranate within thy lockes.

Thy necke is like the tower of Dauid builded for an armorie, whereon there hang a thousand bucklers, all shields of mightie men.

Thy two breasts, are like two yong Roes, that are twinnes, which feed among the lillies.

Untill the day breake, and the shadowes flee away, I will get mee to the mountaines of myrrhe, and to the hill of frankincense.

---

7. Gilead is a mountainous region east of the Jordan River. Its name means "hill of witness." Metaphorically, it may signal eternity; alternatively, it may connote healing, for the Hebrew Bible contains many references to the "balm of Gilead," understanding the balsam carried from Gilead by the caravan of merchants to whom Joseph was sold by his brothers (see Genesis 37.25) as a healing agent (see Jeremiah 8.22).

Thou art all faire, my loue, there is no spot in thee.

Come with me from Lebanon (my spouse,) with me from Lebanon: looke from the top of Amana, from the top of Shenir and Hermon,[8] from the Lions dennes, from the mountaines of the Leopards.

Thou hast rauished my heart, my sister, my spouse; thou hast rauished my heart, with one of thine eyes, with one chaine of thy necke.

How faire is thy loue, my sister, my spouse! how much better is thy loue then wine! and the smell of thine oyntments then all spices!

Thy lips, O my spouse! drop as the hony combe: hony and milke are vnder thy tongue, and the smell of thy garments is like the smell of Lebanon.

A garden inclosed is my sister, my spouse: a spring shut vp, a fountaine sealed.

Thy plants are an orchard of pomegranates, with pleasant fruits, Camphire,° *camphor* with Spikenard, Spikenard and Saffron, Calamus and Cynamom,° *cinnamon* with all trees of Frankincense, Mirrhe and Aloes, with all the chiefe spices.
A fountaine of gardens, a well of liuing waters, and streames from Lebanon.

Awake, O Northwinde, and come thou South, blow vpon my garden, that the spices thereof may flow out: let my beloued come into his garden, and eate his pleasant fruits.

Lucretius
(c. 99–c. 55 b.c.e.)

WITH THIS PRAYER, TITUS Lucretius Carus, known to us as Lucretius, begins his epic philosophical poem *De rerum natura*, or *On the Nature of Things*. It is a noted paradox that Lucretius begins his work with this invocation to Venus, because the poem's stated purpose is to promote an Epicurean physics and to dissuade readers from seeking after supernatural explanations for worldly events. Lucretius argues rather that the operations of the world can be accounted for in terms of natural phenomena, and explains the motions of the universe as the effect of atoms upon one another. Whether Lucretius is merely following a well-established epic convention or allegorizing the

---

8. These names seem to refer to peaks in the Anti-Lebanon range, between Syria and Lebanon.

abundant life-force of nature in the person of the goddess of sexual love and genera-tion, his invocation teems with life, and frames the active world explored in the poem that follows. The translation that appears here, by poet and English Civil War biogra-pher Lucy Hutchinson (1620–1681), may have been the first in English.

from *De rerum natura*
LINES 1–25

Aeneadum genetrix, hominum divomque voluptas,
alma Venus, caeli subter labentia signa
quae mare navigerum, quae terras frugiferentis
concelebras, per te quoniam genus omne animantum
concipitur visitque exortum lumina solis:
te, dea, te fugiunt venti, te nubila caeli
adventumque tuum, tibi suavis daedala tellus
summittit flores, tibi rident aequora ponti
placatumque nitet diffuso lumine caelum.
nam simul ac species patefactast verna diei
et reserata viget genitabilis aura favoni,
aeriae primum volucris te, diva, tuumque
significant initum perculsae corda tua vi.
inde ferae pecudes persultant pabula laeta
et rapidos tranant amnis: ita capta lepore
te sequitur cupide quo quamque inducere pergis.
denique per maria ac montis fluviosque rapacis
frondiferasque domos avium camposque virentis
omnibus incutiens blandum per pectora amorem
efficis ut cupide generatim saecla propagent.
quae quoniam rerum naturam sola gubernas
nec sine te quicquam dias in luminis oras
exoritur neque fit laetum neque amabile quicquam,
te sociam studeo scribendis versibus esse,
quos ego de rerum natura pangere.

Faire Venus mother of Æneas race[9]
Delight of gods and men thou that doest grace
The starrie firmament, the sea, the earth

---

9. The goddess was legendarily the mother of the Trojan hero Æneas, the founder of Rome.

To whom all living creatures owe their birth
By thee conceivd, and brought forth to the day,
When thou (O Goddesse) comest stormes flie away
And heaven is no more obscur'd with showres.
For thee the fragrant earth spreads various flowers
The calmed ocean smiles, and att thy sight
The serene skie shines with augmented light.
Then doth the spring her glorious days disclose
And the releast, life-giving westwind blowes.
Thy power possessing first birds of the ayre
They thy approach with amorous noates declare,
Next when desires the savage heard incite
They swim through streames, and their fat pastures slight
To follow thee, who in seas, rivers, hills
In the birds leavie bowers, and in greene fields
Instilling wanton love into each mind,
Mak'st creatures strive to propagate their kind.
Since all things thus are brought to light by thee,
By whom alone their natures governd bee,
From whom both lovelinesse and pleasure springs,
Assist me while the nature of these things
I sing.

Horace

(65–8 B.C.E.)

QUINTUS HORATIUS FLACCUS was born in Venusia, in the boot-heel of what is now
Italy. His father sent the young Horace to be educated first in Rome and then in Athens.
He joined the army of Brutus after the assassination of Julius Caesar, and fought on
the losing side at the battle of Philippi, against Octavian (later Caesar Augustus). He
returned to Rome, where he was befriended by Virgil, who introduced him to his own
patron, Maecenas. Horace's literary legacy includes early Satires and Epodes, two
books of Epistles, and four monumental books of Odes. Horace's own name for this
last group of lyrics was *carminae,* or songs. Ode 1.31 appears here as translated by
American poet W. S. Merwin (b. 1927); Ode 3.22 by American classicist and poet John
Talbot (b. 1966).

Carmina 1.31

Quid dedicatum poscit Apollinem
vates? Quid orat, de patera novum
      fundens liquorem? Non opimae
        Sardiniae segetes feraces,

non aestuosae grata Calabriae
armenta, non aurum aut ebur Indicum,
      non rura, quae Liris quieta
        mordet aqua taciturnus amnis.

Premant Calena falce quibus dedit
Fortuna vitem, dives et aureis
      mercator exsiccet culillis
        vina Syra reparata merce,

dis carus ipsis, quippe ter et quater
anno revisens aequor Atlanticum
      inpune: me pascust olivae,
        me cichorea levesque malvae.

Frui paratis et valido mihi,
Latoe, dones, at, precor, integra
      cum mente, nec turpem senectam
        degere nec cithara carentem.

Ode 1.31

What does a poet ask at the new temple
to Apollo,[10] and pray to have when pouring
      new wine from the bowl? Not for the piled
        harvests of opulent Sardinia

nor the contented herds in the warm climate
of Calabria, nor Indian gold or
      ivory, nor fields that the Liris
        wears away softly with its wordless flow.

---

10. The son of the nymph Latona, Apollo was the Greek and Roman god of the sun, of light, and of music and poetry, whose temple on the Palatine hill was built and dedicated by Caesar Augustus about five years before the composition of this poem.

Let those for whom Fortune provided it use
the pruning knife of Cales so that the rich
      merchant may drink from a golden bowl
        wine paid for with trade goods from Syria.[11]

The gods seem to love that man. Three or four times
a year he sails out onto the Atlantic
      and survives. My own fare of olives,
        endives and light mallow root suits me best.

Son of Latona, let me take pleasure in
what I have, keeping the health of my body
      and mind through a dignified old age,
        not lacking honor, or songs, to the end.

Carmina 3.22

Montium custos nemorumque, virgo,
quae laborantis utero puellas
ter vocata audis adimisque leto,
      diva triformis,

inminens villae tua pinus esto,
quam per exactos ego laetus annos
verris obliquum meditantis ictum
      sanguine donem.

Ode 3.22

Keeper of mountaintops. Guardian of the groves.
Virgin. By girls in childbirth's hard press
cried out for, thrice. You hear, you spare their lives.
      Three-personed goddess,[12]

---

11. This poem references several place-names from what is now the Italian peninsula to indicate the best
and richest of climates: Calabria in southern Italy, and the Liris or Garigliano River and the town
Cales, both in modern Campania.

12. Diana Nemorensis, or Diana of the Wood, was conceived as having three aspects: as goddess of the
Moon, goddess of the underworld, and the virgin huntress-goddess. She was invoked to aid mothers
in childbirth.

sponsor this pine that overhangs my door.
I'll seal that pledge with annual blood—a little
boar's, still practicing his feint and spar,
        who'll never see battle.

The Gospel According to Luke / τὸ εὐαγγέλιον κατὰ Λουκᾶν
(c. 60–80 c.e.)

THE AUTHOR OF THE GOSPEL of Luke, probably a gentile (that is, Greek) Christian, intended his narrative for the Greek-speaking populations of the ancient world. His report of the life of Jesus is based not on eyewitness experience but on existing sources, including the Gospel of Mark. Luke's Gospel contains a wide variety of literary forms, indicating that its author was a well-read and inventive writer. In the lyric printed here, which contains allusions to a number of Hebrew scriptures (including the books of Genesis, Samuel, Job, the Psalms, Isaiah, and Habakkuk), Mary, the mother of Jesus, meditates in verse on the news that she is to give birth to the Son of God. Also known as the Song or Canticle of Mary, this poem is often included in evening prayer services; its familiar name from long liturgical use is the *Magnificat*, from the first word of the poem in its Latin translation. Again, for its wide familiarity and its influence on the English literary tradition, the 1611 King James Bible is the source of the translation here.

Luke 1.46–55 (The *Magnificat*)

Καὶ εἶπεν Μαριάμ· Μεγαλύνει ἡ ψυχή μου τὸν Κύριον.
καὶ ἠγαλλίασεν τὸ πνεῦμά μου ἐπὶ τῷ Θεῷ τῷ σωτῆρί μου,
ὅτι ἐπέβλεψεν ἐπὶ τὴν ταπείνωσιν τῆς δούλης αὐτοῦ. ἰδοὺ γὰρ ἀπὸ τοῦ νῦν
    μακαριοῦσίν με πᾶσαι αἱ γενεαί.
ὅτι ἐποίησέν μοι μεγάλα ὁ δυνατὸς καὶ ἅγιον τὸ ὄνομα αὐτοῦ,
καὶ τὸ ἔλεος αὐτοῦ εἰς γενεὰς γενεῶν τοῖς φοβουμένοις αὐτόν.
Ἐποίησεν κράτος ἐν βραχίονι αὐτοῦ, διεσκόρπισεν ὑπερηφάνους διανοίᾳ
    καρδίας αὐτῶν·
καθεῖλεν δυνάστας ἀπὸ θρόνων καὶ ὕψωσεν ταπεινούς,

πεινῶντας ἐνέπλησεν ἀγαθῶν καὶ πλουτοῦντας ἐξαπέστειλεν κενούς.
ἀντελάβετο Ἰσραὴλ παιδὸς αὐτοῦ, μνησθῆναι ἐλέους,
καθὼς ἐλάλησεν πρὸς τοὺς πατέρας ἡμῶν, τῷ Ἀβραὰμ καὶ τῷ σπέρματι αὐτοῦ
    εἰς τὸν αἰῶνα.

And Marie said, My soule doth magnifie the Lord.
And my spirit hath reioyced in God my sauiour.
For hee hath regarded the low estate of his handmaiden:
for behold, from hencefoorth all generations shall call me blessed.
For he that is mighty hath done to mee great things, and holy is his Name.
And his mercy is on them that feare him, from generation to generation.
Hee hath shewed strength with his arme, he hath scattered the proud,
in the imagination of their hearts.
He hath put downe the mighty from their seates, and exalted them of low degree.
Hee hath filled the hungry with good things, and the rich hee hath sent emptie away.
Hee hath holpen° his seruant Israel, in remembrance of his mercy,   *helped*
As he spake to our fathers, to Abraham, and to his seed for euer.

2

Early Christian Lyrics Through the Fifteenth Century

WHAT WOULD BECOME, DURING the early modern period, a strong English lyric culture grew out of both classical and Germanic poetic traditions. Though early Christian communities harbored some suspicion about classical poetry, viewing it as idolatrous and its rhetoric as more concerned with self-congratulatory beauty than with truth, nevertheless the rise of religious poetry in the ante-Nicene period was aided by the increasing number of educated Romans converting to Christianity, and by a growing recognition of the literary value of the Bible with its trove of figures and rhetorical flourishes. As Christianity expanded across Europe, its classically inflected poetic repertoire was brought into contact with the rich traditions of oral poetry and song among the Germanic peoples. This cultural exchange ensured that the orally transmitted compositions of northern Europe would be preserved and carried beyond their communities of origin, copied out by hand. Indeed, much of the extant poetry from the second century through the medieval period was written, or written down, by theologians and monks, the work preserved within the scribal culture of monastic Christianity.

In addition to writing prose theological treatises, many theologians of the early medieval period grappled with spiritual concerns in poetry. These poems appear in Latin, but are influenced by vernacular song structures. In the twelfth century, an emphasis on the affective aspects of faith led to an increased priority on expressing spiritual feelings in vernacular poetry. The Franciscan monastic order, which reached

England in the thirteenth century, focused on the heart as the site of primary spiritual experience, and the religious lyric proved an effective tool for moving audiences. The Franciscans wrote for two kinds of audience—the educated clergy and the illiterate lay folk—and devotional poetry, which was increasingly composed in the vernacular rather than in Latin, provided a point of access for listeners across the spectrum of literacy.

The very circumstances that preserved these early poems also produced some instability. The composers of medieval vernacular lyrics were often unknown even to medieval scribes, who frequently worked from memory, incorporating unintentional variations as well as intentional "improvements." In many cases, these poems survive in unique versions, but at times they exist in a number of different versions. In the case of such variants, we have attempted to select here texts that seem to be most nearly complete and readable. And while examples of devotional poetry can be found throughout continental Europe, we have here selected poems with particular connections to the tradition of poetry in English, whether because their authors come from what is now England or because the texts in question, or their authors, were widely influential in the formation of English spirituality. Finally, though the hymnic mode is yet dominant in the aesthetic culture of early and medieval Christianity, we focus here on poems that demonstrate the personal affective negotiations of an emerging lyric tradition.

FURTHER READING

Bestul, Thomas H. *Texts of the Passion: Latin Devotional Literature and Medieval Society.* Philadelphia: University of Pennsylvania Press, 1996.

Brown, Carleton. *English Lyrics of the Thirteenth Century.* Oxford: Clarendon, 1932.

———. *Religious Lyrics of the XIVth Century.* Oxford: Clarendon, 1924.

———. *Religious Lyrics of the XVth Century.* Oxford: Clarendon, 1939.

Curtius, Ernst Robert. *European Literature and the Latin Middle Ages.* Princeton: Princeton University Press, 1991.

Den Boeft, J., and A. Hilhorst, eds. *Early Christian Poetry: A Collection of Essays.* Leiden: E. J. Brill, 1993.

Dronke, Peter. *The Medieval Lyric.* Rochester, N.Y.: Brewer, 1968.

Garde, Judith N. *Old English Poetry in Medieval Christian Perspective: A Doctrinal Approach.* Rochester, N.Y.: Brewer, 1991.

Huppé, Bernard F. *Doctrine and Poetry: Augustine's Influence on Old English Poetry.* Albany: State University of New York Press, 1959.

Jeffrey, David L. *The Early English Lyric and Franciscan Spirituality.* Lincoln: University of Nebraska Press, 1975.

Clement of Alexandria

(c. 150–c. 215)

TITUS FLAVIUS CLEMENS WAS born, according to some ancient sources, in Athens, and converted to Christianity. He became a prominent early Christian theologian, and he taught at the Catechetical School of Alexandria. His major works are theological treatises urging Greeks to adopt Christianity and offering the figure of Jesus as the great teacher of humankind. Appended to one of these long prose works, the Παιδαγωγος, or *Instructor,* was this hymn. Victorian poet Elizabeth Barrett Browning (1806–1861) provides a vivid translation of the first half of the poem; the balance is supplied by nineteenth-century scholars Alexander Roberts (1826–1901) and James Donaldson (1831–1915), from an 1867 translation.

Ὑμνος του σωτηρος Χριστου του αγιου Κλημεντος

Στόμιον πώλων ἀδαῶν,
πτερὸν ὀρνίθων ἀπλανῶν,
οἴαξ νηῶν ἀτρεκής,
ποιμὴν ἀρνῶν βασιλικῶν·
τοὺς σοὺς ἀφελεῖς
παῖδας ἄγειρον,
αἰνεῖν ἁγίως,
ὑμνεῖν ἀδόλως

ἀκάκοις στόμασιν
παίδων ἡγήτορα Χριστόν.
Βασιλεῦ ἁγίων,
λόγε πανδαμάτωρ
πατρὸς ὑψίστου,
σοφίας πρύτανι,
στήριγμα πόνων
αἰωνοχαρές,
βροτέας γενεᾶς
σῶτερ Ἰησοῦ,
ποιμήν, ἀροτήρ,
οἴαξ, στόμιον,
πτερὸν οὐράνιον
παναγοῦς ποίμνης,
ἁλιεῦ μερόπων
τῶν σῳζομένων
πελάγους κακίας,
ἰχθῦς ἁγνοὺς
κύματος ἐχθροῦ
γλυκερῇ ζωῇ δελεάζων.
Προβάτων
λογικῶν ποιμὴν
ἅγιε, ἡγοῦ,
βασιλεῦ παίδων ἀνεπάφων·
ἴχνια Χριστοῦ
ὁδὸς οὐρανία.
Λόγος ἀέναος,
αἰὼν ἄπλετος,
φῶς ἀίδιον,
ἐλέους πηγή,
ῥεκτὴρ ἀρετῆς
σεμνῇ βιοτῇ
θεὸν ὑμνούντων.
Χριστὲ Ἰησοῦ,
γάλα οὐράνιον
μαστῶν γλυκερῶν
νύμφης χαρίτων
σοφίας τῆς σῆς,
ἐκθλιβόμενον.
Οἱ νηπίαχοι

ἀταλοῖς στόμασιν
ἀτιταλλόμενοι,
θηλῆς λογικῆς
πνεύματι δροσερῷ
ἐμπιμπλάμενοι,
αἴνους ἀφελεῖς,
ὕμνους ἀτρεκεῖς
βασιλεῖ Χριστῷ,
μισθοὺς ὁσίους
ζωῆς διδαχῆς,
μέλπωμεν ὁμοῦ.
πέμπωμεν ἁπλῶς
παῖδα κρατερόν,
χορὸς εἰρήνης
οἱ χριστόγονοι,
λαὸς σώφρων,
ψάλλωμεν ὁμοῦ
θεὸν εἰρήνης.

Ode to the Saviour Christ

Curb for wild horses,
Wing for bird-courses
Never yet flown!
Helm, sage for weak ones,
Shepherd, bespeak once,
The young lambs thine own.
Rouse up the youth,
Shepherd and feeder,
So let them bless thee,
Praise and confess thee,—
Pure words on pure mouth,—
Christ, the child-leader!
O, the saints' Lord,
All-dominant word!
Holding, by Christdom,
God's highest wisdom!
Column in place
When sorrows seize us,—

Endless in grace
Unto man's race,
Saving one, Jesus!
Pastor and ploughman,
Helm, curb, together,—
Pinion that now can
(Heavenly of feather)
Raise and release us!
Fisher who catcheth
Those whom he watcheth
From the hateful wave
Of a sea of vices.

Guide, Shepherd
of rational sheep;
guide unharmed children,
O holy King,
O footsteps of Christ,
O heavenly way,
perennial Word,
immeasurable Age,
Eternal Light,
Fount of mercy,
performer of virtue;
noble the life
of those who hymn God,
O Christ Jesus,
heavenly milk
of the sweet breasts
of the graces of the Bride,
pressed out
of Thy wisdom.
Babes nourished
with tender mouths,
filled with the dewy spirit
of the rational pap,
let us sing together
simple praises,
true hymns
to Christ King,

holy fee
for the teaching of life;
let us sing
in simplicity
the powerful Child.
O choir of peace,
the Christ-begotten,
O chaste people,
let us sing together
the God of peace.

Gregory of Nazianzus
(c. 329–c. 390)

GREGORY WAS BORN TO WEALTHY parents in Cappadocia, a Roman province of what is now Turkey. His mother converted the family to Christianity. Gregory studied rhetoric and philosophy in major centers of learning in the ancient world, including Alexandria and Athens. He served as a presbyter in his hometown of Nazianzus, as Bishop of Sasima, and eventually as Archbishop of Constantinople. He wrote a number of theological works, most notably concerning the doctrine of the Trinity and the nature of the Holy Spirit. In addition to his many theological discourses, he wrote several poems. His work was translated into Latin and became influential throughout the early Christian church. The English version here is by Scottish cleric John Brownlie (1857–1925), who translated many books of early Christian verse.

Πρὸς ἑσπέραν θρῆνος

Ἐψευσάμην σε. τὴν ἀλήθειαν, Λόγε,
Σοὶ τὴν παροῦσαν ἡμέραν καθαγνίσας.
Οὐ πάντα φωτεινόν
με νὺξ ἐδέξατο.
Ἦ μὴν προσηυξάμην
τε καὶ τοῦτ᾽ ᾠόμην·
Ἀλλ᾽ ἔστιν οὗ μοι

καὶ προσέπταισαν πόδες.
Ζόφος γὰρ ἦλθε
βάσκανος σωτηρίας.
Λάμποις τὸ φῶς μοι, Χριστὲ,
καὶ πάλιν φανείς.

An Evening Hymn

O Word of Truth! in devious paths
    My wayward feet have trod;
I have not kept the day serene
    I gave at morn to God.

And now 'tis night, and night within;
    O God, the light hath fled!
I have not kept the vow I made
    When morn its glories shed.

For clouds of gloom from nether world
    Obscured my upward way;
O Christ the Light, Thy light bestow
    And turn my night to day!

Ambrose of Milan
(340–397)

AURELIUS AMBROSIUS WAS BORN into a Roman Christian family in what is now western Germany. Educated in Rome, Ambrose served as consular prefect, or governor, of a region of northern Italy, headquartered in Milan. After helping to quell a doctrinal conflict among early Christian sects, he was pressured to become Bishop of Rome, despite never having been baptized. After a hasty baptism, he took up the bishopric. His subsequent theological work helped to stabilize the developing doctrine of an institutional Christian church. He wrote many exegetical treatises on various aspects of theology and doctrine, as well as a number of hymns. Augustine credits Ambrose as an influence upon his own conversion. This translation is by English cleric William John Copeland (1804–1885), and was published in his *Hymns for the Week, &c.* in 1848.

Aeterne rerum conditor,
noctem diemque qui regis,
et temporum das tempora,
ut alleves fastidium;

Praeco diei iam sonat,
noctis profundae pervigil,
nocturna lux viantibus
a nocte noctem segregans.

Hoc excitatus lucifer
solvit polum caligine,
hoc omnis erronum chorus
vias nocendi deserit.

Hoc nauta vires colligit
pontique mitescunt freta,
hoc ipsa petra ecclesiae
canente culpam diluit.

Surgamus ergo strenue!
Gallus iacentes excitat,
et somnolentos increpat,
Gallus negantes arguit.

Gallo canente spes redit,
aegris salus refunditur,
mucro latronis conditur,
lapsis fides revertitur.

Iesu, labantes respice,
et nos videndo corrige,
si respicis, lapsus cadunt,
fletuque culpa solvitur.

Tu lux refulge sensibus,
mentisque somnum discute,
te nostra vox primum sonet
et ore psallamus tibi.

Sit, Christe, Rex piissime,
tibi Patrique gloria
cum Spiritu Paraclito,
in sempiterna saecula. Amen.

Maker of all, eternal King,
who day and night about dost bring:
who weary mortals to relieve,
dost in their times the seasons give:

Now the shrill cock proclaims the day,
and calls the sun's awakening ray,
the wandering pilgrim's guiding light,
that marks the watches night by night.

Roused at the note, the morning star
heaven's dusky veil uplifts afar:
night's vagrant bands no longer roam,
but from their dark ways hie them home.

The encouraged sailor's fears are o'er,
the foaming billows rage no more:
Lo! e'en the very Church's Rock
melts at the crowing of the cock.

O let us then like men arise;
the cock rebukes our slumbering eyes,
bestirs who still in sleep would lie,
and shames who would their Lord deny.

New hope his clarion note awakes,
sickness the feeble frame forsakes,
the robber sheathes his lawless sword,
faith to fallen is restored.

Look in us, Jesu, when we fall,
and with Thy look our souls recall:
if Thou but look, our sins are gone,
and with due tears our pardon won.

Shed through our hearts Thy piercing ray,
our soul's dull slumber drive away:
Thy Name be first on every tongue,
to Thee our earliest praises sung.

All laud to God the Father be;
all praise, Eternal Son, to Thee;
all glory, as is ever meet,
to God the Holy Paraclete. Amen.

Prudentius
(348–c. 413)

AURELIUS PRUDENTIUS CLEMENS was born in what is now northern Spain. He was a lawyer and governor before serving in the court of the Roman emperor Theodosius I, but he retired in later life to become a religious ascetic. His work includes a number of poems and hymns, a few of which are still familiar today, including the Christmas hymn translated as "Of the Father's Love Begotten." His allegorical poem *Psychomachia* would deeply influence the allegorical literature of the medieval period. The poem included below concludes his collection of hymns on the liturgical hours. The translation is by English Wesleyan minister Robert Martin Pope (1865–1944).

Epilogus

Inmolat Deo Patri
pius, fidelis, innocens, pudicus
dona conscientiae,
quibus beata mens abundat intus:
alter et pecuniam
recidit, unde victitent egeni.
Nos citos iambicos
sacramus et rotatiles trochaeos,
sanctitatis indigi
nec ad levamen pauperum potentes;
adprobat tamen Deus
pedestre carmen, et benignus audit.
Multa divitis domo
sita est per omnes angulos supellex.
Fulget aureus scyphus,
nec aere defit expolita pelvis:
est et olla fictilis,
gravisque et ampla argentea est parabsis.
Sunt eburna quaepiam,
nonnulla quercu sunt cavata et ulmo:
omne vas fit utile,
quod est ad usum congruens herilem,

Instruunt enim domum
ut empta magno, sic parata ligno.
Me paterno in atrio
ut obsoletum vasculum caducis
Christus aptat usibus,
sinitque parte in anguli manere.
Munus ecce fictile
inimus intra regiam salutis;
attamen vel infimam
Deo obsequelam praestitisse prodest.
Quidquid illud accidit,
iuvabit ore personasse Christum.

Epilogue

The pure and faithful saint, whose heart is whole,
    To God the Father makes his sacrifice
From out the treasures of a stainless soul,
    Glad gifts of innocence, beyond all price:
Another with free hand bestows his gold,
    Whereby his needy neighbour may be fed.
No wealth of holiness my heart doth hold,
    No store have I to buy my brothers bread:
So here I humbly dedicate to Thee
    The rolling trochee and iambus swift;
Thou wilt approve my simple minstrelsy,
    Thine ear will listen to Thy servant's gift.
The rich man's halls are nobly furnishèd;
    Therein no nook or corner empty seems;
Here stands the brazen laver burnishèd,
    And there the golden goblet brightly gleams;
Hard by some crock of clumsy earthen ware,
    Massive and ample lies a silver plate;
And rough-hewn cups of oak or elm are there
    With vases carved of ivory delicate.
Yet every vessel in its place is good,
    So be it for the Master's service meet;
The priceless salver and the bowl of wood

Alike He needs to make His home complete.
Therefore within His Father's spacious hall
    Christ fits me for the service of a day,
Mean though I be, a vessel poor and small,—
    And in some lowly corner lets me stay.
Lo in the palace of the King of Kings
    I play the earthen pitcher's humble part;
Yet to have done Him meanest service brings
    A thrill of rapture to my thankful heart:
Whate'er the end, this thought will joy afford,
    My lips have sung the praises of my Lord.

Cædmon
(fl. c. 657)

PROBABLY THE EARLIEST SURVIVING Old English poem, Cædmon's Hymn was recorded in the Latin *Historia ecclesiastica gentis Anglorum,* or *Ecclesiastical History of the English People,* by a Northumbrian monk named Bede. In the course of relating the spread of Christianity and the development of the English church, Bede tells how Cædmon, an illiterate Anglo-Saxon who cared for animals at the monastery of Streonæshalch (Whitby Abbey) at the time of St. Hilda (614–680), was miraculously inspired with the gift of song. Legend tells us that the rustic later became a monk and religious poet. Cædmon's poem marries the alliterative meter of vernacular Anglo-Saxon heroic verse to religious themes. There are seventeen different extant manuscripts of Cædmon's Hymn in a number of dialects. This Northumbrian version is the oldest known version of the poem, dating to around 737; it survives in Cambridge University Library's MS. Kk 5.16 ["Moore"].

Cædmon's Hymn

Nu scylun hergan hefaenricaes uard
metudæs maecti end his modgidanc
uerc uuldurfadur sue he uundra gihuaes

eci dryctin or astelidæ.
he aerist scop aelda barnum
heben til hrofe haleg scepen;
tha middungeard moncynnæs uard
eci dryctin æfter tiadæ
firum foldu frea allmectig

Now must we praise heaven-kingdom's guardian,
the measurer's might and his mind-thoughts,
the work of the Gloryfather, how he of each wonder,
Eternal Lord, established a beginning.
He first shaped for men's sons
heaven as a roof, the Holy Shaper;
then middle-earth mankind's guardian
Eternal Lord, afterward made
the earth for men, Lord Almighty.

Alcuin
(c. 735–804)

ALCUIN WAS BORN IN NORTHUMBRIA, an early medieval kingdom in the north-east of what is now England. He came to York at an early age, where he came under the tutelage of Archbishop Ecgbert, who had himself been a disciple of the Venerable Bede. In York, Alcuin became learned in classical poetry, as well as in the classical educative disciplines including grammar, logic, music, mathematics, and astronomy. He later joined Charlemagne's court, where as the head of the Palace School for the last two decades of the eighth century he became a spearhead figure of the Carolingian Renaissance, a period of intellectual and cultural revival in eighth- and ninth-century Europe. Alcuin's poem "De Sancta Cruce," or "On the Holy Cross," reflects his inspiration by classical verse as well as his investment in rigorous intellectual activity. The poem turns upon a number of acrostics (printed in this volume in boldface) along the horizontal and vertical margins of the text, down and across the center axes, and diagonally through each quadrant of the poem, according to the following pattern:

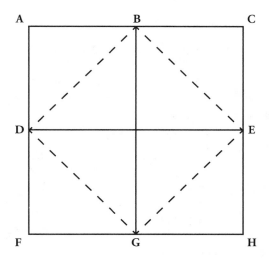

The acrostic lines supplement the linear argument of the poem, both in form and in content.

The frame:

Line 1 (a–c): Crux decus es mundi Iessu de sanguine sancta ("Cross, you are the glory of the world, in Jesus's blood sanctified.")

Line 37 (f–h): Suscipe sic talem rubicundam celsa coronam ("Accept, exalted cross, from me this scarlet crown.")

The initial letters of each line (a–f): Crux pia vera salus partes in quatuor orbis ("Pious cross, true salvation in the four corners of the world.")

The terminal letters of each line (c–h): Alma teneto tuam Christo dominane coronam ("Beneficent, take your crown, Christ being the Lord.")

The cross:

Line 19 (d–e): Rector in orbe tuis sanavit saecla sigillis ("The ruler of the world saved generations by your sign.")

Vertical center line (b–g): Surge lavanda tuae sunt saecula fonte fidei ("Rise, the world is cleansed in the font of faith.")

The diamond upon which the cross is inscribed, representing the world (whose four corners are referenced in the left-marginal acrostic):

Left hemisphere (b–d–g): Salve sancta rubens, fregisti vincula mundi ("Hail holy scarlet, you have shattered the world's shackles")

Right hemisphere (b–e–g): Signa valete novis reserata salutibus orbi ("Wonders are manifest, revealed anew to the world in saving works.")

De Sancta Cruce

```
CRUXDECUSESMUNDIIESSUDESANGUINESANCTA
REXDEUSEXCRUCEDONAVITCAELESTETRIBUNAL
VICTORTOLLENDOMALAREGNATVICITETHOSTEM
XRISTUSNOSTRACRUCIGRANDISENHOSTIAFIXA
PASTOROVESMORIENSDEXTRASANANTEREDEMIT
INCLYTASANCTASALUSLIGNIVENERABILISORE
ABSOLVENDOTRAHITPRAEDAMCARNALELIGAMEN
VINCTUSENIMNOSREXSUMMUSSOLVEBATETIPSE
EXTRADENDOCRUCIVITAMDEMORTETHRIUMPHAT
REGIASANCTAPATETMUNDISICHOSTEPEREMPTO
AMPLIUSHAECTOTOLAUDANDAVIGOREPATEBUNT
SIGNAGERENDABONISNAMCERNANTOMNIASENSU
ALTIUSUTVIDEANTQUOTSOLVITPASSIOSANCTA
LUCTIBUSAETERNISUNUMQUEATEMPOREVICTUM
UTPRESSOSPLAGISSANARETABHOSTISETISTIC
SITNUNCNOSTRASALUSEXCELSUSVERUSIOSEPH
PASSUSINARCECRUCISSICNESEDUCERETERROR
AFFICIENSHOMINESTRUDENSQUEEXLUCEFIDEI
RECTORINORBETUISSANAVITSAECLASIGILLIS
TEMEAVITASALUSTIBITANTUMCANTICACONDET
ETGENEROSACANETVOXSEMPERCARMINAAPERTO
SILICEATPLECTROQUIACLARUSCARMINEDAVID
INSISTENDOPROBATPRETIOSOSANCTACOTURNO
NOBISTESTIFICAREDECENSESSEINDEPARATUM
QUEMPRIMUMINCOEPITUCHRISTISUMESUPERNI
VERASALUSCALAMUMTULUXPIASANCTAQUEDEIN
ALMACRUCISVEXILLACANUNTGENTILIASAECLA
TOTATREMENSTELLUSEFFERTURETUNITENOMEN
TESTIFICATCRUCISENORANSSUBTILIAPANDIT
VISCERANUNCVANUSCONFOSSUSINIQUUSAVETE
OMNIPOTENSFULGETSITCORDEBEATAFIDESNEC
RURSUSYLIDRUSAGATVETERIVTPECTORARETRO
OPTIMUSADREGNUMNOSFIDUSETILLEREDEMTOR
REDDIDITETRIGIDUMSIGNOSUPERAVITINISTO
BELLIGERUMEVERTENSDEREGNISORTESATANAN
INCLYTACRUXMUNDUSDEBETTIBISOLVEREVOTA
SUSCIPESICTALEMRUBICUNDAMCELSACORONAM
```

Crux decus es mundi Iessu de sanguine sancta
Rex dues ex cruce donavit caeleste tribunal
Victor tollendo mala regnat vicit et hostem
Xristus nostra cruci grandis en hostia fixa
Pastor oves moriens dextra sanante redemit
Inclyta sancta salus ligni venerabilis ore
Absolvendo trahit praedam carnale ligamen
Vinctus enim nos rex summus solvebat et ipse
Ex tradendo cruci vitam de morte triumphat
Regia sancta patet mundi sic hoste perempto
Amplius haec toto laudanda vigore patebunt
Signa gerenda bonis nam cernent omnia sensu
Altius ut videant quot solvit passio sancta
Luctibus aeternis unumque a tempore victum
Ut pressos plagis sanaret ab hostis et istic
Sit nunc nostra salus excelsus verus Ioseph
Passus in arce cruces sic ne seduceret error
Afficiens homines trudensque ex luce fidei
Rector in orbe tuis sanavit saecla sigillis
Te mea vita salus. Tibi tantum cantica condet
Et generosa canet vox semper carmina aperto
Si liceat plectro quia clarus carmine David
Insistendo probat pretioso sancta coturno
Nobis testificare decens esse inde paratum
Quem primum incoepi tu Christi sume superni
Vera salus calamum tu lux pia sanctaque. Dein
Alma cruces vexilla canunt gentilia saecla
Tota tremens tellus effertur et unite nomen
Testificat cruces. En orans subtilia pandit
Viscera nunc vanus confossus iniquus avete
Omnipotens fulget. Sit corde beata fides nec
Rursus ylidrus agat veteri ut pectora retro
Optimus ad regnum nos fidus et ille redemtor
Reddidit et rigidum signo superavit in isto
Belligerum evertens de regni sorte Satanan
Inclyta crux mundus debet tibi solvere vota
Suscipe sic talem rubicundam celsa coronam.

On the Holy Cross

Cross, you are the glory of the world, in Jesus's blood sanctified.
God the king from the cross conveyed heaven's judgment.
A victor he reigns, destroying evil and conquering the enemy,
Christ the great sacrifice nailed on the cross for us.
The shepherd by dying redeemed his sheep with his healing right hand.
Glorious, holy salvation from the venerable tree,
he seized the prize, shrugging off the ties of flesh.
Though in bonds the highest king freed us, and he himself
giving his life to the cross triumphed over death.
The kingdom of heaven gaped when the world's enemy was destroyed.
The sign will be more manifest and all good people will wear it,
praising it with all strength; let all discern more profoundly
so that they may see how many his holy passion frees
from eternal sorrow, and see one thrown down by time
to heal those oppressed by the enemy's torments; there
may the highest and true Joseph now be our salvation,[1]
who suffered high upon the cross such that error can't seduce
and poison men and drag them from the light of faith.
The ruler of the world saved generations by your sign.
You, my life, my salvation! For you alone my voice composes hymns,
and shall sing always the highest songs, clear and plain
with the plectrum; for David famous for his song
proves that it is proper for us to testify holiness continually
in elaborate style—accept that which I have just begun, O Christ supernal,
true salvation, great sufferer, you sacred and holy light. Now
the secular nations sing the beneficent sign of the cross,
all the earth trembles and in one accord proclaims
the fame of the cross. In prayer it reveals its inmost heart.
Now hear, vain men, confounded in evil:
The almighty shines forth. May blessed faith fill your hearts
and the serpent not drive them back to their old ways.
The highest and most faithful redeemer has restored us
to his kingdom, and has conquered by this sign the obdurate one,
toppling warlike Satan from the place he hazarded to rule.
Glorious cross, the world should loose its prayers to you.
Accept, exalted cross, from me this scarlet crown.

---

1. Alcuin interprets Joseph of Egypt from the Genesis narrative as a type, or foreshadow, of Christ.

Rabanus Maurus
(c. 776–856)

BORN IN MAINZ, IN WHAT IS now Germany, Rabanus Maurus was a monk who later became the Archbishop of Mainz. A student of Alcuin, Rabanus was the author of the encyclopedia *De rerum naturis* (*On the Nature of Things*), and also wrote treatises on education and a number of commentaries on the Bible. He was one of the most prominent teachers and writers of the Carolingian age, and earned the honorific title *praeceptor Germania*, "the teacher of Germany." Though "Veni, creator spiritus" is properly a hymn rather than a lyric, its influence on the poetic tradition is undeniable, owing in part to its wide familiarity across confessional lines: more than sixty English versions of Maurus's hymn are in use today. English translations appear as early as the last decades of the thirteenth century; the translation provided here dates from 1899, when it was published in the *Yattendon Hymnal* by Robert Bridges (1844–1930), Poet Laureate of England for nearly two decades of the early twentieth century.

[Veni, creator spiritus]

Veni, creator spiritus,
mentes tuorum visita,
imple superna gratia
quae tu creasti pectora.

Qui diceris paraclitus,
altissimi donum dei,
fons vivus, ignis, caritas,
et spiritalis unctio.

Tu, septiformis munere,
digitus paternae dexterae,
tu rite promissum patris,
sermone ditans guttura.

Accende lumen sensibus:
infunde amorem cordibus:
infirma nostri corporis
virtute firmans perpeti.

Hostem repellas longius,
pacemque dones protinus:
ductore sic te praevio
vitemus omne noxium.

Per te sciamus da patrem,
noscamus atque filium;
teque utriusque spiritum
credamus omni tempore.

Deo Patri sit gloria,
et Filio, qui a mortuis
surrexit, ac Paraclito,
in saeculorum saecula.

Come, O Creator Spirit, Come

Come, O Creator Spirit, come,
and make within our heart thy home;
to us thy grace celestial give,
who of thy breathing move and live.

O Comforter, that name is thine,
of God most high the gift divine;
the well of life, the fire of love,
our souls' anointing from above.

Thou dost appear in sevenfold dower[2]
the sign of God's almighty power;
the Father's promise, making rich
with saving truth our earthly speech.

Our senses with thy light inflame,
our hearts to heavenly love reclaim;
our bodies' poor infirmity
with strength perpetual fortify.

Our mortal foes afar repel,
grant us henceforth in peace to dwell;

---

2. An imaginative expansion on Revelation 1.20, which says that "The seven stars are the angels [or messengers] of the seven churches."

and so to us, with thee for guide,
no ill shall come, no harm betide.

May we by thee the Father learn,
and know the Son, and thee discern,
who art of both; and thus adore
in perfect faith for evermore.

Now to the Father and the Son,
Who rose from death, be glory given,
with Thou, O Holy Comforter,
henceforth by all in earth and heaven.

Gottschalk
(803?–867?)

GOTTSCHALK WAS BORN INTO a noble Saxony family. In his childhood he was
given as an oblate, vowed by his parents to monastic life, to the monastery of Fulda (in
modern Germany), which was then an important educational center with Rabanus
Maurus, Alcuin's pupil, serving as head of its school. There, Gottschalk studied classi-
cal literature, the Bible, and the writings of the early church fathers. Gottschalk became
a monk in his young adulthood, but he soon petitioned to be released from orders,
saying he'd been compelled against his will to the vows. Maurus resisted, and though
Gottschalk was released the two men parted acrimoniously. After leaving Fulda,
Gottschalk lived peripatetically for years, traveling from one religious community to
another until he took orders once again at the monastery of Orbais (in modern France).
He was ordained a priest without the knowledge of his bishop, and started preaching
doctrine that the official church found heretical. These actions reignited the ire of his
old teacher Maurus, now an archbishop. Gottschalk was accused of violation of the
monastic regulations, deposed from priesthood, flogged, and compelled to burn his
books. He was sentenced to "eternal silence" and imprisonment at the monastery of
Hautvilliers, where he spent the rest of his days.

Ut quid iubes, pusiole,
quare mandas, filiole,
carmen dulce me cantare,

cum sim longe exsul valde
intra mare?
O cur iubes canere?

Magis mihi, miserule,
flere libet, puerule,
plus plorare quam cantare
carmen tale, iubes quale,
amore care.
O cur iubes canere?

Mallem, scias, pusillule,
ut velles tu, fratercule,
pio corde condolere
mihi atque prona mente
conlugere.
O cur iubes canere?

Scis, divine tiruncule,
scis, superne clientule,
hic diu me exsulare,
multa die sive nocte
tolerare.
O cur iubes canere?

Scis, captivae plebeculae
Israeli cognomine
praeceptum in Babylone
decantare extra longe
fines Iudae.
O cur iubes canere?

Non potuerunt utique
nec debuerunt itaque.
carmen dulce coram gente
aliena nostrae terrae
resonare,
o cur iubes canere?

Sed quia vis omnimode,
consodalis egregie,
canam patri filioque
simul atque procedente

ex utroque.
Hoc cano ultronee.

Benedictus es, Domine,
Pater, nate, paraclite,
Deus trine, Deus une,
Deus summe, Deus pie,
Deus iuste.
Hoc cano spontanee.

Exsul ego diuscule
hoc in mare sum, Domine,
annos nempe duos fere,
nosti fere, sed iamiamque
miserere.
Hoc rogo humillime.

Interim cum, pusiole,
psallam ore, psallam mente,
psallam voce, psallam corde,
psallam die, psallam nocte,
carmen dulce,
tibi, rex piissime.

Why do you ask, little boy,
why do you demand, little son,
that I sing a sweet song
when I am in exile far away
on the sea?
O why do you bid me to sing?

It is better, little wretch,
to weep, little child,
to cry in lamentation
than the sweet song
you request.
O why do you bid me to sing?

You should know, little one,
that I would rather, little brother,
you should with pious heart
and humble spirit

grieve for me.
O why do you bid me to sing?

You know, little disciple,
you know, divine protégé,
this day I am an exile,
many days and many nights
I wear away.
O why do you bid me to sing?

You know the captive people
named Israel
in Babylon
were bid to sing, so far
from the home-borders of Judah.
O why do you bid me to sing?

They were not able,
so they were not obliged.
To sing a sweet song
in the presence of people
foreign to our land,
O why do you bid me to sing?

But because you will it,
my singular companion,
I shall sing of the Father and the Son,
showing forth together
and everywhere.
This I sing most willingly.

Blessed are you, Lord,
Father, Son, and Spirit,
triune God, unified God,
God in the highest, God most holy,
God of justice.
This I sing of my own desire.

I am long an exile,
long upon this sea, Lord,
nearly two years borne,
borne as you know, but at last

take pity!
This I ask most humbly.

In the meantime, little child,
I'll psalm with my mouth, my soul,
I'll psalm with my voice and my heart,
psalm by day and psalm by night,
a sweet song
to you, most holy king.

Bernard of Clairvaux
(1090–1153)

BORN INTO A NOBLE FAMILY in Burgundy, in what is now France, Bernard was instrumental in refocusing ritual worship in Christianity into a personalized and emotionally engaged faith-practice. In contrast to the classically inflected rational approach to worship embraced by many of his contemporaries, Bernard preached an immediate faith, one that transcended or eluded the operations of reason. Bernard came to be known as Doctor Mellifluus, "the honey-sweet theologian," for his eloquence. His treatise on the Song of Songs continues to influence interpretations of that biblical text. The full text of "Iesu, dulcis memoria" ranges from forty-two to fifty-three stanzas, depending upon the manuscript, but its opening stanzas are in wide use across the confessional spectrum. The rendering here is by English hymnist Edward Caswall (1814–1878).

from [Iesu, dulcis memoria]

Iesu, dulcis memoria,
dans vera cordis gaudia,
sed super mel et omnia,
eius dulcis praesentia.

Nil canitur suavius,
nil auditur iucundius,
nil cogitatur dulcius,
quam Iesus Dei Filius.

Iesu, spes paenitentibus,
quam pius es petentibus!
quam bonus te quaerentibus!
sed quid invenientibus?

Nec lingua valet dicere,
nec littera exprimere:
expertus potest credere,
quid sit Iesum diligere.

Sis, Iesu, nostrum gaudium,
qui es futurus praemium:
sit nostra in te gloria,
per cuncta semper saecula.

The Loving Soul's Jubilation

Jesus, the very thought of Thee,
with sweetness fills my breast,
but sweeter far Thy face to see,
and in Thy presence rest.

Nor voice can sing, nor heart can frame,
nor can the memory find
a sweeter sound than Thy blest Name,
o Savior of mankind!

O hope of every contrite heart
o joy of all the meek,
to those who fall, how kind Thou art!
how good to those who seek!

But what to those who find? Ah this
nor tongue nor pen can show:
the love of Jesus, what it is
none but His loved ones know.

Jesu, our only joy be Thou,
As Thou our prize wilt be:
Jesu, be Thou our glory now,
And through eternity.

Thomas Aquinas

(1225–1274)

SON OF A NOBLEMAN, THOMAS of Aquino was educated in classical literature and philosophy before taking orders as a Dominican monk. His prodigious output includes a number of commentaries on Aristotle and the magisterial *Summa Theologiæ*, a compendium of theological teachings and doctrine. His philosophical approach to faith earned him the honorific title "The Angelic Doctor," and he appears in Dante's *Divine Comedy* as an exemplar of religious wisdom. Pope Urban VI commissioned Thomas Aquinas to write the text for the eucharistic liturgy, though this hymn, composed around 1260 (and possibly attributed in error to Thomas Aquinas), was not originally composed for that service, and indeed its confession of interpretive difficulty remains markedly personal and private. This poem appears in many English versions, including a rendering by seventeenth-century poet Richard Crashaw. The translation here is by English poet and Jesuit priest Gerard Manley Hopkins (1844–1889).

[Adoro te devote]

Adoro te devote, latens Deitas,
Quae sub his figuris vere latitas;
Tibi se cor meum totum subiicit,
Quia te contemplans, totum deficit.

Visus, tactus, gustus in te fallitur,
Sed auditu solo tuto creditur;
Credo quidquid dixit Dei Filius,
Nil hoc verbo veritatis verius.

In cruce latebat sola Deitas.
At hic latet simul et humanitas:
Ambo tamen credens, atgue confitens,
Peto quod petivit latro paenitens.

Plagas, sicut Thomas, non intueor,
Deum tamen meum te confiteor:
Fac me tibi semper magis credere,
In te spem habere, te diligere.

O memoriale mortis Domini,
Panis vivus vitam praestans homini:
Praesta meae menti de te vivere,
Et te illi semper dulce sapere.

Pie pellicane Iesu Domine,
Me immundum munda tuo sanguine:
Cuius una stilla salvum facere
Totum mundum quit ab omni scelere.

Iesu, quem velatum nunc aspicio,
Oro, fiat illud, quod tam sitio,
Ut te revelata cernens facie,
Visu sim beatus tuae gloriae.

Lost, All in Wonder

Godhead here in hiding, whom I do adore,
Masked by these bare shadows, shape and nothing more,
See, Lord, at thy service low lies here a heart
Lost, all lost in wonder at the God thou art.

Seeing, touching, tasting are in thee deceived:
How says trusty hearing? that shall be believed;
What God's Son has told me, take for truth I do;
Truth himself speaks truly or there's nothing true.

On the cross thy godhead made no sign to men,
Here thy very manhood steals from human ken:
Both are my confession, both are my belief,
And I pray the prayer of the dying thief.

I am not like Thomas, wounds I cannot see,
But can plainly call thee Lord and God as he;
Let me to a deeper faith daily nearer move,
Daily make me harder hope and dearer love.

O thou our reminder of Christ crucified,
Living Bread, the life of us for whom he died,
Lend this life to me then: feed and feast my mind,
There be thou the sweetness man was meant to find.

Bring the tender tale true of the Pelican;[3]
Bathe me, Jesu Lord, in what thy bosom ran—
Blood whereof a single drop has power to win
All the world forgiveness of its world of sin.

Jesu, whom I look at shrouded here below,
I beseech thee send me what I thirst for so,
Some day to gaze on thee face to face in light
And be blest for ever with thy glory's sight.

Medieval Lyrics
(THIRTEENTH—SIXTEENTH CENTURIES)

THE LATE MEDIEVAL PERIOD saw an explosion of lyrics, both secular and sacred. Thousands of lyrics from the thirteenth century on are preserved in manuscripts, varying widely in both theme and style. In an age in which literary production was for the most part anonymous, lyrics circulated in manuscript from hand to hand, and were gathered in compilations by monks. Religious orders in England were increasingly devoting themselves to preaching in the vernacular, and many lyrics seem to have been written or collected to embellish sermons, to liven them up with a few lines of pithy vernacular poetry. Though informed by traditions of common prayer and worship, the medieval religious lyric begins to represent with more frequency the private, affective response of the individual worshipper. Exploring thus the subjective and mystical dynamics of devotion, and imagining the poem as arising out of a particular occasion, the eternal *now* of the poetic moment, the medieval lyric distinguishes itself radically from the more narrative and celebratory modes of hymnody. The anonymous texts collected here are identified by the manuscripts in which they appear. Original spelling has been maintained, accompanied by modernized text for clarity; these "translations" become increasingly unnecessary as we enter the sixteenth century and are replaced by marginal glosses. We have indicated passages where the manuscripts are illegible with a bracketed ellipsis ([. . .]).

---

3. The pelican is understood as an allegorical figure for Christ, based on a belief that the mother pelican will, in time of famine, pierce her own breast with her beak to feed her young with her blood.

Bodleian MS Arch. Selden supra 74, fol. 55v (c. 1240)

Nou goth sonne vnder wod,
me reweth, marie, þi faire Rode.
Nou goþ sonne vnder tre,
me reweþ, marie, þi sone and þe.

Now goes sun under wood°   *trees, cross*
I pity, Mary, thy fair rood.°   *cross, countenance*
Now goes sun under tree,
I pity, Mary, thy son and thee.

Ashmole MS 360 (c. 1300)

Þe minde of þi passion, suete ihesu,
þe teres it tolled,
þe heine it bolled,
þe neb it wetth,
in herte sueteth.

The mind° of thy passion, sweet Jesus,   *thought*
the tears it draws forth,
the eyes it makes swollen,
the face it wets,
in the heart it sweetens.

Cambridge, St. John's College MS 15 (c. 1300)

Wenne hic soe on rode idon
ihesus mi leman,
and bi him stoned
maria and johan,
his herte duepe i-stunge,
his body þis scurge i-ssuenge,
for þe sunne of man,
Hiþe hi mai wepen
and selte teres leten,
ief hic of luue chan.

When I see on the cross hung
Jesus my lover,
and by him standing
Mary and John,
his heart deeply stung,
his body with a scourge beaten
for the sin of man,
easily I may weep
and shed salt tears,
if I know anything of love.

Harley MS 2253 (c. 1310)

Wynter wakeneþ al my care,
nou þis leues waxeþ bare;
ofte y sike and mourne sare
    when hit comeþ in my þoht
    of þis worldes joie hou hit geþ al to noht.

Nou hit is and nou hit nys,
also hit ner nere ywys,
þat moni mon seiþ soþ hit ys:
    al goþ bote Godes wille,
    alle we shule deye þah vs like ylle.

al þat grein me graueþ grene,
nou hit faleweþ al bydene;
Iesu, help þat hit be sene,
    ant shild vs from helle,
    for y not whider y shal ne hou longe her duelle.

Winter wakens all my care,
now these leaves wax bare;
often I sigh and mourn sore
    when it comes in my thought
    of this world's joy how it goes all to naught.

Now it is and now it isn't,
as if it never were indeed,
that many moan, say sooth° it is   *true*

all goes but God's wille,
all we shall die though we like it ill.

All that grain I grew green
Now it fades all straightaway;
Jesus help that it be seen,
    and shield us from hell,
      For I [know] not whither I shall, nor how
    long here, dwell.

Harley MS 2253 (c. 1310)

I syke when y singe
    for sorewe þat y se
when y wiþ wypinge
    biholde vpon þe tre
ant se Iesu þe suete
is herte blod forlete
    for þe loue of me;
ys woundes waxen wete,
þei wepen stille ant mete.
    Marie, reweþ þe.

Heȝe vpon a doune,
    Þer al folk hit se may,
a mile from vch toune,
    aboute þe midday,
þe rode is vp arered,
his frendes aren afered
    ant clyngeþ so þe clay.
þe rode stond in stone;
Marie stont hire one,
    ant seiþ "Weilawei!"

When y þe biholde
    wiþ eyȝen bryhte bo,
ant þi bodi colde,
    þi ble waxeþ blo;
þou hengest al of blode

so heȝe vpon þe rode,
    bituene þeues tuo—
who may syke more?
Marie wepeþ sore
    ant siht al þis wo.

Þe naylles beþ to stronge,
    þe smyþes are to sleye,
þou bledest al to longe,
    þe tre is al to heyȝe,
þe stones beoþ al wete;
Alas! Iesu þe suete,
    for non frend hast þou non
bote seint Iohan mournynde
ant Marie wepynde
    for pyne þat þe ys on.

Ofte when y syke
    ant makie my mon,
wel ille þah me like
    wonder is hit non;
when y se honge heȝe
ant bittre pynes dreȝe
    Iesu, my lemmon,
his wondes sore smerte,
þe spere al to is herte
    ant þourh is sydes gon.

Ofte when y syke
    wiþ care y am þourhsoht;
when y wake, y wyke,
    of serewe is al mi þoht.
Alas! Men beþ wode
þat suereþ by þe Rode
    ant selleþ him for noht
þat bohte vs out of synne.
He bring vs to wynne
    þat haþ vs duere boht.

I sigh when I sing
    for sorrow that I see
when I with weeping
    behold upon the tree
and see Jesus the sweet
his heart-blood forth let
    for the love of me;
his wounds wax wet,
they weep still and plenty.
    Mary, pity thee.

High upon a down,°   *hill*
    where all folk may see it,
a mile from out of town,
    about the midday,
the rood° is up-reared,   *cross*
his friends are afraid,
    and clingeth as the clay.
The rood stands in stone;
Mary stands here alone,
    and sayeth "Wail away!"

When I thee behold
    with eyes bright both,
and thy body cold,
    thy color waxes gray;
thou hangest all a'blood
so high upon the rood,
    between thieves two—
who may sigh more?
Mary weeps sore
    and sighs at this woe.

The nails be too strong,
    the blacksmiths are too sly,°   *skilled*
thou bleeds all too long,
    the tree is all top high,
the stones be all wet.
Alas! Jesu the sweet,
    for no friend has thou none
but saint John mourning

and Marie weeping
    for pine that thee is on.[4]

Oft when I sigh
    and make my moan
well ill though I like it
    wonder is it none;
when I see hung high
and with bitter pines° drawn   *torments*
    Jesu, my beloved,
his woundes sore smart,
the spear all through his heart
    and through his sides gone.

Oft when I sigh
    with care I am throughshot;
when I wake, I weaken,
    of sorrow is all my thought.
Alas! Men be wood°   *crazy*
that swear by the Rood
    and sell him for naught
that bought us out of sin.
He brings us to win
    that hath us dear bought.

Merton College Oxford MS 248 (Fourteenth Century)

Steddefast crosse, immong alle oþer
þow art a tre mykel of prise,
in brawnche and flore swylke a-noþer
I ne wot non in wode no rys.
Swete be þe nalys,
and swete be þe tre,
and sweter be þe birdyn þat hangis vppon the!

Steadfast cross, among all other
thou art a tree mighty of price,
in branch and flower such another

---

4. For the sorrow that is upon you.

I know of none in wood nor thicket.
Sweet be the nails,
and sweet be the tree,
and sweeter be the bird that hangs upon thee![5]

New College Oxford MS 88 (Fourteenth Century)

Louerd, þou clepedest me
And ich nagt ne ansuarede þe
Bute wordes scloe and sclepie:
"þole yet! þole a litel!"
Bute "yiet" and "yiet" was endelis
And "þole a litel" a long wey is.

Lord, thou called me
And I naught answered thee
But words slow and sleepy:
"Wait yet! Wait a little!"
But "yet" and "yet" was endless
And "wait a little" a long way is.

Eton College MS 36 Pt. II (c. 1350)

Al oþer loue is lych þe mone
þat wext and wanet as flour in plein,
as flour þat fayret and fawyt sone,
as day þat scwret and endt in rein.

Al oþer loue begint bi blisse,
in wep and wo mak is hendyng,
no loue þer nis þat oure halle lyses,
bot wat areste in hevene kyng,

Wos loue ys [. . .] & eure grene,
and eure ful wyth-oute wanyyng;

---

5. The Middle English term "byrden" creates a pun in the last line of this poem, simultaneously signifying *bird*, *burden* in the sense of load or weight, and *bourden* in the self-referential sense of low musical harmony.

is loue suetyth wyth-oute tene,
is loue is hendles and a-ring.

Al oþer loue y flo for þe;
tel me, tel me, wer þou lyst?
"In marie mylde an fre
i schal be founde, ak mor in crist."

Crist me founde, nouht y þe, hast:
hald me to þe with al þi meyn;
help geld þat mi loue be stedfast,
lest þus sone it turne ageyn.

Wan nou hyet myn hert is sor,
y-wys hie spilt myn herte blod:
god canne mi lef, y care na mor—
hyet y hoppe hys wil be god.

Allas! what wole y a Rome?
seye y may in lore of loue,
"vndo y am by manne dome
bot he me help þat syt a-boue."

All other love is like the moon
That waxes and wanes as flower on plain,
as flower that fairs and fades soon,
as day that showers and ends in rain.

All other love begins by bliss,
in weep and woe makes his ending:
no love there is that's our all-bliss,
but what rests in heaven's king,

What love is [. . .] & ever green,
and ever full with-out waning;
is love [that] sweetens without teen,°   *suffering*
is love [that] is endless and a ring.

All other love I fled for thee;
tell me, tell me, where thou liest?
"In Mary mild and free
I shall be found, and more in Christ."

Christ me found, not I thee, has:
hold me to thee with all thy main;°   *might*

help grant that my love be steadfast,
lest thus soon it turn again.

When now yet mine heart is sore
indeed it spills my heart blood,
God can me leave, I care no more—
Yet I hope his will be good.

Alas! What will I [do] in Rome?
Say I may in words of love,
"Undone I am by man's doom,
but he me help that sits above."

Advocates Library 18.7.21 (Fourteenth Century)

Gold & al þis werdis wyn
Is nouth but cristis rode;
I wolde ben clad in cristis skyn,
þat ran so longe on blode,
& gon t'is herte & taken myn In—
þer is a fulsum fode.
þan ȝef I litel of kith or kyn,
For þer is alle gode. Amen.

Gold and all this world's win°   *gain*
Is nothing but Christ's rood;°   *cross*
I would be clad in Christ's skin,
That ran so long with blood,
& gone to his heart & taken mine in—
There is a fulsome food.
Then give I little for kith or kin,
For there is all good. Amen.

Harley MS 2316 (Late Fourteenth Century)

Ihesu cryst, myn leman swete,
ȝat for me deye-des on rode tre,
with al myn herte i ȝe bi-seke
for ȝi wndes to and thre,
ȝat al so faste in myn herte

3i loue roted mute be,
as was 3e spere in-to 3i side,
whan 30w suffredis ded for me.

Jesu Christ, my beloved sweet,
That for me died on the rood-tree,°   *cross*
with all mine heart I thee beseech
for thy woundes two and three,
that all so fast in mine heart,
thy love rooted might be,
as was the spear into thy side,
when thou suffered dead for me.

Sloane MS 2593 (c. 1430)

I Syng of a myden þat is makelees,
kyng of alle kynges To here sone she ches.

he cam also stylle þer his moder was
as dewe in aprylle þat fallyt on þe gras.

he cam also stylle his moderes bowr
as dewe in aprylle þat fallyt on þe flour.

he cam also stylle þer his moder lay
as dewe in aprylle þat fallyt on þe spray.

moder and mayden was neuer non but che—
wel may swych a lady godes moder be.

I Sing of a maiden that is matchless,
king of all kings to° her son she chose.   *as*

he came as still to where his mother was
as dew in April that falleth on the grass.

he came as still to his mother's bower
as dew in April that falleth on the flower.

he came as still to where his mother lay
as dew in April that falleth on the spray°   *sea*

mother and maiden was never one but she—
well may such a lady god's mother be.

Arundel MS 286 (Fifteenth Century)

Ihesus woundes so wide
ben welles of lif to þe goode,
Namely þe stronde of hys side,
þat ran ful breme on þe rode.

ȝif þee liste to drinke,
to fle fro þe fendes of helle,
Bowe þu doun to þe brinke
& mekely taste of þe welle.

Jesus's wounds so wide
been wells of life to the good,
Namely the stream of his side,
that ran full fierce on the rood.°   *cross*

If ye list° to drink,   *want*
to flee from the fiends of hell,
Bow thou down to the brink
& meekly taste of the well.

Bodleian Addition MS 39574 (Wheatley MS) (Fifteenth Century)

God, þat madist al þing of nouȝt
And with þi precious blood us bouȝt
Mercy, helpe and grace!
As þou art verry god and man,
And of þi side þi blood ran,
fforȝeue us oure trespace!
þe world, oure flesch, þe feend oure fo
Makiþ us mys-þinke, mys-speke, mys-do—
Al þus we falle in blame.
Of alle oure synnes, lasse and moore,
Swete ihĉ, us ruweþ soore,
Mercy! for þin holy name.

God, that made all things of naught
And with thy precious blood us bought
Mercy, help and grace!
As thou art very god and man,

And of thy side thy blood ran,
forgive us our trespass!
The world, our flesh, the fiend our foe
Makes us mis-think, mis-speak, mis-do—
All thus we fall in blame.
Of all our sins, less and more,
Sweet Jesus, us rue sore,[6]
Mercy! for thine holy name.

Bodleian Addition MS 37049 (Fifteenth Century)

Ihū, my luf, my ioy, my reste,
þi perfite luf close in my breste
þat I þe luf & neuer reste;
And mak me luf þe of al þinge best,
And wounde my hert in þi luf fre,
þat I may reyne in ioy euer-more with þe.

Jesu, my love, my joy, my rest,
thy perfect love close in my breast
that I thee love & never rest;
And make me love thee of all things best,
And wound my heart in thy love free
that I may reign in joy evermore with thee.

Frontispiece to the Book of Hours, Sarum Primer, 1514

God be in my heed°   *head*
And in myn understandynge
God be in myn eyen°   *eyes*
And in my lokynge°   *looking*
God be in my mouthe
And in my spekynge
God be in my herte
And in my thynkynge
God be at myn ende
And my departynge

------

6. Sweet Jesus, pity us deeply.

3

Psalm Translations of
the English Renaissance

THE BIBLE AS ART

MILES COVERDALE (1488–1569), who produced the first complete printed translation of the Bible into English, also published in 1535 the first vernacular psalter, *Goostly Psalmes and Spiritual Songes Drawen out of the Holy Scripture,* which contained English versions of thirteen psalms. Coverdale's translations were not the first renderings of psalmic texts into English (the tenth-century Paris Psalter contains some fifty psalms in Old English), but they were the first to be printed and disseminated widely, and were thus available for use in worship services.

The Reformation of the sixteenth century put an increased priority on vernacular worship—that is, on making scriptural and liturgical texts, so long the province of Latinists and clerics, accessible to all worshippers in their own tongues. As English Bibles were adopted for use in public and private devotions (and as tools for cultivating literacy), the Book of Psalms comprised the most widely known poetic texts in Renaissance English culture. Beginning in the 1530s, a widespread interest in the psalms took hold in England, in which theologians, poets, and devout amateurs experimented with translating and adapting, paraphrasing and improvising on the biblical poems, a phenomenon that identified in ancient scriptural texts a vibrant contemporary relevance and explored the personal resonances of its poetry.

From the first, the psalm translations that were incorporated into public worship often used a ballad stanza, also called common meter, an easily memorized quatrain form with alternating lines borrowed from folksongs. But translation projects undertaken by poets were less concerned with being appropriated by congregations and more concerned with the ways in which the psalms enabled an individuated consideration of spiritual concerns. Within the predetermined arc of each biblical poem, translators discovered rich opportunities for invention in both style and content. Renaissance psalms provide the ground for extravagant formal innovation, and their arguments exhibit surprising elaborations and extensions of their originals, blurring the line between original poetry and translation.

Moreover, psalm translation provided a space for the cultivation of voices that might otherwise have been silent. Women, who were discouraged from asserting their authority in both religious and literary matters during the period, were encouraged to translate religious works, for the development of language skills as well as virtue. Under the authorizing auspices of the biblical psalmists, Renaissance women exercised their eloquence, their artistic accomplishment, and—because translation is always also interpretation—their authority over the texts they translated.

The examples in this section show the variety of forms and styles used by sixteenth- and seventeeth-century translators. That many of the translators here collected are familiar for their own poetry indicates how urgent a literary concern psalm translation was in this period of increasingly vernacular spirituality.

FURTHER READING

Austern, Linda Phyllis, Kari Boys McBride, and David L. Orvis, eds. *Psalms in the Early Modern World*. Surrey, U.K.: Ashgate, 2011.

Baroway, Israel. "The Bible as Poetry in the English Renaissance: An Introduction." *Journal of English and Germanic Philology,* 32 (1933): 447–480.

Greene, Roland. "Sir Philip Sidney's Psalms, the Sixteenth-Century Psalter, and the Nature of Lyric." *Studies in English Literature, 1500–1900,* 30, no. 1 (1990): 19–40.

Hamlin, Hannibal. *Psalm Culture and Early Modern English Literature*. Cambridge: Cambridge University Press, 2004.

Hannay, Margaret P. "'So May I with the Psalmist Truly Say': Early Modern Englishwomen's Psalm Discourse." In *Write or Be Written: Early Modern Women Poets and Cultural Constraints,* ed. Barbara Smith and Ursula Appelt. Aldershot, U.K.: Ashgate, 2001.

———. "'Wisdome the Wordes': Psalm Translation and Elizabethan Women's Spirituality." *Religion & Literature,* 23, no. 3 (1991): 65–82.

Sidney, Sir Philip, and Mary Sidney Herbert. *The Sidney Psalter,* ed. Hannibal Hamlin, Michael G. Brennan, Margaret P. Hannay, and Noel J. Kinnamon. Oxford: Oxford University Press, 2009.

Smith, Hallett. "English Metrical Psalms in the Sixteenth Century and Their Literary Significance." *Huntington Library Quarterly*, 9 (1946): 249–271.

Twombly, Robert G. "Thomas Wyatt's Paraphrase of the Penitential Psalms of David." *Texas Studies in Literature and Language: A Journal of the Humanities*, 12 (1970): 345–380.

Thomas Sternhold
(1500–1549)

and John Hopkins
(d. 1570)

GROOM OF THE ROBES TO BOTH Henry VIII and Edward VI of England, Thomas Sternhold published his first, short collection of *Certayn Psalmes,* containing nineteen psalms and dedicated to Edward VI, sometime between 1547 and 1549. Shortly after his death, an expanded volume, *Al such psalms of David as Thomas Sternehold late grome of the kinges Majesties Robes, didde in his life time draw into english Metre,* was shepherded into publication by clergyman John Hopkins, who added seven of his own psalm translations to Sternhold's thirty-seven. Their translations were included in most editions of the Geneva Bible and adopted for use in worship services in the *Book of Common Prayer.* The Sternhold and Hopkins psalter expanded over a number of subsequent editions until the 1562 appearance of the *Whole Booke of Psalmes,* which included several previously unpublished translations by Sternhold, Hopkins, and other writers. This volume provided tunes for each psalm, most of which were composed in interchangeable common meter. Combining the personal devotional stance of the lyric with the utility of a practical psalter to be sung, the Sternhold and Hopkins volume was continuously in print, in close to a thousand editions, until the late seventeenth century, and their translations remained in regular liturgical use until the late eighteenth century.

Psalm 3—Domine quid multiplicati.[1] (Thomas Sternhold)

O Lord how are my foes increast,
>which vexe me more & more,
They kil my hart when as they say,
>God can him not restore.

But thou, O Lord, art my defence,
>when I am harde bestead:
My worship and my honor bothe
>and thou hold'st up my hed.

Then with my voyce vpon the Lorde
>I did bothe call and cry:
And he out of his holy hill,
>did heare me by and by.

I layde me downe, and quyetly,
>I slept and rose agayne:
For why? I know assuredly,
>The Lorde will me sustayn,

If ten thousande had hemde me in,
>I could not be afrayde:
For thou art still my Lorde my God,
>my sauiour and mine ayde.

Rise up therfore, saue me, my God
>for now to thee I call:
For thou hast broke the cheekes and teeth,
>of these wicked men all.

Saluation only doth belong,
>to thee, O Lorde above:
Thou doest bestowe vpon thy folke,
>thy blessing and thy loue.

---

1. Sternhold and Hopkins, like many of their contemporaries, title each of their psalm translations with the opening words in the Latin version of the Bible. Here, the Latin reads *Lord, why have those been multiplied [who trouble me]*.

Psalm 70—Deus in adiutorium.[2] (John Hopkins)

O God, to me take hede,
   of help I thee require:
O Lorde of hosts with hast and spede
   helpe, helpe, I thee desire.

With shame confound them all,
   that seke my soule to spill:
Rebuke them backe with blame to fall
   that thinke and wish me ill.

Confounde them that applye,
   and seke to worke me shame:
And at my harme, do laugh and crye,
   so, so, there goth the game.[3]

But let them ioyfull be,
   in thee with ioy and wealth:
Which only trust and seke to thee,
   and to thy sauing health:

That they may say always,
   in mirth and one accorde:
All glory, honor, laud and prayse,
   be geuen to thee (O Lorde.)

But I am weake and poore,
   come Lorde thine ayde I lacke:
Thou art my stay and helpe therefore,
   make spede and be not slack.

---

2. Latin: *God in help.*

3. The speaker imagines being hunted by his enemies, as if they were pursuing wild game.

Sir Thomas Wyatt the Elder
(1503–1542)

THOMAS WYATT WAS BORN into a family connected to English royalty; his father had served as one of Henry VII's Privy Council members, and the poet himself served as an ambassador under Henry VIII. He was part of the embassy to petition Pope Clement VII to annul Henry VIII's marriage to Catherine of Aragon so that Henry could marry Anne Boleyn. Wyatt was knighted in 1535, but in 1536 he was imprisoned for suspicion of adultery with Anne Boleyn. His favor at court rose and fell for his remaining years, and he was once again serving as an ambassador when he died of illness. Wyatt's poetry was deeply influenced by his familiarity with continental literature; he produced imitations of classical poetry and experimented in French verse forms, but his most significant literary contribution may lie in his translation of sonnets from Petrarch and his appropriation of the Italian poet's form into original English sonnets. Wyatt's poetry was not published during his lifetime; the first book to feature his verse was the popular and influential 1557 volume published by Richard Tottel and now known as *Tottel's Miscellany*, the first anthology of poetry in English.

Psalm 38—Domine ne in furore tuo.[4]

O Lord as I haue ye° both prayed and praye,	*thee*
Although in the° be no alteracyon	*thee*
But that we men, like as our selfes we saye	
Mesuryng thy Iustyce, by our mutacyon,	
Chastice me not (oh lorde) in thy furor	
Nor me correcte, in wrathful castygacyon.	
For that thy arrowes, of feare, of Terror	
Of sword, of sycknes, of famine, of fyre	
Stickes depe in me, I (loo°) from myne errour	*lo!*
Am plucked vp, as horse out of the myre	
With stroke of spurre; such is thy hande on me	
That in my flesshe, for terror of thy yre	
Is not one poynt of firme stabilytye	
Nor in my bones, ther is no stedfastnes:	

---

4. Wyatt's title is taken from the Latin translation of Psalm 38: *Lord, not in your anger.*

Suche is my dreade of mutabylytye°   *changefulness*

For that I knowe my fraylfull wyckednes.

For why? my synnes aboue my hed are bounde

Lyke heuy weightes, that doth my force oppresse

Under the whych I stoupe, and bowe to the grounde

As wyllow plante, haled by violence;

And of my fleshe, eche not well cured wounde

That festered is by folye° and neclygence,°   *folly / negligence*

By secrete luste, hath rankled vnder skynne

Not duely cured, by my penytence.

Perceyuynge° thus the tyrannye of synne   *Perceiving*

That with weyght, hath humbled and deprest

My pryde by grudgyng of the worme within

That neuer dyeth, I lyue wyth outen° rest   *live without*

So are myne entrayles Infect with feruent° sore   *fevered*

Fedynge° my harme, that hath my welth° oppreste   *feeding / well-being*

That in my fleshe, is left no health therefore.

So wonderous great hath ben my vexacyon

That it forced my harte to cry and rore.

O lorde thou knowest th'inwarde contemplacyon

Of my desire, thou knowest my syghes and plaints,

Thou knowest the teares of my lamentacyon

Cannot expresse my hartes inwarde restrayntes.

My harte pantethe, my force I feele it quayle,[5]

My sight, my eyes, my loke° decayes and fayntes,   *appearance*

And when myne enemyes dyd me most assayle

My frendes most sure, wherein I set most trust—

Myne owne vertues—sonest then dyd fayle

And stode aparte. Reason & wytt vniuste

As kyn vnkynde, were fardeste° gone at need.   *farthest*

So had they place ther venume° out to thruste   *venom*

That sought my death by naughty worde and deade.

Ther tonges reproche, their wit dyd frawde applye

And I lyke deafe & dom forthe my waye yede°   *went*

Lyke one that heres not, nor hath to replye

Not one worde agayne. Knowyng that from thyne hande

These thynges procede, & thou lorde shalte replye°   *repay*

My truste in that wherein I stycke and stande,

---

5. I feel my force quail, or faint.

Yet haue I had, greate cause to dreade and feare
That thou wouldeste geue° my foes the ouer hande.°   *give / upper hand*
For in my fal they shewed suche pleasaunt chere,
That there withal,° I alway in the lashe   *therefore*
Abyde the stroke, and wythe me euery where
I beare my faulte, that greatly doth abashe
My dolefull cheare; for I my fault confesse,
And my deserte dothe al my comfort dashe.[6]
In the mene while mine enemies styll encrease
And my prouokers hereby doe augmente,
That without cause to hurt me do not cease.
In euell for good agaynste me they be bente[7]
And hynder shal, my good presente° of grace.   *pursuit*
Loo° nowe my god, that seest my whole entente,   *lo*
My lord I am thou knowest in what case.[8]
Forsake me not, be not far from me gone
Haste to my helpe, haste lorde, & hast apace,
O lord, the lord, of al my helth alone.

Henry Howard, Earl of Surrey

(1517–1547)

SURREY WAS BORN INTO A noble family, descended from kings through both pa-
rental lines. He was raised at Windsor Castle with Henry VIII's illegitimate son as his
friend and companion, and two of his cousins (Anne Boleyn and Katherine Howard)
were among Henry VIII's six wives. For voicing a series of impolitic opinions in the
fragile early years of young Edward VI's reign, Surrey was condemned for treason
and executed. Together with Sir Thomas Wyatt, Surrey introduced the sonnet into
English. Surrey's poetry circulated in manuscript form among courtiers. It was pub-
lished posthumously in Richard Tottel's 1557 *Miscellany;* the full title of that anthol-
ogy testifies to the esteem in which Surrey was held, both as a poet and for his social

---

6. What I deserve dashes all my comfort.

7. Returning evil for my good, they are bent against me.

8. My lord, you know in what condition I am.

position: *Songs and Sonnets written by the Right Honorable Lord Henry Howard late Earl of Surrey and other.* Surrey's loose translations—what he called "paraphrases"—of five psalms seem to have been composed during his final imprisonment.

Psalm 55

Give ear to my suit, Lord! fromward° hide not thy face.	*averted*
Beholde, herking in grief, lamenting how I praye.	
My fooes that bray so lowde, and eke° threpe° on so fast,	*also / press*
Buckeled° to do me scathe,° so is their malice bent.	*girded / harm*
Care perceth my entrayls, and trauayleth° my spryte;°	*troubles / spirit*
The greslye° feare of death enuyroneth° my brest;	*grisly / encompasses*
A tremblynge cold of dred clene ouerwhelmeth my hert.	
"Oh!" thinke I, "hadd I wings like to the symple doue,	
This peryll myght I flye, and seke some place of rest	
In wylder woods, where I might dwell farr from these cares."	
What speady way of wing my playnts° shold thei lay on,	*complaints*
To skape° the stormye blast that threatned is to me?	*escape*
Rayne those vnbrydled tungs! breake that coniured° league!	*conspiring*
For I decyphred haue amydd our towne the stryfe:	
Gyle° and wrong kept the walles, they ward° both day and night,	*guile / guard*
Whiles myscheif with care doth keep the market stede,°	*marketplace*
Whilst wickidnes with craft in heaps swarme through the strete.	
Ne my declared foo wrought me all this reproche:[9]	
By harme so loked for, yt wayeth halfe the lesse,[10]	
For, though myne ennemyes happ° had byn for to prevaile,	*fortune*
I cold haue hidd my face from uenym° of his eye.	*venom*
It was a friendly foo, by shadow° of good will,	*disguise*
Myne old fere° and dere frende, my guyde, that trapped me,	*companion*
Where I was wont to fetche the cure of all my care,	
And in his bosome hyde my secret zeale to God.	
Such sodden surprys quicke may them hell deuoure,[11]	
Whilst I inuoke the Lord, whose power shall me defend.	
My prayer shall not cease from that° the sonne disscends	*when*
Till he his haulture° wynn° and hyde them in the see.	*prominence / gain*

---

9. Nor has only my known foe worked me all this injury.

10. The harm I expected to experience weighs less than half my burden.

11. With such sudden surprise may hell devour them quickly.

With words of hott effect,° that moueth from hert contryte,   *passionate words*
Such humble sute, O Lord, doth pierce thy pacyent eare.
It was the Lord that brake the bloody compackts of those
That pricked on with yre to slaughter me and myne.
The euerlasting God whose kingdom hath no end,
Whome, by no tale to dred he cold divert from synne,[12]
The conscyence vnquiet he stryks with heuy hand,
And proues their force in fayth whome he sware to defend.
Butter fales° not so soft as doth hys pacyence longe,   *falls*
And ouer passeth° fine oyle, running not halfe so smothe;   *overruns*
But when his suffraunce fynds that brydled wrath prouoks,[13]
He thretneth wrath, he whets more sharppe then any toole can fyle.
Friowr,° whose harme and tounge presents the wicked sort   *Friar*
Of those false wolues, with cootes which doo their ravin hyde,[14]
That sweare to me by heauen, the fotestole of the Lord,[15]
Who though force had hurt my fame, they did not touch my life;
Such patching care[16] I lothe as feeds the welth with lyes.
But in thother Psalme of David fynd I ease:[17]
Iacta curam tuam super dominum et ipse te enutriet.[18]

Anne Askew (Ayscough)
(1521–1546)

BORN INTO A FAMILY OF landed gentry, Askew was married off by her father at the
age of fifteen to Thomas Kyme, as a proxy for an older sister for whom the marriage
had originally been arranged. Her refusal to take her husband's name indicates the
friction between them, due in part to her strong Protestantism. She spoke out publicly
against Catholic doctrine, and in 1545 was arrested as a heretic, though her examiners

---

12. Those sinners whom by no cautionary tale God could divert from sin.

13. But when God's patience finds that which provokes his bridled wrath.

14. Of those false wolues, with coats which do their fierceness hide (i.e., wolves in sheep's clothing).

15. See Matthew 5.35.

16. Ignoble concern (ignoble, that is, as a patch that hides a hole).

17. Perhaps Psalm 55.23?

18. Latin: *Cast thy care upon the Lord, and He shall sustain thee.*

could not prove their charges against her and she was released. She was arrested and interrogated again in 1546; according to her own account, she parried her examiners using scriptural authorization for her position. Though her defense was eloquent and made use of deft logic, she was burned at the stake in July 1546. The first-person account of her trial was published in John Foxe's 1563 *Acts and Monuments,* a hagiography of Protestant martyrs that was installed in every cathedral in England. This psalm translation was appended to Askew's autobiographical account.

The voice of Anne Askewe out of the 54. Psalme of David, called Deus in nomine tuo.[19]

For thy names sake, be my refuge,
     And in thy truthe, my quarell judge.
Before the (lorde) lete me be hearde,
     And with faver my tale regarde
Loo, faythlesse men, agaynst me ryse,
     And for thy sake, my deathe practyse.°   *intend*
My lyfe they seke, with mayne° and might   *force*
     Whych have not the,° afore their sight   *thee*
Yet helpest thu° me, in thys dystresse,   *thou*
     Savynge my sowle, from cruelnesse.
I wote° thu wylt revenge my wronge,   *know*
     And vysyte° them, ere it be longe.   *visit*
I wyll therfor, my whole hart bende,
     Thy gracyouse name (lorde) to commende.
From evyll thu hast delyvered me,
     Declarynge what, myne enmyes be.
     Prayse to God.

---

19. The Latin title here reads *God by your name.*

Anne Lok

(c. 1530–after 1590)

ANNE LOK (SOMETIMES LOCKE) was the daughter of a merchant. In her childhood, her father was governor of the Merchant Adventurers' factory in Antwerp, where the family converted to Protestantism. After the family returned to London in the 1540s, Anne married mercer Henry Lok, a committed Protestant. In Henry's household, Anne met Scottish theologian John Knox, with whom she developed a lifelong friendship. When Knox was in exile in Geneva, Anne went with her children, and with her husband's apparent blessing, to live chastely in Knox's company. In Geneva, Anne translated Calvin's sermons on the song of Hezekiah, as well as a metrical paraphrase of the fifty-first psalm, which she published in 1560. After the death of Henry Lok, Anne married firebrand Protestant preacher Edward Dering. In 1590 she published a translation of a French religious text. In Lok's poem below, her direct translation of the Latin text of Psalm 51 is interspersed between the meditation's stanzas.

A Meditation of a Penitent Sinner: Written in Maner of a Paraphrase upon the 51 Psalme of Dauid.

THE PREFACE, EXPRESSING THE PASSIONED MINDE OF THE PENITENT SINNER.

The hainous gylt of my forsaken ghost	
So threates, alas, vnto my febled sprite	
Deserved death, and (that me greveth most)	
Still stand so fixt before my daseld° sight	*dazzled*
The lothesome filthe of my disteined° life,	*stained*
The mighty wrath of myne offended Lorde,	
My Lord whos wrath is sharper than the knife,	
And deper woundes than dobleedged° sworde,	*double-edged*
That, as the dimmed and fordulled eyen°	*dulled eyes*
Full fraught with teares & more & more opprest	
With growing streames of the distilled bryne	
Sent from the fornace of a grefefull° brest,	*grief-full*
Can not enioy the comfort of the light,	
Nor finde the waye wherin to walke aright:	

So I blinde wretch, whome Gods enflamed ire
With pearcing stroke hath throwne vnto the ground,
Amidde my sinnes still groueling in the myre,
Finde not the way that other oft haue found,
Whome cherefull glimse of gods abounding grace
Hath oft releued and oft with shyning light
Hath brought to ioy out of the vgglye place,
Where I in darke of euerlasting night
Bewayle my woefull and vnhappy case,
And fret my dyeng soule with gnawing paine.
Yet blinde, alas, I groape about for grace.
While blinde for grace I groape about in vaine,
My fainting breath I gather vp and straine,
Mercie, mercie to crye and crye againe.

But mercy while I sound with shreking crye
For graunt° of grace and pardon while I pray,   *grant*
Euen then despeir before my ruthefull° eye   *rueful*
Spredes forth my sinne & shame, & semes to saye
In vaine thou brayest forth thy bootlesse noyse
To him for mercy, O refused wight,°   *person*
That heares not the forsaken sinners voice.
Thy reprobate and foreordeined sprite,
For damned vessell of his heauie wrath,
(As selfe witnes of thy beknowyng° hart,   *knowing*
And secrete gilt of thine owne conscience saith)
Of his swete promises can claime no part:
But thee, caytif,° deserued curse doeth draw   *wretch*
To hell, by iustice, for offended law.

This horror when my trembling soule doth heare,
When markes and tokens of the reprobate,
My growing sinnes, of grace my senslesse cheare,[20]
Enforce the profe° of euerlastyng hate,   *give evidence*
That I conceiue the heauens king to beare
Against my sinfull and forsaken ghost:
As in the throte of hell, I quake for feare,

---

20. As my awareness of my sin grows, so too grows my senseless, or ignorant, awareness of grace.

And then in present perill to be lost
(Although by conscience wanteth to replye,
But with remorse enforcing myne offence,
Doth argue vaine my not auailyng crye)
With woefull sighes and bitter penitence
To him from whom the endlesse mercy flowes
I cry for mercy to releve my woes.

And then not daring with presuming eye
Once to beholde the angry heauens face,
From troubled sprite I send confused crye,
To craue the crummes of all sufficing grace.
With foltring knee I fallyng to the ground,
Bendyng my yelding handes to heauens throne,
Poure forth my piteous plaint with woefull sound,
With smoking sighes, & oft repeted grone,
Before the Lord, the Lord, whom synner I,
I cursed wretch, I haue offended so,
That dredyng, in his wrekefull° wrath to dye,   *vengeful*
And damned downe to depth of hell to go,
Thus tost with panges and passions of despeir,
Thus craue I mercy with repentant chere.

Haue mercie vpon me (o God) after thy great merci

Haue mercy, God, for thy great mercies sake.
O God: my God, vnto my shame I say,
Beynge° fled from thee, so as I dred to take   *being*
Thy name in wretched mouth, and feare to pray
Or aske the mercy that I haue abusde.
But, God of mercy, let me come to thee:
Not for iustice, that iustly am accusde:
Which selfe word Iustice so amaseth me,
That scarce I dare thy mercy sound againe.
But mercie, Lord, yet suffer me to craue.
Mercie is thine: Let me not crye in vaine,
Thy great mercie for my great fault to haue.
Haue mercie, God, pitie my penitence
With greater mercie than my great offence.

And according vnto the multitude of thy mercies do away myne offences.

My many sinnes in nomber are encreast,
With weight wherof in sea of depe despeire
My sinking soule is now so sore opprest,
That now in peril and in present fere,
I crye: susteine me, Lord, and Lord I pray,
With endlesse nomber of thy mercies take
The endlesse nomber of my sinnes away.
So by thy mercie, for thy mercies sake,
Rue° on me, Lord, releve me with thy grace.   *pity*
My sinne is cause that I so nede to haue
Thy mercies ayde in my so woefull case:
My synne is cause that scarce I dare to craue
Thy mercie manyfolde, which onely may
Releve my soule, and take my sinnes away.

Wash me yet more from my wickednes, and clense me from my sinne.

So foule is sinne and lothesome in thy sighte,
So foule with sinne I see my selfe to be,
That till from sinne I may be washed white,
So foule I dare not, Lord, approche to thee.
Ofte hath thy mercie washed me before,
Thou madest me cleane: but I am foule againe.
Yet washe me Lord againe, and washe me more.
Washe me, O Lord, and do away the staine
Of vggly sinnes that in my soule appere.
Let flow thy plentuous streames of clensing grace.
Washe me againe, yea washe me euery where,
Bothe leprous bodie and defiled face.
Yea washe me all, for I am all vncleane,
And from my sin, Lord, cleanse me ones againe.

For I knowledge my wickednes, and my sinne is euer before me.

Haue mercie, Lord, haue mercie: for I know
How muche I nede thy mercie in this case.
The horror of my gilt doth dayly growe,
And growing weares my feble hope of grace.
I fele and suffer in my thralled brest
Secret remorse and gnawing of my hart.
I fele my sinne, my sinne that hath opprest

My soule with sorrow and surmounting smart.
Drawe me to mercie: for so oft as I
Presume to mercy to direct my sight,
My Chaos and my heape of sinne doth lie,
Betwene me and thy mercies shining light.
What euer way I gaze about for grace,
My filth and fault are euer in my face.

Against thee onelye haue I sinned, & don euill in thy sight.

Graunt thou me mercy, Lord: thee thee alone
I haue offended, and offendyng thee,
For mercy loe, how I do lye and grone.
Thou with allpearcing eye beheldest me,
Without regard that sinned in thy sight.
Beholde againe, how now my spirite it rues,°   *regrets*
And wailes the tyme, when I with foule delight
Thy swete forbearing mercy did abuse.
My cruell conscience with sharpned knife
Doth splat° my ripped hert, and layes abrode   *split*
The lothesome secretes of my filthy life,
And spredes them forth before the face of God.
Whom shame from dede shamelesse cold° not restrain,   *could*
Shame for my dede is added to my paine.

That thou mightest be founde iust in thy sayinges, and maiest ouer come when thou art
   iudged.

But mercy Lord, O Lord some pitie take,
Withdraw my soule from the deserved hell,
O Lord of glory, for thy glories sake:
That I may saued of thy mercy tell,
And shew how thou, which mercy hast behight°   *promised*
To sighyng sinners, that haue broke thy lawes,
Performest mercy: so as in the sight
Of them that iudge the iustice of thy cause
Thou onely iust be demed, and no moe,[21]
The worldes vniustice wholy to confound:
That damning me to depth of during° woe   *enduring*

———————————

21. Only you are deemed just, and none other.

Iust in thy iudgement shouldest thou be found:
And from deserved flames relevyng° me *relieving*
Iust in thy mercy mayst thou also be.

For loe, I was shapen in wickednes, and in sinne my mother conceiued me.

For lo, in sinne, Lord, I begotten was,
With sede° and shape my sinne I toke also, *birth*
Sinne is my nature and my kinde° alas, *race*
In sinne my mother me conceiued: Lo
I am but sinne, and sinfull ought to dye,
Dye in his wrath that hath forbydden sinne.
Such bloome and frute loe sinne doth multiplie,
Such was my roote, such is my iuyse° within. *juice*
I plead not this as to excuse my blame,
On kynde or parentes myne owne gilt to lay:
But by disclosing of my sinne, my shame,
And nede of helpe, the plainer to displaye
Thy mightie mercy, if with plenteous grace
My plenteous sinnes it please thee to deface.

But lo, thou haste loued trueth, the hidden and secrete thinges of thy wisedome thou haste opened vnto me.

Thou louest simple sooth,° not hidden face *truth*
With trutheles visour of deceiving showe.
Lo simplie, Lord, I do confesse my case,
And simplie craue thy mercy in my woe.
This secrete wisedom hast thou graunted me,
To se my sinnes, & whence my sinnes do growe:
This hidden knowledge haue I learnd of thee,
To fele my sinnes, and howe my sinnes do flowe
With such excesse, that with vnfained hert,
Dreding to drowne, my Lorde, lo howe I flee,
Simply with teares bewailyng my desert,
Releved simply by thy hand to be.
Thou louest truth, thou taughtest me the same.
Helpe, Lord of truth, for glory of thy name

Sprinkle me, Lorde, with hisope and I shalbe cleane: washe me and I shalbe whiter then snow.

With swete Hysope besprinkle thou my sprite:[22]
Not such hysope, nor so besprinkle me,
As law vnperfect shade of perfect lyght
Did vse as an apointed signe to be
Foreshewing figure of thy grace behight.° *promised*
With death and bloodshed of thine only sonne,
The swete hysope, cleanse me defyled wyght,
Sprinkle my soule. And when thou so haste done,
Bedeawd with droppes of mercy and of grace,
I shalbe cleane as cleansed of my synne.
Ah wash me, Lord: for I am foule alas:
That only canst, Lord, wash me well within,
Wash me, O Lord: when I am washed soe,
I shalbe whiter than the whitest snowe.

Thou shalt make me heare ioye and gladnesse, al the bones which thou hast broken shal
    reioyse

Long haue I heard, & yet I heare the soundes
Of dredfull threates and thonders of the law,
Which Eccho of my gylty minde resoundes,
And with redoubled horror doth so draw
My listening soule from mercies gentle voice,
That louder, Lorde, I am constraynde to call:
Lorde, pearce myne eares, & make me to reioyse,
When I shall heare, and when thy mercy shall
Sounde in my hart the gospell of thy grace.
Then shalt thou geue° my hearing ioy againe, *give*
The ioy that onely may releve my case.
And then my broosed bones, that thou with paine
Hast made to weake my febled corps to beare,
Shall leape for ioy, to shewe myne inward chere.

Turne away thy face from my sinnes, and do away all my misdedes.

Loke on me, Lord: though trembling I beknowe,
That sight of sinne so sore offendeth thee,
That seing sinne, how it doth ouerflowe
My whelmed soule, thou canst not loke on me,

---

22. Hyssop: a purgative herb.

But with disdaine, with horror and despite.
Loke on me, Lord: but loke not on my sinne.
Not that I hope to hyde it from thy sight,
Which seest me all without and eke° within.   *also*
But so remoue it from thy wrathfull eye,
And from the iustice of thyne angry face,
That thou impute it not. Looke not how I
Am foule by sinne: but make me by thy grace
Pure in thy mercies sight, and, Lord, I pray,
That hatest sinne, wipe all my sinnes away.

Create a cleane hart within me, O God: and renew a stedfast spirit within my bowels.

Sinne and despeir haue so possest my hart,
And hold my captiue soule in such restraint,
As of thy mercies I can fele no part,
But still in languor do I lye and faint.
Create a new pure hart within my brest:
Myne old can hold no liquour of thy grace.
My feble faith with heauy lode opprest
Staggring doth scarcely creepe a reeling pace,
And fallen it is to faint to rise againe.
Renew, O Lord, in me a constant sprite,
That stayde with mercy may my soule susteine,
A sprite so setled and so firmely pight°   *placed*
Within my bowells, that it neuer moue,
But still vphold th'assurance of thy loue.

Cast me not away from thy face, and take not thy holy spirit from me.

Loe prostrate, Lorde, before thy face I lye,
With sighes depe drawne depe sorow to expresse.
O Lord of mercie, mercie do I crye:
Dryve me not from thy face in my distresse,
Thy face of mercie and of swete relefe,
The face that fedes angels with onely sight,
The face of comfort in extremest grefe.
Take not away the succour of thy sprite,
Thy holy sprite, which is myne onely stay,
The stay that when despeir assaileth me,
In faintest hope yet moueth me to pray,
To pray for mercy, and to pray to thee.

Lord, cast me not from presence of thy face,
Nor take from me the spirite of thy grace.

Restore to me the comforte of thy sauing helpe, & stablishe me with thy free spirit.

But render me my wonted ioyes againe,
Which sinne hath reft, and planted in theyr place
Doubt of thy mercy ground of all my paine.
The tast, that thy loue whilome° did embrace   *formerly*
My chearfull soule, the signes that dyd assure
My felyng° ghost of fauor in thy sight,   *feeling*
Are fled from me, and wretched I endure
Senslesse of grace the absence of thy sprite.
Restore my ioyes, and make me fele againe
The swete retorne of grace that I haue lost,
That I may hope I pray not all in vayne.
With thy free sprite confirme my feble ghost,
To hold my faith from ruine and decay
With fast affiance and assured stay.

I shal teach thy waies vnto the wicked, & sinners shall be tourned vnto thee.

Lord, of thy mercy if thou me withdraw
From gaping throte of depe deuouring hell,
Loe, I shall preach the iustice of thy law:
By mercy saued, thy mercy shall I tell.
The wicked I wyll teache thyne only way,
Thy wayes to take, and mans deuise° to flee,   *scheming*
And suche as lewd delight hath ledde astray,
To rue theyr errour and returne to thee.
So shall the profe° of myne example preache   *testimony*
The bitter frute of lust and foule delight:
So shall my pardon by thy mercy teache
The way to finde swete mercy in thy sight.
Haue mercy, Lorde, in me example make
Of lawe and mercy, for thy mercies sake.

Deliuer me from bloud o God, God of my helth & my tong shall ioyfullye talke of thy
    iustice.

O God, God of my health, my sauing God,
Haue mercy Lord, and shew thy might to saue,
Assoile° me, God, from gilt of giltlesse blod,   *absolve*

And eke from sinne that I ingrowing haue
By fleshe and bloud and by corrupted kinde.
Vpon my bloud and soule extende not, Lorde,
Vengeance for bloud, but mercy let me finde,
And strike me not with thy reuengyng sworde.
So, Lord, my ioying tong shall talke thy praise,
Thy name my mouth shall vtter in delight,
My voice shall sounde thy iustice, and thy waies,
Thy waies to iustifie thy sinfull wight.
God of my health, from bloud I saued so
Shall spred thy prayse for all the world to know.

Lord, open thou my lippes, and my mouth shal shewe thy praise.

Lo straining crampe of colde despeir againe
In feble brest doth pinche my pinyng hart,
So as in greatest nede to cry and plaine°   *complain*
My speache doth faile to vtter thee my smart.
Refreshe my yeldyng hert, with warming grace,
And loose my speche, and make me call to thee.
Lord open thou my lippes to shewe my case,
My Lord, for mercy Loe to thee I flee.
I can not pray without thy mouyng ayde,
Ne can I ryse, ne° can I stande alone.   *nor*
Lord, make me pray, & graunt when I haue praide,
Lord loose my lippes, I may expresse my mone,
And findyng grace with open mouth I may
Thy mercies praise, and holy name display.

If thou haddest desired sacrifice, I wold haue geuen: thou delytest not in burnt offringes.

Thy mercies praise, instede of sacrifice,
With thankfull minde so shall I yeld to thee.
For if it were delitefull in thine eyes,
Or hereby mought° thy wrath appeased be,   *might*
Of cattell slayne and burnt with sacred flame
Vp to the heauen the vaprie smoke to send:
Of gyltlesse beastes, to purge my gilt and blame,
On altars broylde the sauour shold ascend,
To pease thy wrath. But thy swete sonne alone,
With one sufficing sacrifice for all
Appeaseth thee, and maketh the° at one   *thee*

With sinfull man, and hath repaird our fall.
That sacred hoste is euer in thine eyes.[23]
The praise of that I yeld for sacrifice.

The sacrifice to God is a trobled spirit: a broken and an humbled hart, o god, thou wilt not despise.

I yeld my self, I offer vp my ghoste,
My slayne delightes, my dyeng hart to thee.
To God a trobled sprite is pleasing hoste.
My trobled sprite doth drede° like him to be,   *fear*
In whome tastlesse languor with lingring paine
Hath febled so the starued appetite,
That foode to late is offred all in vaine,
To holde in fainting corps the fleing sprite.
My pining soule for famine of thy grace
So feares alas the faintnesse of my faithe.
I offre vp my trobled sprite: alas,
My trobled sprite refuse not in thy wrathe.
Such offring likes thee, ne wilt thou despise
The broken humbled hart in angry wise.

Shew fauour, o lord in thy good will vnto Sion, that the walles of Hierusalem may be bylded.

Shew mercie, Lord, not vnto me alone:
But stretch thy fauor and thy pleased will,
To sprede thy bountie and thy grace vpon
Sion, for Sion is thy holly hyll:
That thy Hierusalem with mighty wall
May be enclosed vnder thy defense,
And bylded so that it may neuer fall
By myning° fraude or mighty violence.   *undermining*
Defend thy chirch, Lord, and aduaunce it soe,
So in despite of tyrannie to stand,
That trembling at thy power the world may know
It is vpholden by thy mighty hand:
That Sion and Hierusalem may be
A safe abode for them that honor thee.

---

23. Refers to the eucharistic *host*, the sacramental bread and wine that represents Christ.

Then shalt thou accept the sacrifice of righteousnesse, burnt offringes and oblations. then
    shall they offre yonge bullockes vpon thine altare.

Then on thy hill, and in thy walled towne,
Thou shalt receaue the pleasing sacrifice,
The brute shall of thy praised name resoune[24]
In thankfull mouthes, and then with gentle eyes
Thou shalt behold vpon thine altar lye
Many a yelden° host of humbled hart,   *yielded*
And round about then shall thy people crye:
We praise thee, God our God: thou onely art
The God of might, of mercie, and of grace.
That I then, Lorde, may also honor thee,
Releue my sorow, and my sinnes deface:
Be, Lord of mercie, mercifull to me:
Restore my feling of thy grace againe:
Assure my soule, I craue it not in vaine.

George Gascoigne
(c. 1535–1577)

THE ELDEST SON OF SIR JOHN Gascoigne, George was intended for a career in the law. Whether he persisted in this profession is unclear, but his exploits were notorious; by his own account he sold his inheritance to pay his debts. He served as a Member of Parliament for a time, but his election was later refused on charges that he was "a defamed person," "a common Rymer," and "a notorious rufilanne [ruffian]." Considering himself a devotee of Chaucer, Gascoigne in 1573 published his most well-known work, *A Hundredth Sundry Flowres*, a collection of poems that hinted, in satiric style, at courtly scandals and intrigues. Gascoigne's fluid prosody finds a reflective expression in "Certayne Notes of Instruction concerning the making of verse or ryme in English" (1575), the first essay on English versification.

---

24. The noise (bruit) shall resound with your praised name.

The introduction to the Psalme of De profundis.[25]

The Skies gan° scowle, orecast with misty clowdes,	*began*
When (as I rode alone by London waye,	
Cloakelesse, vnclad) thus did I sing and say:	
Behold quoth I, bright *Titan*° how he shroudes	*the sun*
His head abacke, and yelds the raine his reach,°	*sphere of authority*
Till in his wrath, *Dan Ioue* have soust the soile,[26]	
And washt me wretch which in his trauaile° toile.	*difficulty; journey*
But holla° (here) doth rudenesse me appeach,°	*wait / accuses me*
Since *Ioue* is Lord and king of mighty power,	
Which can commaund the Sunne to shewe his face,	
And (when him lyst)° to give the raine his place.	*(when he likes)*
Why doe not I my wery° muses frame,	*weary*
(Although I bee well soused in this showre,)	
To write some verse in honour of his name?	

Gascoignes De profundis.

From depth of doole° wherein my soule doth dwell,	*sorrow*
From heauy heart which harbours in my brest,	
From troubled sprite which sildome taketh rest.	
From hope of heauen, from dreade of darkesome hell.	
O gracious God, to thee I crye and yell.	
My God, my Lorde, my louely Lord aloane,	
To thee I call, to thee I make my moane.	
And thou (good God) vouchsafe in gree° to take,	*with good will*
This woefull plaint,	
Wherein I faint.	
Oh heare me then for thy great mercies sake.	

Oh bende thine eares attentiuely to heare,
Oh turne thine eyes, behold me how I wayle,
O hearken Lord, give eare for mine auaile,
O marke in minde the burdens that I beare:
See howe I sinke in sorrowes euerye where.

---

25. *De profundis* refers to the first words in Latin of Psalm 130: *From the depths.*
26. Don [Sir] Jove, Roman sky god: metaphoric for the rain, which has soused the soil.

Beholde and see what dollors° I endure,   *sorrows*
Give eare and marke what plaintes I put in vre.°   *into action*
Bende wylling eare: and pittie therewithall,
My wayling voyce,
Which hath no choyce.
But euermore vpon thy name to call.

If thou good Lorde shouldest take thy rod in hande,
If thou regard what sinnes are daylye done,
If thou take holde where wee our workes begone,°   *begun*
If thou decree in Judgement for to stande,
And be extreame to see our scuses skande,[27]
If thou take note of euery thing amysse,
And wryte in rowles° howe frayle our nature is,   *rolls*
O gloryous God, O King, O Prince of power,
What mortall wight,°   *person*
Maye then have lyght,
To feele thy frowne, if thou haue lyst to lowre?[28]

But thou art good, and hast of mercye store,
Thou not delyghtst to see a sinner fall,
Thou hearknest first, before we come to call.
Thine eares are set wyde open euermore,
Before we knocke thou commest to the doore.
Thou art more prest° to heare a sinner crye,   *inclined*
Then he is quicke to climbe to thee on hye.
Thy mighty name bee praysed then alwaye,
Let fayth and feare,
True witnesse beare.
Howe fast they stand which on thy mercy staye.

I looke for thee (my louelye Lord) therefore.
For thee I wayte, for thee I tarrye styll,
Myne eyes doe long to gaze on thee my fyll.
For thee I watche, for thee I prye and pore.°   *look carefully*
My Soule for thee attendeth euermore.
My Soule doth thyrst to take of thee a taste,

---

27. And be severe to see our excuses judged.
28. To feel thy frown, if you wish to scowl?

My Soule desires with thee for to bee plaste.°   *placed*
And to thy worde (which can no man deceyve)
Myne onely trust,
My loue and lust
In confidence continuallye shall cleave.

Before the breake or dawning of the daye,
Before the lyght be seene in loftye Skyes,
Before the Sunne appeare in pleasaunt wyse,°   *aspect*
Before the watche (before the watche I saye)[29]
Before the warde that waytes therefore alwaye:
My soule, my sense, my secreete thought, my sprite,
My wyll, my wishe, my joye, and my delight:
Unto the Lord that sittes in heauen on highe,
With hastye wing,
From me doeth fling,
And stryueth styll, vnto the Lorde to flye.

O Israell, O housholde of the Lorde,
O *Abrahams* Brattes,° O broode of blessed seede,   *children*
O chosen sheepe that loue the Lord in deede:
O hungrye heartes, feede styll vpon his worde,
And put your trust in him with one accorde.
For he hath mercye euermore at hande,
His fountaines flowe, his springes doe neuer stande.
And plenteouslye hee loueth to redeeme,
Such sinners all,
As on him call,
And faithfully his mercies most esteeme.

Hee wyll redeeme our deadly drowping state,
He wyll bring home the sheepe that goe astraye,
He wyll helpe them that hope in him alwaye:
He wyll appease our discorde and debate,
He wyll soone save, though we repent vs late.
He wyll be ours if we continewe his,
He wyll bring° bale° to joye and perfect blisse.   *transform / woe*
He wyll redeeme the flocke of his electe,
From all that is,

---

29. That is, before the dawn changing of the guard.

Or was amisse.

Since *Abrahams* heyres dyd first his Lawes reject.

Euer or neuer.[30]

Sir Philip Sidney
(1554–1586)

and Mary Sidney Herbert
(1561–1621)

ARISTOCRATIC SIBLINGS PHILIP and Mary Sidney were connected with nearly all aspects of English culture in the late sixteenth century. Philip was appointed the Royal Cupbearer in 1576, and served as an ambassador to continental imperial courts in the late 1570s. Though his relationship with Queen Elizabeth varied with political and interpersonal frictions of his time, he was knighted in 1583. Philip's zeal for the Protestant cause led him to participate in the war against Spanish forces in the Netherlands, where he was shot in the thigh. He died twenty-six days later, at the age of thirty-one. At the time of his death, Philip had been engaged in translating the Psalms, of which he had completed forty-three. Mary, who supervised the posthumous publication of Philip's works, translated the remaining one hundred and seven poems and revised many of Philip's. As a woman, Mary could not attend university, but she was educated at home in classical and contemporary languages and literature as well as the Bible. At sixteen, after having served as a lady-in-waiting to Elizabeth I, she married the Earl of Pembroke. In addition to translating the lion's share of what became known as the Sidney Psalter, she also composed a number of original poems and was a major figure in the literary patronage system throughout her life, supporting the work of many other writers, including Edmund Spenser. The Sidney Psalter was not published until the nineteenth century, but it circulated vigorously in manuscript, copied over and over again and passed from hand to hand. Poetically accomplished and formally innovative, with a vivid personal style, the Sidney Psalter influenced not only subsequent psalm translations but also the work of Henry Vaughan and Christopher Harvey, as well as Sidney relatives Lady Mary Wroth and George Herbert. John Donne praised the Sidneys' translation as a shared masterwork: "They tell us *why,* and teach us *how* to sing."

---

30. Ever or never: a declaration of faithfulness.

Psalm 13—Usquequo, Domine?[31] (Philip Sidney)

How long, O Lord, shall I forgotten be?
      What, ever?
How long wilt Thou Thy hidden face from me
      Dissever?
How long shall I consult with carefull sprite
      In anguish?
How long shall I with foes' triumphant might
      Thus languish?
Behold me, Lord, let to Thy hearing creep
      My crying;
Nay, giue me eyes and light, least that I sleep
      In dying:
Least my foe bragg, that in my ruin hee
      Prevailed,
And at my fall they joy that trouble me
      Assailed.
No, no! I trust on Thee, and joy in Thy
      Great pity;
Still, therfore, of Thy mercies shall be my
      Song's ditty.

Psalm 43—Judica me, Deus[32] (Philip Sidney)

Judg of all, judg me,
      And protector bee
Of my cause, oppressed
      Of most cruel sprites;
Saue me from bad wights°   *persons*
In false colours dressed.

For, my God, Thy sight
      Giveth me my might;
Why then hast Thou left me?
      Why walk I in woes,

---

31. The Sidneys title each of their psalm translations with the opening words in the Latin version of the Bible. Here, the Latin reads *How long, Lord?*
32. Latin: *Judge me, God.*

While prevayling foes
    Haue of joyes bereft me?

Send Thy truth and light,
       Let them guide me right
From the paths of folly;
       Bringing me to Thy
Tabernacles high,
In Thy hill most holy.

To God's altars tho
       I will boldly go,
Shaking off all sadnes;
       To that God that is
God of all my blisse,
God of all my gladness.

Then lo, then I will,
       With sweet musick's skill,
Gratefull meaning show Thee:
       Then, God, yea, my God,
I will sing abroad
What great thanks I ow Thee.

Why art thou, my soul,
       Cast down in such dole?
What ayles thy discomfort?
       Wait on God, for still
Thank my God, I will,
My onely aide and comfort.

Psalm 111—Confitebor tibi[33] (Mary Sidney Herbert)

At home, abroad most willingly I will
Bestow on God my praises uttmost skill:
Chaunting his workes, workes of unmatched might,
Deem'd so by them, who in their search delight.
Endlesse the honor to his powre pertaines:
From end as farre his justice eake° remaines,   *also*

---

33. Latin: *I will confess to you.*

Gratious and good and working wonders soe
His wonders never can forgotten goe.
In hungry waste he fedd his faithful Crue,
Keeping his league,° and still in promise true.   *fellowship*
Lastly his strength he caus'd them understand,
Making them lords of all the heathens land.
Now what could more each promise, doome, decree,
Of him confirme sure, just, unmov'd to be!
Preserv'd his folk, his league eternall fram'd:
Quake then with feare when holy he is nam'd.
Reverence of him is Perfect wisdoms well:
Stand in his lawe, so understand you well.
The praise of him (though wicked hartes repine)
Unbounded bides, noe time can it define.

Psalm 117—Laudate Dominum[34] (Mary Sidney Herbert)

Praise him that ay°   *always*
Remaines the same:
All tongues display
Iehovas fame.
Sing all that share
This earthly ball:
His mercies are
Expos'd to all:
Like as the word
Once he doth give
Rold° in record,   *enrolled*
Doth tyme outlive.

Psalm 139—Domine, probasti[35] (Mary Sidney Herbert)

O Lord in me there lieth nought,
    But to thy search revealed lies:
        For when I sitt

---

34. Latin: *Praise the Lord.*
35. Latin: *Lord, you have searched me.*

Thou markest it:
   No lesse thou notest when I rise:
      Yea closest closett of my thought
        Hath open windowes to thine eyes.

Thou walkest with me when I walk,
   When to my bed for rest I go,
      I find thee there,
      And ev'ry where:
   Not yongest thought in me doth grow,
No not one word I cast to talk,
   But yet unutt'red thou dost know.

If forth I march, thou goest before,
   If back I torne, thou com'st behind:
      Soe foorth nor back
      Thy guard I lack,
   Nay on me too, thy hand I find.
Well I thy wisdom may adore,
   But never reach with earthy mind.

To shunn thy notice, leave thine ey,
   O whither might I take my way?
      To starry spheare?
      Thy throne is there.
   To dead mens undelightsome stay?
There is thy walk, and there to ly
   Unknown, in vain I should assay.

O Sun, whome light nor flight can match,
   Suppose thy lightfull flightfull wings
      Thou lend to me,
      And I could flee
   As farr as thee the ev'ning brings:
Ev'n ledd to West he would me catch,
   Nor should I lurk with western things.

Doe thou thy best, O secret night,
   In sable vaile to cover me:
      Thy sable vaile
      Shall vainly faile:

With day unmask'd my night shall be,
For night is day, and darkness light,
   O father of all lights, to thee.

Each inmost peece in me is thine:
   While yet I in my mother dwelt,
      All that me cladd
      From thee I hadd.
   Thou in my frame hast strangly° delt: *wondrously*
Needes° in my praise thy workes must shine   *necessarily*
   So inly them my thoughts have felt.

Thou, how my back was beam-wise laid,
   And raftring of my ribbs, dost know:
      Know'st ev'ry point
      Of bone and joynt,
   How to this whole these partes did grow,
In brave embrod'ry faire araid,
   Though wrought in shopp both dark and low.

Nay fashionles, ere forme I toke,
   Thy all and more beholding ey
      My shapelesse shape
      Could not escape:
All these[36] tyme fram'd successively
Ere one had beeing, in the booke
   Of thy foresight, enrol'd did ly.

My God, how I these studies prize,
   That doe thy hidden workings show!
      Whose summ is such,
      Noe suume soe much:
   Nay summ'd as sand they summlesse grow.
I lye to sleepe, from sleepe I rise,
   Yet still in thought with thee I goe.

My God if thou but one wouldst kill,
   Then straight would leave my further chase
      This cursed brood
      Inur'd to blood:

---

36. That is, my form and shape.

Whose gracelesse tauntes at thy disgrace
Have aimed oft: and hating still
 Would with proud lies thy truth outface.[37]

Psalm 142—Voce mea ad Dominum[38] (Mary Sidney Herbert)

My voice to thee it self extreamly strayning,
 Cries praying, Lord, againe it cryeng praieth:
Before thy face the cause of my complayning,
 Before thy face my cases° mapp it laieth   *condition's*
Wherein my soule is painted
 In doubtfull way a stranger:
But, Lord, thou art acquainted,
 And knowst each path, where stick the toiles of danger.
For me, mine ey to ev'ry coast directed
 Lights not on one that will soe much as know me:
My life by all neglected,
 Ev'n hope of help is now quite perish'd from me.
Then with good cause to thee my spiritt flieth,
 Flieth, and saith: O Lord my safe abiding
Abides in thee: in thee all-only lieth
 Lott of my life, and plott of my residing.
Alas, then yeeld me hearing,
 For wearing woes have spent me:
And save me from their tearing,
 Who hunt me hard, and daily worse torment me.
O change my state, unthrall my soule enthralled:
 Of my escape then will I tell the story:
And with a crown enwalled
 Of godly men, will glory in thy glory.

---

37. This stanza suggests that if God would kill just one among the speaker's enemies, the others would
   grow desensitized to blood and leave off the pursuit.
38. Latin: *My voice to God*.

George Herbert
(1593–1633)

IN 1630, HERBERT LEFT BEHIND political ambitions and a brief career in Parliament to take orders in the Church of England. He spent the rest of his short life serving as the minister of a small parish in Bemerton St. Andrew, near Salisbury. In 1633, Herbert completed a book of poems entitled *The Temple,* in which his translation of the famous Twenty-Third Psalm appears. More work from *The Temple* can be found in the next section of this anthology.

The 23 Psalme

The God of love my shepherd is,
       And he that doth me feed:
While he is mine, and I am his,
       What can I want or need?

He leads me to the tender grasse,
       Where I both feed and rest;
Then to the streams that gently passe:
       In both I have the best.

Or if I stray, he doth convert
       And bring my minde in frame:
And all this not for my desert,
       But for his holy name.

Yea, in deaths shadie black abode
       Well may I walk, not fear:
For thou art with me; and thy rod
       To guide, thy staff to bear.

Nay, thou dost make me sit and dine,
       Ev'n in my enemies sight:
My head with oyl, my cup with wine
       Runnes over day and night.

Surely thy sweet and wondrous love
          Shall measure all my dayes;
And as it never shall remove,
          So neither shall my praise.

John Milton
(1608–1674)

MILTON WAS BORN THE SON OF a scrivener in London. Educated at Cambridge, he was preparing to take orders in the Anglican Church, but became involved instead in politics. After the English Civil War, he served as Secretary for Foreign Tongues—a sort of official multilingual letter-writer—under Oliver Cromwell during the Commonwealth. Of his many works, his first datable compositions are two psalm translations, produced at school when he was fifteen. Other poems by Milton are included in the next section of this anthology.

Psalm 88

Lord God that dost me save and keep,
          All day to thee I cry;
And all night long, before thee *weep*
          Before thee *prostrate lie*.
Into thy presence let my praier
          With sighs devout ascend;
And to my cries, that *ceaseless are*,
          Thine ear with favour bend.
For cloy'd with woes and trouble store
          Surcharg'd my Soul doth lie,
My life *at deaths uncherful dore*
          Unto the grave draws nigh.
Reck'n'd I am with them that pass
          Down to the *dismal* pit;
I am a man, but weak alas
          And for that name unfit.

From life discharg'd and parted quite
        Among the dead *to sleep,*
And like the slain *in bloody fight*
        That in the grave lie *deep.*
Whom thou rememberest no more,
        Dost never more regard,
Them from thy hand deliver'd o're
        Deaths hideous house hath barr'd.
Thou in the lowest pit *profound*
        Hast set me *all forlorn,*
Where thickest darkness *hovers round,*
        In horrid deeps *to mourn.*
Thy wrath *from which no shelter saves*
        Full sore doth press on me;
Thou break'st upon me all thy waves,
        And all thy waves break me.
Thou dost my friends from me estrange,
        And mak'st me odious,
Me to them odious, *for they change,*
        And I here pent up thus.
Through sorrow, and affliction great
        Mine eye grows dim and dead,
Lord all the day I thee entreat,
        My hands to thee I spread.
Wilt thou do wonders on the dead,
        Shall the deceas'd arise
And praise thee *from their loathsom bed*
        With pale and hollow eyes?
Shall they thy loving kindness tell
        On whom the grave *hath hold,*
Or they *who* in perdition *dwell*
        Thy faithfulness *unfold?*
In darkness can thy mighty *hand*
        Or wondrous acts be known,
Thy justice in the *gloomy* land
        Of *dark* oblivion?
But I to thee O Lord do cry
        E're yet my life be spent,
And *up to thee* my praier *doth hie*
        Each morn, and thee prevent.°   *anticipate*

Why wilt thou Lord my soul forsake,
   And hide thy face from me,
That am already bruis'd, and shake
   With terror sent from thee;
Bruz'd, and afflicted and *so low*
   As ready to expire,
While I thy terrors undergo
   Astonish'd with thine ire.
Thy fierce wrath over me doth flow
   Thy threatnings cut me through:
All day they round about me go,
   Like waves they me persue.
Lover and friend thou hast remov'd
   And sever'd from me far.
They *fly me now* whom I have lov'd,
   And as in darkness are.

Richard Crashaw
(1613–1649)

CRASHAW WAS THE SON OF William Crashaw, a staunchly anti-Catholic preacher
who had officiated at the death of Mary, Queen of Scots. Richard, perhaps in rebellion
against his father, converted to Catholicism in adulthood. In 1646, the exiled English
Queen Henrietta Maria helped Crashaw to secure a position in Rome, but he died after
only three years in Italy. Crashaw's major works of poetry are the collections *Steps to
the Temple* and *The Delights of the Muses;* more of his work can be found in the next
section of this anthology.

Psalme 23

Happy me! o happy sheepe!
Whom my God vouchsafes to keepe;
Even my God, even he it is,
That points me to these wayes of blisse;
On whose pastures cheereful spring,

All the yeare doth sit and sing,
And rejoicing smiles to see
Their green backs wear his liverie:
Pleasure sings my soule to rest,
Plenty weares me at her brest,
Whose sweet temper teaches me
Not wanton, nor in want to be.
At my feet the blubb'ring Mountaine
Weeping, melts into a Fountaine,
Whose soft silver-sweating streames
Make high Noon forget his beames:
When my waiward breath is flying,
Hee calls home my soule from dying,
Strokes and tames my rabid Griefe,
And does woe° me into life: *woo*
When my simple weaknesse strayes,
(Tangled in forbidden wayes)
Hee (my Shepheard) is my Guide,
Hee's before me, on my side;
And behind me, he beguiles
Craft in all her knotty wiles:
Hee expounds the giddy wonder
Of my weary steps, and under
Spreads a Path cleare as the Day,
Where no churlish rub° saies nay   *impediment*
To my joy-conducted Feet,
Whil'st they Gladly goe to meet
Grace and peace, to learn new laies°   *songs*
Tun'd to my great Shepheards praise.
Come now all yee terrors, sally,
Muster forth into the valley,
Where triumphant darknesse hovers
With a sable wing, that covers
Brooding Horror. Come thou Death,
Let the damps of thy dull Breath
Overshadow even that shade,
And make darknesse selfe afraid;
There my feet, even there shall find
Way for a resolved mind.
Still my Shepheard, still my God

Thou art with me, Still thy rod,
And thy staffe, whose influence
Gives direction, gives defence.
At the whisper of thy Word
Crown'd abundance spreads my Bord:°   *table*
While I feast, my foes doe feed
Their rank malice not their need,
So that with the self-same bread
They are starv'd, and I am fed.
How my head in ointment swims!
How my cup orelooks her Brims!
So, even so still may I move
By the Line of thy deare Love;
Still may thy sweet mercy spread
A shady Arme above my head,
About my Paths, so shall I find
The faire Center of my mind
Thy Temple, and those lovely walls
Bright ever with a beame that falls
Fresh from the pure glance of thine eye,
Lighting to Eternity.
There I'le dwell for ever, there
Will I find a purer aire
To feed my Life with, there I'le sup
Balme and Nectar in my Cup,
And thence my ripe soule will I breath
Warme into the Armes of Death.

The Bay Psalm Book
(1640)

THE FIRST BOOK PRINTED IN America was a psalter, published in Cambridge, Massachusetts, by Stephen Day. Though the Puritan separatists who settled the Massachusetts Bay Colony had brought a number of psalm books with them, including the Sternhold and Hopkins translation, they wished for a psalter that would forgo poetic invention and hew more closely to the Hebrew originals. A number of ministers, including Richard Mather (father to Increase and grandfather to Cotton), presented this new volume of translated psalms, to be sung to familiar tunes from existing psalters. The book's full title page reads *The Whole Booke of Psalmes Faithfully* TRANSLATED *into* ENGLISH *Metre. Whereunto is prefixed a discourse declaring not only the lawfullnes, but also the necessity of the heavenly Ordinance of singing Scripture Psalmes in the Churches of God.* Over the next century, the Bay Psalm Book went through nine editions.

Psalm 141

A psalme of David
O God, my Lord, on thee I call
        doe thou make haste to mee:
and harken thou unto my voice,
        when I cry unto thee.
And let my pray'r directed be
        as incense in thy sight:
and the up-lifting of my hands
        as sacrifice at night.
Iehovah, oh that thou would'st set
        a watch my mouth before:
as also of my lips with care
        o doe thou keepe the dore.
Bow not my heart to evill things,
        to doe the wicked deed
with wicked workers: & let not
        mee of their daintees° feed.   *delicacies*
Let just-men smite mee, kindenes 'tis,
        let him reprove mee eke,°   *also*
it shall be such a pretious oyle,
        my head it shall not breake:
For yet my prayr's ev'n in their woes.
        When their judges are cast
on rocks, then shall they heare my words,
        for they are sweet to taste.
Like unto one who on the earth
        doth cutt & cleave the wood,
ev'n so our bones at the graves mouth
        are scattered abroad.

But unto thee o God, the Lord
          directed are mine eyes:
my soule o leave not destitute,
          on thee my hope relyes.
O doe thou keepe mee from the snare
          which they have layd for mee;
& also from the grins of those
          that work iniquitee.
Together into their owne nets
          o let the wicked fall:
untill such time as I escape
          may make from them withall.°

furthermore

4

The Flourishing of the Devotional Lyric
in the Post-Reformation Era

IN CHARTING THE HISTORICAL development of the devotional lyric, we might think of the period from the middle sixteenth century through the late seventeenth century as standing at the convergence of a number of intellectual and theological developments, a sort of poetic perfect storm.

The end of the fifteenth century had seen the accession to the throne of Henry VII, under whose monarchy the government of England became centralized, consolidated, and strengthened. This increased stability led to the growth of national and cultural infrastructures, including the expansion of universities.

As the intellectual culture of England developed, the island nation increasingly felt the influence of the movement that had begun in Italy in the fourteenth century and spread across the European continent: the Renaissance—a transformation whose scope was made possible by the invention of the printing press in the middle of the fifteenth century. Affecting all spheres of intellectual inquiry, including art, literature, religion, science, and politics, the Renaissance sought to revive the values expressed in ancient Greek and Roman artistic and philosophical texts. Inspired by the moral and literary legacy of the classical world, scholars, writers, and educators known today as humanists reformed education to emphasize the deep connection they saw between eloquence and critical thinking on the one hand and the cultivation of virtue on the other hand.

Not coincidentally, the intellectual revolution of the Renaissance dovetailed in the sixteenth century with a series of theological challenges against the Catholic Church which would become known as the Reformation. There had always been theological divisions within the institutional church, and some of its key doctrines had been disputed in fourteenth-century England by the Lollards, led by early biblical translator John Wycliffe. But the reform movement that began in 1517 with Martin Luther in Germany ramified throughout continental Europe, again assisted in its spread by the now-easy dissemination of ideas in print. Luther argued that the conscience was the central site of worship, and advocated for personal responsibility in reading and interpreting scripture rather than relying on the interpretive authority of clergy. With its emphasis on individual engagement with scriptural text, the Reformation fueled a hunger for vernacular Bibles, which led to a widespread familiarity with biblical stories and language. Moreover, as theological debate and controversy multiplied over the course of the Reformation, with clerics and philosophers from various and sometimes conflicting doctrinal positions publishing treatises and exegeses at rapid rates, religion registered increasingly in the wider culture as a point of conflict largely centered around questions of language and interpretation. It was only natural that the poetry written during this period would respond to these conflicts.

The increased focus on the individual in the discourses of both Renaissance humanism and Reformation theology corresponds to an efflorescence of lyric poetry in the sixteenth and seventeenth centuries. The lyric, generically invested in approximating the motions of an individual mind, provided a literary cognate for the shifting priorities of early modern culture. The lyric poems of the Italian poet Petrarch (1304–1374), vernacular treatments of the ideals of love and beauty that fused classical philosophy with a Christian perspective, inspired imitations across the continent, and sparked a culture of lyric poetry in England that would dominate that nation's literary landscape for nearly two centuries.

FURTHER READING

Davies, Horton. *Worship and Theology in England: From Cranmer to Baxter and Fox, 1534–1690.* Grand Rapids, Mich.: William B. Eerdmans, 1996.

Healy, Thomas. "Performing the Self: Reformation History and the English Renaissance Lyric." In *Performances of the Sacred in Late Medieval and Early Modern England,* ed. Susanne Rupp and Tobias Döring. Amsterdam: Rodopi, 2005: 65–79.

Lewalski, Barbara Kiefer. *Protestant Poetics and the Seventeenth-Century Religious Lyric.* Princeton: Princeton University Press, 1984.

Martz, Louis. *The Poetry of Meditation: A Study in English Religious Literature of the Seventeenth Century.* New Haven: Yale University Press, 1976.

Roberts, John R., ed. *New Perspectives on the Seventeenth-Century English Religious Lyric*. Columbia: University of Missouri Press, 1994.

Ross, Malcolm Mackenzie. *Poetry and Dogma: The Transformation of Eucharistic Symbols in Seventeenth Century English Poetry*. New York: Octagon, 1969.

Shuger, Debora Kuller. *The Renaissance Bible: Scholarship, Sacrifice, and Subjectivity*. Berkeley: University of California Press, 1994.

John Skelton
(c. 1460–1529)

EDUCATED AT OXFORD AND Cambridge, Skelton was the first significant poet of the Tudor period. He was a favorite of Henry VII's mother, the Countess of Richmond. Under her influence, he participated in the royal household and served as a tutor to the child who would become Henry VIII. He may have been appointed Poet Laureate when his pupil became King. Skelton was ordained a priest of the Catholic Church in the last years of the fifteenth century, and later retired from courtly circles to serve as rector of a small town in Norfolk. He was perhaps best known for his biting satires against court culture and the clergy, though he also wrote ballads, morality plays, and other poems, which were collected and published around 1520.

A Prayer to the Father of Heauen

O radiant luminary of light interminable!
Celestiall father, potenciall God of might
Of heauen and earth. O Lorde incomperable!
Of al perfections the essenciall most perfight;°   *perfect*
O Maker of mankind, that formed day and night
Whose power imperial, comprehendeth euery place!
Mine hart, my mind, my thought, my hole delite
Is after this lyfe, to se thy glorious face.

Whose magnificence is incomprehensible,
Al arguments of reason, which far doth excede;
Whose deite° doutles, is indiuisible,   *deity*
From whom al goodnes, and vertue doth procede
Of thy support, al creatures haue nede
Assist me, good Lord, and graunt me of thy grace
To liue to thy pleasure, in word thought and dede,
And after this lyfe, to see thy glorious face.

William Baldwin
(1515–1563?)

WILLIAM BALDWIN IS PERHAPS best known as one of the original compilers of the
1559 *Mirrour for Magistrates,* a collection of didactic and moralistic poems narrating the
lives and tragic ends of various historical figures, with the intention that magistrates
and other persons in power would learn from the ethical examples—and especially
from the errors—of the famous. Born in the southwest of England and educated at
Oxford, Baldwin published a number of works, including *A Treatise of Morall Phyloso-
phie* (1547) and the verse translation *Canticles or Balades of Salomon* (1549).

Christ my Beloved

Christe my Beloved whiche styl° doth fede   *still*
Among the flowers, having delight
        Among his faythful lilies:[1]
Doeth take great care for me in dede,
And I agayne with all my might
        Wyll do what so his wyl is.

My love in me, and I in hym,
Conioyned by love wyll styl abyde
        Among the faythful lilies:

---

1. See Song of Songs 2.1–2, 2.16, and 6.2.

Tyll day doe breake, and truth do dym
All shadowes darke, and cause them slyde,
    According as his wyll is.

Elizabeth I
(1533–1603)

ELIZABETH TUDOR ASSUMED the throne of England after her sister Mary's death in 1558. Her mother, Anne Boleyn, had been Henry VIII's second wife, whom he married after his split from the Roman Catholic Church and his divorce from Mary's mother, Catherine of Aragon. But Anne Boleyn had been executed when Elizabeth was a young child, and she was declared illegitimate. Elizabeth brought a savvy and pragmatic political sensibility to her reign, and governed England with relative religious tolerance, though as Supreme Governor of the Church of England she established Protestantism as the official state religion. It was long expected that Elizabeth would marry and produce an heir, but she refused her suitors, and near the end of her life proclaimed that James VI of Scotland would succeed her as England's monarch. Elizabeth was educated by the most prominent humanist thinkers of her time, and she was trained in classical and modern languages, rhetoric, theology, and philosophy, among other fields of study. She conducted her own diplomatic exchanges in fluent Latin. Throughout her life, Elizabeth composed original poems and translations from the Bible and from classical and contemporary literary and philosophical texts. The following poem, attributed to Elizabeth, celebrates the defeat of the Spanish Armada by the underdog English navy.

A songe made by her Majestie and songe before her at her cominge from white hall to Powles through Fleete streete in Anno domini 1588. Songe in December after the scatteringe of the Spanishe Navy.[2]

Lok° and bowe downe thyne eare o Lorde   *Look*
from thy bright spheare behould and see
Thy hand maide[3] and thy handy worke
Amongest thy pristes offeringe to thee
zeale for incense Reachinge the skyes
my selfe and septer sacryifise

My sowle assende this holy place
Ascribe him strengthe and singe his prayse
For he Refraynethe peryures spyrite°   *restrains perjurers' spirits*
And hathe done wonders in my Daies
he made the wynds and waters rise
To scatter all myne enemyes

This Josephes Lorde and Israells god
the fyry piller and dayes clowde[4]
That saved his saincts from wicked men
And drenchet° the honor of the prowde   *drowned*
And hathe preserved in tender love
The spirit of his Turtle Dove.

Richard Stanihurst
(1545–1618)

BORN IN DUBLIN, STANIHURST was the first major Irish writer to compose in English. He was friendly with scholar and Latinist Gabriel Harvey and poet Sir Philip Sidney. Educated at Oxford, Stanihurst, after completing training in the law, moved to

---

2. As the title indicates, this poem was written by Queen Elizabeth and sung as she rode from Whitehall Palace to St. Paul's Cathedral through Fleet Street in London, after the defeat of the Spanish Armada by the English navy in 1588.
3. See Luke 2.28.
4. See Exodus 13.21.

Leiden and took holy orders. He served as chaplain to Albert, Archduke of Austria, who was then governor of the Spanish Netherlands. Stanihurst's Latin works in poetry and prose are numerous, and he also published translations of Virgil's *Æneid* and several psalms.

A Prayer to the Trinitie

Trinitee blessed, deitee coequal,
Unitie sacred, God one eeke° in essence,   *also*
Yeeld to thy servaunt, pitifullye calling,
     Merciful hearing.

Vertuus living dyd I long relinquish,
Thy wyl and precepts misirablye scorning,
Graunt toe mee, sinful pacient, repenting,
     Helthful amendment.

Blessed I judge him, that in hart is healed:
Cursed I know him, that in helth is harmed:
Thy physick° therefore, toe° me, wretch unhappye,   *medicine / to*
     Send, mye Redeemer.

Glorye toe God, the father, and his onlye
Soon,° the protectoure of us earthlye sinners,   *son*
Thee sacred Spirit, laborers refreshing,
     Still be renowned. Amen.

Edmund Spenser
(1552–1599)

AN ENGLISH POET BEST KNOWN for his allegorical fantasy epic *The Faerie Queene*, Spenser was a man of high ambition, aspiring to become the greatest poet of his time. He was born to a family whose bloodlines were not noble, but he received a strong education and became the secretary to noblemen, including the Earl of Leicester, Queen Elizabeth's favorite. In 1580, Spenser was in service to the Lord Deputy of Ireland, and he wrote the bulk of his literary output in that country, including a pastoral called *Colin*

Clouts Come Home Again, *The Faerie Queene*, and his sonnet sequence *Amoretti*, or "little loves." His sonnet cycle departs from the sonneteering tradition in that it celebrates a successful love relationship, rather than lamenting an inaccessible beloved.

from *Amoretti*
68

Most glorious Lord of lyfe that on this day,[5]
Didst make thy triumph ouer death and sin:
and hauing harrow'd hell didst bring away
captiuity thence captiue, vs to win.
This ioyous day, deare Lord, with ioy begin,
and grant that we for whom thou diddest dye
being with thy deare blood clene washt from sin,
may liue for euer in felicity.
And that thy loue we weighing worthily,
may likewise love thee for the same again:
and for thy sake, that all lyke deare didst buy,[6]
with loue may one another entertayne.
So let vs loue, dear loue, lyke as we ought,
loue is the lesson which the Lord vs taught.

Fulke Greville, Lord Brooke
(1554–1628)

BORN THE ONLY SON OF A noble family, Fulke Greville attended school with Philip Sidney, who became his close friend. Sidney's father offered the youth a post, but he chose instead to follow Philip to Elizabeth I's court. After Sidney's death, Greville wrote an elegy to the poet, and later a biography of his friend. Greville served in Parliament, and held high governmental positions under both Elizabeth I and James I. Greville was murdered by a servant who believed he had been cheated in Greville's

---

5. "This day": Easter.
6. That bought all at the same cost.

will. All of Greville's works were published posthumously, including his biography of
Sidney, a few plays, and his most famous work, the sonnet cycle *Cælica*, a series of love
poems as well as verses on religious and philosophical themes.

from *Cælica*
99

Downe in the depth of mine iniquity,
That vgly centre of infernall spirits,
Where each sinne feeles her owne deformity,
In these peculiar torments she inherits,
      Depriu'd of humane graces, and diuine,
      Euen there appeares this *sauing God* of mine.

And in this fatall mirrour of transgression,
Shewes man as fruit of his degeneration,
The errours° ugly infinite impression,   *error's*
Which beares the faithlesse doome to desperation;
      Depriu'd of humane graces, and diuine,
      Euen there appeares this *sauing God* of mine.

In power and truth, Almighty and eternall,
Which on the sinne reflects strange desolation,
With glory scourging all the Spr'its infernall,
And vncreated hell with vnpriuation;°   *deprivation*
      Depriu'd of humane graces, not diuine,
      Euen there appeares this *sauing God* of mine.

For on this sp'ritual Crosse condemned lying,
To paines infernall by eternal doome,
I see my Sauiour for the same sinnes dying,
And from that hell I fear'd, to free me, come;
      Depriu'd of humane graces, not diuine,
      Thus hath his death rais'd up this soule of mine.

Sir Philip Sidney
(1554–1586)

PHILIP SIDNEY WAS BORN AT Penshurst, his family's ancestral manor, the eldest
son of Sir Henry Sidney, Lord Deputy of Ireland, and nephew of Robert Dudley, Earl
of Leicester. He attended Oxford, but left without taking a degree to travel through
Europe. After his return, Sidney became a prominent figure in Elizabethan culture,
both as a courtier to Elizabeth I and as a patron of the arts, encouraging such authors as
Edward Dyer, Fulke Greville, and Edmund Spenser, who dedicated *The Shepheardes
Calender* to him. Sidney's works include translations of the Psalms (see Part 3 of this
anthology), the long sonnet cycle *Astrophil and Stella,* an influential work of early lit-
erary criticism (*The Defence of Poesy*), and the elaborate prose romance *Arcadia,* which
he dedicated to his sister, Mary Sidney Herbert, the Countess of Pembroke. Mary
reworked the *Arcadia* after Philip's death from a musketball wound; a number of his
sonnets are included in the volume she published.

from *Certaine Sonets*
(printed in *The Countesse of Pembrokes Arcadia. Written by Sir Philip Sidney Knight,* 1598)

Leaue me o Loue, which reachest but to dust,
And thou my mind aspire to higher things:
Grow rich in that which neuer taketh rust:
What euer fades, but fading pleasure brings.

Draw in thy beames, and humble all thy might,
To that sweet yoke, where lasting freedomes be:
Which breakes the clowds, and opens forth the light,
That doth both shine and giue us sight to see.

O take fast hold, let that light be thy guide,
In this small course which birth drawes out to death,
And thinke how euill becommeth him to slide,[7]
Who seeketh heau'n, and comes of heau'nly breath.

---

7. And think how poorly it becomes him to err.

Then farewell, world, thy uttermost I see,
Eternall Loue maintaine thy life in me.

Splendidis longum valedico nugis.[8]

Robert Southwell
(1561–1595)

IN 1584, SOUTHWELL, AN Englishman living in Rome, was ordained a priest. That
same year, an English law was enacted that forbade any English-born subject who had
entered into Roman Catholic orders to remain in England longer than forty days on
pain of death. Southwell requested that he be sent to England in 1586 as a Jesuit mis-
sionary. He went from one Catholic family to another, administering Catholic rites,
and in 1589 became domestic chaplain to Ann Howard, whose husband, the first Earl of
Arundel, was in prison convicted of treason. After he had spent six years in England,
Southwell's activities were reported to the authorities; he was arrested and tortured,
and spent some years imprisoned in the Tower of London, during which period he
likely composed the bulk of his poems. Southwell was hanged for treason. A volume of
his poems was published posthumously, initially without the author's name, and was
reprinted thirteen times during the next forty years.

Christs bloody sweate

Fatt soyle,	full springe,	sweete olive,	grape of blisse	
That yeldes,	that streames,	that powres,°	that dost distil	*pours*
Untild,°	undrawne,	unstamped,	untouched of presse	*untilled*
Deare fruit,	cleare brooks,	fayre oyle,	sweete wine at will	

Thus Christ unforc'd preventes in shedding bloode
the whippes the thornes the nailes the speare and roode.

He Pelican he Phenix[9] fate doth prove
Whome flames consume whom streames enforce to die

8. Latin: *A long farewell to shining trifles.*

9. According to legend, in a time of famine a mother pelican would draw blood from her own chest and
give the blood to her chicks; thus, the pelican became a symbol for Christ in his Eucharistic function.
Similarly, Christ is associated with the mythical phoenix, which dies and is reborn from its own ashes.

How burneth bloud howe bleedeth burning love
Can one in flame and streame both bathe and frye
How coulde he joyne a Phenix fyerye paynes
In faynting pelicans still bleeding vaynes

Elias once to prove gods soveraigne powre
By ppraire° procur'd a fier of wondrous vorce°   *prayer / force*
That blood and wood and water did devoure
Yea stones and dust beyond all natures course[10]
Such fire is love that fedd with gory bloode
Doth burne no lesse then in the driest woode

O sacred Fire come shewe thy force on me
That sacrifice to Christe I maye retorne
If withered wood for fuell fittest bee
If stones and dust yf fleshe and blood will burne
I withered am and stonye to all good.
A sacke of dust a masse of fleshe and bloode

A childe my Choyce

Let folly praise that phancy loves I praise and love that childe
Whose hart no thought, whose tong no word, whose hand no deed defilde

I praise him most I love him best all prayse and love is his
While him I love in him I live and cannot lyve amisse

Loves sweetest mark lawd's highest theme mans most desired light
To love him life to leave him death to live in him delighte.

He myne by gift I his by debt thus ech to other Dewe
First frende he was best frende he is all tymes will try him trewe.

Though yonge yet wise though small yet strong though man yet God he is
As wise he knows, as stronge he can as God he loves to blisse°   *bless*

His knowledge rules his strength defendes his love doth cherish all
His birth our joye, his life our light, his death our end of thrall

---

10. For the narrative of Elijah's altar, see 2 Kings 1.

Alas he weeps he sighes he pantes yet do his Angells singe
Out of his teares his sighes and throbbs doth bud a joyfull springe

Almightie babe whose tender armes can force all foes to flye
Correct my faultes, protect my life direct me when I die.

The Burning Babe

As I in hoary Winters night stoode shyveringe in the snowe
Surpris'd I was with sodayne° heat, which made my hart to glowe   *sudden*
And lifting upp a fearefull eye to vewe what fire was nere
A pretty babe all burning bright did in the ayre appeare
Who scorched with excessive heate such floodes of teares did shedd
As though his floodes should quench his flames, which with his tears were fedd.
Alas, quoth he, but newly borne in fiery heates I frye
Yet none approach to warme their hartes or feele my fire but I.
My faultles brest the furnace is, the fuell woundinge thornes
Love is the fire and sighs the smoke, the ashes shame and scornes;
The fewell° Justice layeth on and Mercy blowes the coales,   *fuel*
The metall in this furnace wrought are mens defiled soules
For which as nowe on fire I am to worke them to their good
So will I melt into a bathe to wash them in my bloode.
With this he vanisht out of sight and swiftly shronke awaye
And straight I called unto mynde, that it was Christmas daye.

William Alabaster
(1567–1640)

BORN THE ELDEST OF SIX children, Alabaster was descended from an ancient Norman line, though by the time of his birth the family worked mostly in trade. William was educated at Cambridge, where he produced poems in Latin, Greek, and English. He served as chaplain to Robert Devereux, Earl of Essex, and sailed with the earl on his martial expedition against the Spaniards in Cadiz. On this voyage, Alabaster was converted to Roman Catholicism. His conversion, and his zealous defense of the Roman faith, led him to be imprisoned several times. Years later, with apparent vacillation and spiritual turmoil, Alabaster denounced Rome, reverted to the Church of England, and became chaplain to King James I. His *Divine Meditations,* a series of religious sonnets, were composed in the period of his conversion to Catholicism. Though they were never published, Alabaster was well known as an accomplished Latinist; his Latin tragedy *Roxana* appeared in 1595, and he also published a number of mystical readings of biblical texts in Latin.

A Divine Sonnet

Jesu, thy love within me is so main,°   *mighty*
And my poor heart so narrow of content,
That with thy love my heart wellnigh is rent,
And yet I love to bear such loving pain.
O take thy Cross and nails and therewith strain
My heart's desire unto his full extent,
That thy dear love may not therein be pent,
But thoughts may have free scope thy love to explain.
O now my heart more paineth than before,
Because it can receive and hath no more,
O fill this emptiness or else I die,
Now stretch my heart again and now supply,
Now I want space, now grace. To end this smart,
Since my heart holds not thee, hold thou my heart.

Upon the Ensigns of Christ's Crucifying: The Sponge

O sweet and bitter monuments of pain,
Bitter to Christ who all the pain endured,
But sweet to me whose death my life procured,
How shall I full express such loss, such gain?
My tongue shall be my pen, mine eyes shall rain
Tears for my ink, the place where I was cured
Shall be my book, where, having all abjured,
And calling heavens to record in that plain,
Thus plainly will I write: no sin like mine.
When I have done, do thou, Jesu divine,
Take up the tart sponge of thy Passion

And blot it forth; then be thy spirit the quill,
Thy blood the ink, and with compassion
Write thus upon my soul: thy Jesu still.

The Epiphany

O strangest thing that God doth now begin,
      In being which, he hath no godheads grace:
      O strangest Roome, this subject takes his place,
In want of Roome, for none was in his Inne.

O strangest colour to be viewed in,
      For humane darknesse vailed hath his face.
      O strangest middle of respective space,
Where as a starre more than the sunne could win.

O strangest starre that must reveale this sight
That by disorder from the rest gives light.

O strangest eyes that saw him by this starre,
Who when by-standers saw not, saw so farre.

And since such wonders were in seeing him
No wonder if my wondring thought grow dim.

A Sonnet on the Resurrection

Sink down, my soul, into the lowest cell,
Into the anguish of thy sins descend,
There think how Christ for thee his blood did spend,
And afterward went down as low as hell.
Rise up, my soul, as high as God doth dwell,
Unto the hope of heaven, and there expend
How Christ did from the gates of hell ascend,
In height of glory which no thought can tell.
Descend in patience with him to die,
Ascend in confidence with him to reign,
And upwards, downwards by humility.
Since man fell upwards, down by Satan's train,
Look for no fairer way unto thy crown,
Than that that Christ went up, by going down.

Thomas Campion

(1567–1620)

CAMPION, WHOSE PARENTS died in his childhood, studied law, medicine, and music. He was a practicing physician in London. Additionally, he became a prominent theorist of poetry as well as music, publishing both a book on prosody, *Observations in the Art of English Poesie* (1602), and a technical treatise on music, *A New Way of Making Fowre Parts in Counterpoint* (1613). He wrote masques and songs, and poems in both Latin and English. His religious lyrics appear in a book of "airs," or poems set to music; they were originally published along with a score for performance.

1

Avthor of light, revive my dying spright,
Redeeme it from the snares of all-confounding night.
      Lord, light me to thy blessed way:
      For blinde with worldly vaine desires, I wander as a stray:
            Sunne and Moone, Starres and vnderlights I see,
      But all their glorious beames are mists and darknesse being compar'd to thee.

Fountain of health my soules deep wounds recure,
Sweet showres of pitty raine, wash my vncleannesse pure.
      One drop of thy desired grace
      The faint and fading hart can raise, and in ioyes bosome place.
      Sinne and Death, Hell and tempting Fiends may rage;
But God his owne will guard, and their sharp paines and griefe in time asswage.

9

Most sweet and pleasing are thy wayes O God,
Like Meadowes deckt with Christall streames and flowers:
Thy paths no foote prophane hath euer trod:
      Nor hath the proud man rested in thy Bowers.
There liues no Vultur, no deuouring Beare,
But only Doues and Lambs are harbor'd there.

The Wolfe his young ones to their prey doth guide;
    The Foxe his Cubbs with false deceit endues;
The Lyons Whelpe suckes from his Damme his pride;
    In hers the Serpent malice doth infuse:
The darksome Desart all such beasts contaynes,
Not one of them in Paradice remaynes.

Aemilia Lanyer
(1569–1645)

THE FIRST ENGLISHWOMAN to publish her poetry as a professional writer, Lanyer
was the daughter of one of Elizabeth I's royal musicians. She was educated among no-
bility and, although she married her cousin, was also a mistress to a noble kinsman of
Elizabeth's. In 1611, she published *Salve Deus Rex Judaeorum*, a long religious poem
that addresses the mistreatment of women throughout history, an error for which she
blames a misunderstanding both of the scriptures and of Christian doctrine. Her de-
fense of women revisits biblical episodes to demonstrate how their female characters
serve as models for devotion. The passage included here is excerpted from the poem's
description of the Passion; the "deare Lady" mentioned in the last stanza is the Lady
Margaret, Countess Dowager of Cumberland, with whom Lanyer lived for some time
and to whom Lanyer dedicates her poem.

from *Salve Deus Rex Judaeorum*[11]
LINES 265–328

These high deserts invites my lowely Muse
To write of Him, and pardon crave of thee,
For Time so spent, I need make no excuse,
Knowing it doth with thy faire Minde agree
So well, as thou no Labour wilt refuse,
That to thy holy Love may pleasing be:
His Death and Passion I desire to write,
And thee to reade, the blessed Soules delight.

---

11. Latin: *Hail to God, King of the Jews.*

But my deare Muse, now whither wouldst thou flie,
Above the pitch of thy appointed straine?
With Icarus thou seekest now to trie,
Not waxen wings, but thy poore barren Braine,[12]
Which farre too weake, these siely° lines descrie;   *silly*
Yet cannot this thy forward Mind restraine,
But thy poore Infant Verse must soare aloft,
Not fearing threat'ning dangers, happening oft.

Thinke when the eye of Wisdom shall discover
Thy weakling Muse to flie, that scarce could creepe,
And in the Ayre above the Clowdes to hover,
When better 'twere mued° up, and fast asleepe;   *mewed*
They'l thinke with Phaeton, thou canst neare recover,
But helplesse with that poore yong Lad to weepe:
The little World of thy weake Wit on fire,
Where thou wilt perish in thine owne desire.[13]

But yet the Weaker thou doest seeme to be
In Sexe, or Sence, the more his Glory shines,
That doth infuze such powerfull Grace in thee,
To shew thy Love in these few humble Lines;
The Widowes Myte, with this may well agree,
Her little All more worth than golden mynes,
Beeing more deerer to our loving Lord,
Than all the wealth that Kingdoms could affoard.[14]

Therefore I humbly for his Grace will pray,
That he will give me Power and Strength to Write,
That what I have begun, so end I may,
As his great Glory may appeare more bright;
Yea in these Lines I may no further stray,
Than his most holy Spirit shall give me Light:

---

12. In Greek mythology, Icarus attempted to fly on wings made from feathers and wax. He ignored cautions about flying too close to the sun; when the sun's heat melted the wax on his wings, he fell into the sea and drowned.

13. Phaeton was the son of Helios, the ancient Greek sun god. He took his father's chariot one day but could not control it; Zeus had to strike him down with a lightning bolt to prevent him from burning the earth.

14. For the story of the widow's mite, see Luke 21.1–4.

That blindest Weakenesse be not over-bold,
The manner of his Passion to unfold.

In other Phrases than may well agree
With his pure Doctrine, and most holy Writ,
That Heavens cleare eye, and all the World may see,
I seeke his Glory, rather than to get
The Vulgars breath, the seed of Vanitie,
Nor Fames lowd Trumpet care I to admit;
But rather strive in plainest Words to showe,
The Matter which I seeke to undergoe.

A Matter farre beyond my barren skill,
To shew with any Life this map of Death,
This Storie; that whole Worlds with Bookes would fill,
In these few Lines, will put me out of breath,
To run so swiftly up this mightie Hill,
I may behold it with the eye of Faith;
But to present this pure unspotted Lambe,
I must confesse, I farre unworthy am.

Yet if he please t'illuminate my Spirit,
And give me Wisdom from his holy Hill,
That I may Write part of his glorious Merit,
If he vouchsafe to guide my Hand and Quill,
To shew his Death, by which we doe inherit
Those endlesse Joyes that all our hearts doe fill;
Then will I tell of that sad blacke fac'd Night,
Whose mourning Mantle covered Heavenly Light.

John Donne
(1572–1631)

JOHN DONNE WAS BORN INTO a financially comfortable family of London Catholics. Donne's father was an iron merchant, and his mother was the daughter of writer John Heywood and the great-niece of Sir Thomas More. Donne studied law and anticipated a political career. He was later appointed private secretary to Sir Thomas

Egerton, Lord Keeper of the Great Seal, but Donne's career aspirations were derailed when, in 1601, he secretly married Ann More, Lady Egerton's seventeen-year-old niece. Donne was dismissed from Egerton's service and committed by the bride's father to Fleet Prison for several weeks. For more than a decade after his release, Donne's financial position was precarious, but his work won him a number of influential patrons. His prose treatise *Pseudo-Martyr* (1610), which argued that English Catholics could pledge an oath of allegiance to the Protestant English monarch but maintain religious loyalty to the Pope, won James I's favor. In 1607, Donne was urged to enter into the Anglican clergy, but he refused, replying that he was unworthy. But King James continued to encourage Donne in the direction of the church—somewhat forcefully, for in the end he announced that Donne would receive no position or preferment from the King except in the church. In 1615, Donne took orders and was appointed Royal Chaplain. In 1621 he was appointed Dean of St. Paul's, a post he retained until his death. Though he was widely known and admired for the wit and elegance of his sermons, Donne's poetry remained unpublished until two years after his death.

Goodfriday, 1613. Riding Westward.

Let mans Soule be a Spheare, and then, in this,
The intelligence that moves, devotion is,
And as the other Spheares, by being growne
Subject to forraigne motion, lose their owne,
And being by others hurried every day,
Scarce in a yeare their naturall forme obey:
Pleasure or businesse, so, our Soules admit
For their first mover, and are whirld by it.[15]
Hence is't, that I am carryed towards the West
This day, when my Soules forme bends toward the East.
There I should see a Sunne, by rising set,
And by that setting endlesse day beget;
But that Christ on this Crosse, did rise and fall,
Sinne had eternally benighted all.
Yet dare I'almost be glad, I do not see
That spectacle of too much weight for mee.
Who sees Gods face, that is selfe life, must dye;
What a death were it then to see God dye?

---

15. Like the heavenly spheres, which are influenced by gravities not their own, man's soul is moved by the foreign motion of pleasure or business.

9

If poysonous mineralls, and if that tree,
Whose fruit threw death on (else immortall) us,
If lecherous goats, if serpents envious
Cannot be damn'd, alas, why should I be?
Why should intent or reason, borne in mee,
Make sinnes, else equall, in me more hainous?
And mercy being easie, and glorious
To God, in his sterne wrath, why threatens hee?
But who am I, that dare dispute with thee?
O God, oh! of thine onely worthy blood,
And my teares, make a heavenly Lethean flood,[23]
And drowne in it my sinnes blacke memorie,
That thou remember them, some claime as debt,
I thinke it mercy, if thou wilt forget.

13

What if this present were the worlds last night?
Marke in my heart, ô Soule, where thou dost dwell,
The picture of Christ crucifi'd, and tell
Whether his countenance can thee affright,
Teares in his eyes quench the amazing light,
Blood fils his frownes, which from his pierc'd head fell.
And can that tongue adjudge thee unto hell,
Which pray'd forgivenesse for his foes fierce spight?
No, no; but as in my idolatrie
I said to all my profane mistresses,
Beauty, of pitie, foulnesse onely is
A signe of rigour: so I say to thee,
To wicked spirits are horrid shapes assign'd,
This beauteous forme assures a pitious minde.

---

23. In classical mythology, the River Lethe was the river of forgetfulness in the land of the dead.

14

Batter my heart, three person'd God; for, you
As yet but knocke, breathe, shine, & seeke to mend;
That I may rise, and stand, o'rthrow mee,'and bend
Your force, to breake, blowe, burn, & make me new.
I, like an usurpt towne, to'another due,
Labour to admit you, but oh, to no end,
Reason your Viceroy in me, me should defend,
But is captiv'd, and proves weake or untrue,
Yet dearly'I love you, and would be lov'd faine,°   *eagerly*
But am betroth'd unto your enemie,
Divorce me,'untie, or breake that knot againe,
Take me to you, imprison me, for I
Except you'enthrall me, never shall be free,
Nor ever chaste, except you ravish me.

Ben Jonson
(1572–1637)

PERHAPS BEST KNOWN FOR his many plays and masques, Ben Jonson boldly published a volume of his *Works* in 1616, containing drama and poetry that manifested his determination to revive classical forms and themes. In 1640, an expanded folio volume appeared, containing among its catalogue of Jonson's verse some few religious works. Jonson's influence on his contemporaries was profound: many of the so-called Cavalier poets (those whose work is marked by grace and a neoclassical aesthetic, many of whom were courtiers and supported King Charles I during the English Civil War) described themselves as his "sons" or his "tribe"; their inheritance was to continue Jonson's classical interests, his subtle melodies, and his canny deployment of wit. Born into a Protestant family, Jonson converted to Roman Catholicism during a period of strong anti-Catholic sentiment in England; twelve years later, he rejoined the Church of England. In his large body of surviving work are only a handful of devotional poems.

To Heaven

Good, and great God, can I not think of thee,
But it must, straight, my melancholy bee?
Is it interpreted in mee disease,
That, laden with my sinnes, I seeke for ease?
O, be thou witnesse, that the reines[24] dost know
And hearts of all, if I be sad for show,
And judge mee after: if I dare pretend
To ought but grace, or ayme at other end.
As thou art all, so be thou all to mee,
First, midst, and last, converted one, and three;
My faith, my hope, my love: and in this state,
My judge, my witnesse, and my advocate.
Where have I been this while exil'd from thee?
And whither rapt, now thou but stoup'st° to mee?   *stoops*
Dwell, dwell here still: O, being every-where,
How can I doubt to finde thee ever, here?
I know my state, both full of shame, and scorne,
Conceiv'd in sinne, and unto labour borne,
Standing with feare, and must with horror fall,
And destin'd unto judgement, after all.
I feele my griefes too, and there scarce is ground,
Upon my flesh t'inflict another wound.
Yet dare I not complaine, or wish for death
With holy Paul,[25] lest it be thought the breath
Of Discontent; or that these prayers bee
For wearinesse of life, not love of thee.

A Hymne to God the Father

Heare mee, O God!
A broken hart,
   Is my best part:
Use still thy rod,
That I may prove
   Therein, thy Love.

---

24. The kidneys, thought to be the seat of affections.
25. See Romans 7.24.

If thou hadst not
  Beene stern to mee,
  But left me free,
I had forgot
  My selfe and thee.

For sin's so sweet,
  As minds ill bent
  Rarely repent,
Until they meet
  Their punishment.

Who more can crave
  Than thou hast done:
  That gav'st a Sonne,
To free a slave?
  First made of nought;
  With All since bought.

Sinne, Death, and Hell,
  His glorious Name
  Quite overcame,
Yet I rebell,
  And slight the same.

But, i'le come in,
  Before my losse,
  Me farther tosse,
As sure to win
  Under his Crosse.[26]

---

26. But I'll return before my sins toss me farther, as I am certain to win by means of the cross. Jonson's
language evokes the story of the soldiers casting lots for Jesus's clothes after his death; see Matthew
27.35.

Sir John Beaumont

(1583–1627)

JOHN BEAUMONT WAS THE brother of the playwright Francis Beaumont. Born into a noble family, John went to Oxford and later studied law. A Catholic, he was fined for his refusal to attend Anglican services. Nevertheless, he seems to have been active at court and was made the First Baronet Beaumont in 1627. He began to publish verse when he was still in his teens, and counted the poet Michael Drayton among his friends. His reputation as a writer rested on an early mock-heroic work called *The Metamorphosis of Tobacco*. His long poem in twelve books, *The Crown of Thornes*, was never published but circulated in manuscript. A modest selection of his work was published after his death, in 1629.

In Desolation

O Thou, Who sweetly bend'st my stubborne will,
Who send'st Thy stripes to teach, and not to kill!
Thy chearefull face from me no longer hide;
Withdraw these clouds, the scourges of my pride;
I sinke to hell, if I be lower throwne:
I see what man is, being left alone.
My substance, which from nothing did begin,
Is worse then nothing by the waight of sin:
I see my selfe in such a wretched state,
As neither thoughts conceiue, nor words relate.
How great a distance parts vs! for in Thee
Is endlesse good, and boundlesse ill in mee.
All creatures proue me abiect, but how low
Thou onely know'st, and teachest me to know:
To paint this basenesse, Nature is too base;
This darknesse yeelds not but to beames of grace.
Where shall I then this piercing splendor find?
Or found, how shall it guide me, being blind?
Grace is a taste of blisse, a glorious gift,
Which can the soule to heau'nly comforts lift:
It will not shine to me, whose mind is drown'd

In sorrowes, and with worldly troubles bound:
It will not daigne within that house to dwell,
Where drinesse raignes, and proud distractions swell.
Perhaps it sought me in those lightsome dayes
Of my first fervour, when few winds did raise
The waues, and ere they could full strength obtaine,
Some whisp'ring gale straight charm'd them downe again:
When all seem'd calme, and yet the virgin's Child
On my deuotions in His manger smild;
While then I simply walkt, nor heed could take
Of Complacence, that slye deceitfull snake;
When yet I had not dang'rously refus'd
So many calls to vertue, nor abus'd
The spring of life, which I so oft enioy'd,
Nor made so many good intentions voyd;
Deseruing thus that grace should quite depart,
And dreadfull hardnesse should possesse my heart:
Yet in that state this onely good I found,
That fewer spots did then my conscience wound,
Though who can censure,° whether in those times,   *judge*
The want of feeling seem'd the want of crimes?
If solid verities dwell not but in paine,
I will not wish that golden age againe
Because it flow'd with sensible delights
Of heauenly things: God hath created nights
As well as dayes, to decke the varied globe;
Grace comes as oft clad in the dusky robe
Of desolation, as in white attire,
Which better fits the bright celestiall quire.
Some in foule seasons perish through despaire,
But more through boldnesse when the daies are faire.
This then must be the med'cine for my woes,
To yeeld to what my Sauiour shall dispose:
To glory in my basenesse, to reioyce
In mine afflictions, to obey His voyce,
As well when threatnings my defects reproue
As when I cherisht am with words of loue,
To say to Him in eu'ry time and place,
"Withdraw Thy comforts, so thou leaue Thy grace."

William Drummond of Hawthornden
(1585–1649)

BORN THE SON OF THE FIRST Laird of Hawthornden in Midlothian, Scotland, Drummond was educated at the newly founded University of Edinburgh. He became Laird in 1610 upon the death of his father, who had served as gentleman-usher to James VI of Scotland (later James I of England). Many of his poems respond in some way to the Stuart monarchy: Drummond's first publication, in 1613, was an elegy upon Prince Henry, and he published *A Panegyricke to the King's Most Excellent Majestie* in 1617. He also spent many years researching and writing a prose *History of Scotland during the Reigns of the Five Jameses*. His several books of poems include pastorals, madrigals, courtly love lyrics, and religious works. These two sonnets are from his 1623 volume of devotional poems.

from *Flowres of Sion*
10—AMAZEMENT AT THE INCARNATION OF GOD

To spread the azure Canopie of Heauen	
And make it twinkle with those spangs° of Gold,	*spangles*
To stay this ponderous Globe of Earth so euen,	
That it should all, and nought should it vphold;	
To giue strange motions to the Planets seuen,	
Or Ioue to make so meeke, or Mars so bold,[27]	
To temper what is moist, drie, hote, and cold,	
Of all their Iarres° that sweete accords are giuen:	*conflicts*
LORD, to thy Wisedome's nought, nought to thy Might,	
But that thou shouldst (thy Glorie laide aside)	
Come meanelie in mortalitie to bide,	
And die for those deseru'd eternall plight,	
A wonder is so farre aboue our wit,	
That Angels stand amaz'd to muse on it.	

---

27. The planets Jove/Jupiter and Mars, which like other planets were thought to affect human disposition.

Beneath a sable vaile, and Shadowes deepe,
Of vnaccessible and dimming light,
In Silence ebane° cloudes more blacke than Night,   *ebony*
The Worlds great Minde his secrets hidde doth keepe:
Through those thicke Mists when any mortall Wight°   *person*
Aspires, with halting pace, and Eyes that weepe
To prye, and in his Misteries to creepe,
With Thunders hee and Lightnings blasts their Sight.
O Sunne invisible, that dost abide
Within thy bright abysmes, most faire, most darke,
Where with thy proper Rayes thou dost thee hide,
O euer-shining, neuer full seene marke,
To guide mee in Lifes Night, thy light mee show,
The more I search of thee, the lesse I know.

Robert Herrick
(1591–1674)

HERRICK WAS BORN IN LONDON to a prosperous goldsmith, and in his youth he apprenticed to his uncle, who served as King James's jeweler. But Herrick left the family trade to attend college, and took orders in the Church of England in 1623. His Royalist position caused him to lose his vicarage in the wake of the English Civil War, and he spent the years of the Commonwealth living in London and preparing poems for publication. His book *Hesperides,* containing sacred and secular poems, appeared in 1648. After the monarchy was restored, Herrick was reinstalled at his vicarage, where he lived out his days.

To His Saviour. The New yeers Gift.

That little prettie bleeding part
Of Foreskin send to me:
And Ile return a bleeding Heart,
For New-yeers gift to Thee.

Rich is the Jemme° that Thou did'st send,   *gem*
Mine's faulty too, and smal;
But yet this Gift Thou wilt commend
Because I send Thee *all*.

His Prayer for Absolution.

For Those my unbaptised Rhimes,
Writ in my wild unhallowed Times;
For every sentence, clause and word,
That's not inlaid with Thee, (my Lord)
Forgive me God, and blot each Line
Out of my Book, that is not Thine.[28]
But if, 'mongst all, thou find'st here one
Worthy thy Benediction;
That One of all the rest, shall be
The Glory of my Work, and Me.

To God.

Lord, I am like to *Misletoe*,
Which has no root, and cannot grow
Or prosper, but by that same tree
It clings about; so I by Thee.
What need I then to feare at all,
So long as I about Thee craule?
But if that Tree sho'd fall and die,
Tumble shall heav'n, and down will I.

To God.

Do with me, God! As Thou didst deal with *Iohn*,[29]
(Who writ that heavenly *Revelation*)
Let me (like him) first cracks of thunder heare;
Then let the Harps inchantments strike mine eare;

---

28. See Revelation 20.12.
29. John of Patmos, author of the Book of Revelation.

Here give me thornes; there, in thy Kingdome, set
Upon my head the golden coronet;
There give me day; but here my dreadfull night:
My sackcloth here; but there my *Stole* of white.

His Ejaculation to God.

My God! Looke on me with thine eye
Of pittie, not of scrutinie;
For if thou dost, thou then shalt see
Nothing but loathsome sores in mee.
O then! For mercies sake, behold
These my irruptions manifold;
And heale me with thy looke, or touch:
But if thou wilt not deigne so much,
Because I'me odious in thy sight,
Speak but the word, and cure me quite.

To God.

I'le come, I'le creep, (though Thou dost threat)
Humbly unto Thy Mercy-seat:
When I am there, this then I'le do,
Give Thee a Dart, and Dagger too;
Next, when I have my faults confest,
Naked I'le shew a sighing brest;
Which if that can't Thy pittie wooe,
Then let Thy Justice do the rest,
        And strike it through.

His Wish to God.

I Would to God, that mine old age might have
Before my last, but here a living grave,
Some one poore Almes-house; there to lie, or stir
Ghost-like, as in my meaner sepulchre;
A little piggin° and a pipkin° by,   *drinking cup / clay pot*
To hold things fitting my necessity;

Which rightly us'd, both in their time and place,
Might me excite to fore, and after-grace.[30]
Thy Crosse, my *Christ*, fix'd 'fore mine eyes sho'd° be,   *should*
Not to adore that, but to worship Thee.
So, here the remnant of my dayes I'd spend,
Reading Thy Bible, and my Book; *so end.*

Francis Quarles
(1592–1644)

ORPHANED AS A CHILD, Francis Quarles gained an education at Cambridge and
Oxford. He studied law, and was a part of the Earl of Arundel's mission to Heidelberg
escorting Elizabeth, the daughter of King James, to marry the Elector Palatine. Quarles
was a dedicated Royalist, but his religious writings earned him great favor among the
Puritan opponents of Charles I. Quarles produced a significant body of work over his
lifetime, including a number of verse-paraphrases of different books of the Bible, sup-
plemented by moral commentary. These were republished together in the 1630 volume
Divine Poems. Another volume of religious poems, *Divine Fancies,* appeared in 1632.
Quarles's best-known work, and indeed one of the most popular works of the century,
was his *Emblemes* (1635), which contained five books of meditative verse. In accor-
dance with the fashionable emblem-poem genre, each of these poems is accompanied
by an allegorical illustration (many of Quarles's were borrowed from a well-known
emblem book from the Netherlands); in addition, each poem is introduced by a scrip-
tural motto and is followed by both a set of exegetical quotations from early Church
Fathers and a short didactic epigram. Quarles claimed that "an emblem is but a short
parable." In 1637, Quarles published another equally successful book of emblems,
Hieroglyphics of the Life of Man.

from *Divine Fancies*
2.1—TO ALMIGHTY GOD

LORD, Thou requir'st the first of all our *Time,*
The first of all our *Actions,* and the prime
Of all our *Thoughts;* And, *Lord,* good reason, we,

---

30. "Fore, and after-grace": prayers before and after a meal.

When Thou giv'st all, should give the *first* to Thee:
But O, we often rob thee of thy due,
Like *Elies* Children, whom thy vengeance slue:[31]
Wee pinch thy *Offring* to enlarge our *Fee;*
We keepe the *Fat,* and carve the *Leane* to Thee:
We thrust our three-tooth'd *Flesh-hook*[32] in thy *Pot,*
That only, what the *Flesh-hook* taketh not,
We share to thee: Lord, we are still deceiving;
We take the *Prime,* and feed thee with our *leaving:*
Our Sluttish *Bowles* are cream'd with soile & filth,
Our Wheat is full of *Chaffe; of Tares,* our Tilth:
Lord, what in *Flesh* and *Blood* can there be had,
That's worth the having, when the best is bad:
Here's nothing *good,* vnlesse thou please to make it;
O, then, if ought be worth the taking, take it.

3.17——ON MANS GREATEST ENEMY

Of all those mortall enemies, that take part
Against my Peace, *Lord,* keep me from my *Heart.*

3.75——ON THE LIFE OF MAN

A thousand yeares, with God (the Scriptures say)
Are reckon'd but a *Day;*[33]
By which accompt,° this measur'd Life of our   *account*
Exceeds not much an *hower;*
The *halfe* whereof Nature does claime and keepe
As her owne debt for sleepe:
A full *sixt part* or what remaines, we ryot°   *indulge*
In more then needfull Dyet:
Our *Infancy,* our *Child-hood,* and the most
Of our *greene youth* is lost:
The *little* that is left, we thus divide;
One *part* to cloathe our Pride,

---

31. See 2 Kings 2.23–25.
32. An instrument for lifting cooked meat from a pot; see 1 Samuel 2.13–14.
33. See 2 Peter 3.8.

An other Share we lavishly deboyse°   *debauch*
To *vaine,* or *sinfull* Ioyes;
If then, at most, the measur'd life of Man
Be counted but a *Span,*
Being half'd and quarter'd, and disquarter'd thus,
What, what remaines for us?
Lord, if the *Totall* of our dayes doe come
To so-so poore a *summe;*
And if our shares so small, so nothing be,
Out of that *Nothing,* what remaines to *Thee?*

from *Emblemes,* Book Five

Bring my ſoule out of Priſon that I may praiſe
thy Name : Ps:142.7. will:ſimpſon. ſculpſit

10—PSALM 142.7: BRING MY SOULE OUT OF PRISON, THAT I
MAY PRAISE THY NAME.

My Soule is like a Bird; my Flesh, the Cage;
Wherein, she weares her weary Pilgrimage
Of houres as few as evill, daily fed

With sacred Wine, and Sacramentall Bread;
The keyes that lock her in, and lets her out,
Are Birth, and Death; 'twixt both, she hopps about
From perch to perch; from Sense to Reason; then,
From higher Reason, downe to Sense agen:
From Sense she climbes to Faith; where, for a season,
She sits and sings; then, down againe to Reason;
From Reason, back to Faith; and straight, from thence
She rudely flutters to the Perch of Sense;
From Sense, to Hope; then hopps from Hope to Doubt;
From Doubt, to dull Despaire; there, seeks about
For desp'rate Freedome; and at ev'ry Grate,
She wildly thrusts, and begs th'untimely date
Of unexpired thraldome, to release
Th'afflicted Captive, that can find no peace:
Thus am I coop'd within this fleshly Cage,
I weare my youth, and waste my weary Age,
Spending that breath which was ordain'd to chaunt
Heav'ns praises forth, in sighs and sad complaint:
Whilst happier birds can spread their nimble wing
From Shrubs to Cedars, and there chirp and sing
In choice of raptures, the harmonious story
Of mans Redemption and his Makers Glory:
You glorious Martyrs; you illustrious Troopes,
That once were cloyster'd in your fleshly Coopes
As fast as I, what Reth'rick° had your tongues?   *rhetoric*
What dextrous Art had your Elegiak Songs?
What *Paul*-like pow'r had your admir'd devotion?
What shackle-breaking Faith infus'd such motion
To your strong Pray'rs, that could obtaine the boone
To be inlarg'd, to be uncag'd so soone?
When I (poore I) can sing my daily teares,
Growne old in Bondage, and can find no eares:
You great partakers of eternall Glory,
That with your heav'n-prevailing Oratory,
Releas'd your soules from your terrestriall Cage,
Permit the passion of my holy Rage
To recommend my sorrowes (dearely knowne
To you, in dayes of old; and, once, your owne)
To your best thoughts, (but oh't does not befit ye

To moove our pray'rs; you love and joy; not pitie:
Great Lord of soules, to whom should prisners flie,
But Thee? Thou hadst thy Cage, as well as I:
And, for my sake, thy pleasure was to know
The sorrowes that it brought, and feltst them too;
O set me free, and I will spend those dayes,
Which now I wast in begging, in Thy praise.

Anselm. in Protolog. Cap. 1.[34]

O miserable condition of mankind, that has lost that for which he was created! Alas!
What has hee left? And what has hee found? He has lost happinesse for which he was
made, and found misery for which he was not made: What is gone? and what is left?
That thing is gone, without which hee is unhappy; that thing is left, by which he is
miserable: O wretched men! From whence are we expell'd? To what are we impell'd?
Whence are we throwne? And whether are we hurried? From our home into banish-
ment; from the sight of God into our owne blindnesse; from the pleasure of immor-
tality to the bitternesse of death: Miserable change? From how great a good, to how
great an evill? Ah me: What have I enterpriz'd? What have I done? Whither did I
goe? Whither am I come?

Epigram
Pauls Midnight voice prevail'd; his musicks thunder
Unhing'd the prison doores; split bolts in sunder:[35]
And fitst thou here? and hang'st the feeble wing?
And whin'st to be enlarg'd? Soule, learn to sing.

George Herbert
(1593–1633)

George Herbert was born in Wales to a literarily connected noble family: his
mother, Magdalen Herbert, was an influential literary patron to John Donne and other
poets, and he was related by marriage to Mary Sidney Herbert. His first poems, which
argued that God is a worthier subject for verse than romance, he sent as a gift to his

---

34. Anselm, Benedictine monk and Archbishop of Canterbury in the late eleventh century; the reference
    is to the first chapter of his *Proslogion*.
35. See Acts 16.26–27.

mother. Herbert served as rector at Bemerton in Wiltshire, where he was admired for his diligence and humility. When he realized he was dying of consumption, he sent a collection of his poems in manuscript to his friend Nicholas Ferrar to judge whether to burn them or publish them. This book was *The Temple,* a series of religious lyrics whose organization is modeled after a cathedral, from front door to communion at the altar, and which explored the glories and difficulties of devotion. *The Temple* was published to enormous popular acclaim, printed in thirteen editions by 1680. The influence of this volume is felt widely in the later poetic tradition, and is especially clear in the work of Henry Vaughan, Richard Crashaw, Edward Taylor, and Emily Dickinson. Also published after his death, in 1652, Herbert's prose treatise *A Priest to the Temple: Or the Country Parson, his Character and Rule of Life* gently dispensed homely advice on both spiritual and practical matters to country clerics.

The Altar

A broken ALTAR, Lord, thy servant rears,
Made of a heart and cemented with tears;
    Whose parts are as thy hand did frame;
    No workman's tool hath touch'd the same.
        A HEART alone
        Is such a stone,
        As nothing but
        Thy pow'r doth cut.
        Wherefore each part
        Of my hard heart
        Meets in this frame
        To praise thy name.
    That if I chance to hold my peace,
    These stones to praise thee may not cease.
Oh, let thy blessed SACRIFICE be mine,
And sanctify this ALTAR to be thine.

The Reprisall

I Have consider'd it, and finde
There is no dealing with thy mighty passion:
For though I die for thee, I am behinde;
    My sinnes deserve the condemnation.

O make me innocent, that I
May give a disentangled state and free:
And yet thy wounds still my attempts defie,
    For by thy death I die for thee.

Ah! was it not enough that thou
By thy eternall glorie didst outgo me?
Couldst thou not griefs sad conquests me allow,
    But in all vict'ries overthrow me?

Yet by confession will I come
Into the conquest. Though I can do nought
Against thee, in thee I will overcome
    The man, who once against thee fought.

Good Friday

O My chief good,
How shall I measure out thy bloud?
How shall I count what thee befell,
    And each grief tell?

Shall I thy woes
Number according to thy foes?
Or, since one starre show'd thy first breath,
    Shall all thy death?

Or shall each leaf,
Which falls in Autumn, score a grief?
Or can not leaves, but fruit, be signe
    Of the true vine?

Then let each houre
Of my whole life one grief devoure;
That thy distresse through all may runne,
    And be my sunne.

Or rather let
My severall sinnes their sorrows get;
That as each beast his cure doth know,
    Each sinne may so.

Since bloud is fittest, Lord, to write
Thy sorrows in, and bloudie fight;
My heart hath store, write there, where in
One box doth lie both ink and sinne:

That when sinne spies so many foes,
Thy whips, thy nails, thy wounds, thy woes,
All come to lodge there, sinne may say,
No room for me, and flie away.

Sinne being gone, oh fill the place,
And keep possession with thy grace;
Lest sinne take courage and return,
And all the writings blot or burn.

The Quidditie

My God, a verse is not a crown,
No point of honour, or gay suit,
No hawk, or banquet, or renown,
Nor a good sword, nor yet a lute:

It cannot vault, or dance, or play;
It never was in *France* or *Spain;*
Nor can it entertain the day
With my great stable or demain:°   *demesne*

It is no office, art, or news,
Nor the Exchange, or busie Hall;[36]
But it is that which while I use
I am with thee, and *Most take all.*[37]

Deniall

> When my devotions could not pierce
> > Thy silent eares;
> Then was my heart broken, as was my verse;

---

36. Places of commerce and business activities.
37. An alternative form of "Winner take all," from a card game.

My breast was full of fears
And disorder:

My bent thoughts, like a brittle bow,
Did flie asunder:
Each took his way; some would to pleasures go,
Some to the warres and thunder
Of alarms.

As good go any where, they say,
As to benumme
Both knees and heart, in crying night and day,
Come, come, my God, O come,
But no hearing.

O that thou shouldst give dust a tongue
To crie to thee,
And then not heare it crying! all day long
My heart was in my knee,
But no hearing.

Therefore my soul lay out of sight,
Untun'd, unstrung:
My feeble spirit, unable to look right,
Like a nipt blossome, hung
Discontented.

O cheer and tune my heartlesse breast,
Deferre no time;
That so thy favours granting my request,
They and my minde may chime,
And mend my ryme.

Iesu

IESU is in my heart, his sacred name
Is deeply carved there: but th'other week
A great affliction broke the little frame,
Ev'n all to pieces: which I went to seek:
And first I found the corner, where was *I*,
After, where *ES*, and next where *U* was graved,
When I had got these parcels, instantly

I sat me down to spell them, and perceived
That to my broken heart he was *I ease you,*
    And to the whole is *I E S U.*

Love-joy

As on a window late I cast mine eye,
I saw a vine drop grapes with *J* and *C*
Anneal'd on every bunch. One standing by
Ask'd what it meant. I (who am never loth
To spend my iudgement) said, It seem'd to me
To be the bodie and the letters both
Of *Joy* and *Charitie;* Sir, you have not miss'd,
The man reply'd; It figures *JESUS CHRIST.*

The Pulley

        When God at first made man,
Having a glasse of blessings standing by;
Let us (said he) poure on him all we can:
Let the worlds riches, which dispersed lie,
        Contract into a span.

        So strength first made a way;
Then beautie flow'd, then wisdome, honour, pleasure:
When almost all was out, God made a stay,
Perceiving that alone, of all his treasure,
        Rest in the bottome lay.

        For if I should (said he)
Bestow this jewell also on my creature,
He would adore my gifts in stead of me,
And rest in Nature, not the God of Nature:
        So both should losers be.

        Yet let him keep the rest,
But keep them with repining restlesnesse:
Let him be rich and wearie, that at least,
If goodnesse leade him not, yet wearinesse
        May tosse him to my breast.

A true Hymne

My joy, my life, my crown!
My heart was meaning all the day,
    Somewhat it fain° would say,   *eagerly*
And still it runneth muttering up and down
With only this, *My joy, my life, my crown!*

    Yet slight not those few words;
    If truly said, they may take part
    Among the best in art:
The fineness which a hymn or psalm affords
Is, when the soul unto the lines accord.

    He who craves all the mind,
    And all the soul, and strength, and time,
    If the words only rhyme,
Justly complains that somewhat is behind
To make His verse, or write a hymn in kind.

    Whereas if the heart be moved,
    Although the verse be somewhat scant,
    God doth supply the want;
As when the heart says, sighing to be approved,
O, could I love! and stops, God writeth, *Loved*.

Love (III)

Love bade me welcome: yet my soul drew back,
    Guiltie of dust and sinne.
But quick-ey'd Love, observing me grow slack
    From my first entrance in,
Drew nearer to me, sweetly questioning,
    If I lack'd any thing.

A guest, I answer'd, worthy to be here:
    Love said, You shall be he.
I the unkinde, ungratefull? Ah my deare,
    I cannot look on thee.
Love took my hand, and smiling did reply,
    Who made the eyes but I?

Truth Lord, but I have marr'd them: let my shame
Go where it doth deserve.
And know you not, sayes Love, who bore the blame?
My deare, then I will serve.
You must sit down, sayes Love, and taste my meat:
So I did sit and eat.

Christopher Harvey
(1597–1663)

CLERGYMAN CHRISTOPHER Harvey was himself the son of a clergyman. He is today best known as the author of *The Synagogue, or, The shadow of The Temple*, a set of poems that was published anonymously in 1640 in a single volume along with George Herbert's *The Temple*. The influence of Herbert is obvious throughout Harvey's work. A later edition of Harvey's poems appeared in 1647, augmented by poems on festivals and church ornaments and intended to defend the doctrines of the Church of England against Puritan attacks. Harvey also published, anonymously, an emblem book called *Schola cordis* (*School of the Heart*), which he adapted from a version written in Latin and published on the European continent; this work was ascribed by some to Francis Quarles, but an inscription in its 1674 printing gave credit, posthumously, to Harvey.

Confusion

Oh! how my minde
is gravel'd!°   *disarrayed*
not a thought
That I can finde,
but's ravel'd°   *tangled*
all to nought.
Short ends of threds,
and narrow shreds
of lists,
Knots snarled ruffes,
loose broken tufts
of twists,

Are my torne meditations ragged clothing;
Which wound and woven shape a suit for nothing.
One while I think, and then I am in paine
To think how to unthink that thought againe.

How can my soule
    but famish
        with this food?
Pleasures full bowle
    tastes rammish,°   *rank*
        taints the blood:
Profit picks bones,
    and chewes on stones
        that choak:
Honour climbes hils;
    fats not, but fils
        with smoak.
And whilst my thoughts are greedy upon these,
They passe by pearles, and stoop to pick up pease.°   *trifles*
Such wash and draffe° is fit for none but swine;   *waste and dregs*
And such I am not, Lord, if I am thine.
        Cloth me anew, and feed me then afresh;
        Else my soule dyes famisht and starv'd with flesh.

The Sabbath. Or Lords day.

Haile   Vaile°   *respect*
Holy   Wholly
King of days   To thy praise,
The Emperour,   For evermore,
Or universal   Must the rehersal
Monarch of time, the weeks   Of all, that honour seeks
Perpetual Dictatour.   Under the worlds creator.

Thy   My
Beauty   Duty
Far exceeds   Yet must needs
The reach of art,   Yield thee mine heart,
To blazon fully,   And that not dully:

And I thy light ecclipse,
When I most strive to raise thee.

What
Nothing
Else can be,
Thou only art;
The extracted spirit
Of all Eternitie,
By favour antedated.

Spirits of souls, not lips
Alone, are fit to praise thee.

That
Slow thing
Time by thee
Hath got the start,
And doth inherit
That immoralitie
Which sin anticipated.

O
That I
Could lay me
This body so,
That my soul might be
Incorporate with thee,
And no more to six dayes ow.

Invitation.

Turn in, my Lord, turn in to me;
     Mine heart's an homely place:
But thou canst make corruption flee,
     And fill it with thy grace.
So furnished it will be brave,
And a rich dwelling thou shalt have.

It was thy lodging once before,
     It builded was by thee:
But I to sin set ope the door,
     It render'd was by me.
And so thy building was defac'd
And in thy roome another plac'd.

But he usurps, the right is thine:
     O dispossesse him, Lord.
Do thou but say, this heart is mine,
     Hee's gone at the first word.
Thy word's thy will, thy will's thy power,
Thy time is always, now's mine hour.

Now say to sin, depart:
And, *son give me thine heart.*
Thou, that by saying, *Let it be,* didst make it,
Canst, if thou wilt, by saying, *Give't me,* take it.

Richard Flecknoe
(c. 1600–c. 1678)

NOT MUCH IS KNOWN ABOUT Flecknoe's origins, though he seems to have been
born in England to an Irish family. It was suggested that he was a Jesuit priest, though
there is no clear corroboration for that claim. The few biographical details that can be
determined about Flecknoe are based upon his *Relation of Ten Years' Travels in Europe,
Asia, Afrique and America* (c. 1655), a volume that brings together letters he wrote
during his travels. He was a Royalist and a Catholic, and he seems to have begun his
voyages to escape the English Civil War. Flecknoe's circle of acquaintance included
Andrew Marvell and John Dryden—indeed, his name may be most familiar from the
satiric poems each of these writers composed about him. Besides his epistolary travel-
ogue, Flecknoe wrote many works of prose, poetry, and drama.

On the Death of Our Lord

O God! and wouldst Thou die for me,
And shall I nothing do for Thee?
But still continue to offend
So good a Lord, so dear a Friend.
—Had any prince done this for thee,
My soul, what wondering would there be!
But since 'tis God that does it, thou
Dost never wonder at it now.
Strange, that one should more esteem
A grace or gift that's given to him
By earthly kings, than what is given
Unto him by the King of heaven!

Thomas Washbourne
(1606–1687)

WASHBOURNE WAS BORN IN Worcestershire and educated at Oxford. He was an English clergyman and poet, and gained moderate renown for his 1654 book *Divine Poems*. His work, and his reputation as a poet, was revived by the republication of his religious verse in the nineteenth century.

Upon Divine Love

How strong is Love, what tongue expresse it can,
Or heart conceive, since it made God a man?
How strong is Love, which made that God-Man dye,
That man might live with God eternally?
Lord, let this love of thine my heart inspire
With love again, as sparks rise from the fire.
Thy love's a Sun, give me a beam from thence,
Which may both light and heat alike dispence,
Light to direct others the surest way
That leads to heaven and everlasting joy:
Heat to preserve in me a constant motion
Of fervent Zeal to thee, and pure devotion;
That all my thoughts, words, actions may prove
There is no passion half so strong as Love.
A passion is't? a divine vertue rather,
Which from a Deity springs, and calls God Father;
Yea, Love is God, and God is love; O then
Adore, but not profane it with thy pen!

John Milton
(1608–1674)

MILTON WAS A POET, A SCHOLAR, a polemicist for the cause of political and religious reform, and a civil servant who was appointed to be Secretary for Foreign Tongues during Oliver Cromwell's Protectorate. He wrote a number of prose tracts against episcopacy and in support of personal and religious liberty, which led him to argue publicly for the execution of King Charles I. A warrant for his arrest was issued upon the restoration of the monarchy to Charles II, but he was released from his brief imprisonment at the intervention of a few influential friends, including Andrew Marvell. Milton's first published poem, an elegy on Shakespeare, was published in the Second Folio edition of Shakespeare's works. His masque *Comus* was published anonymously in 1637, and a pastoral elegy on a school friend, "Lycidas," in 1638. In 1645, a small collection of Milton's youthful poetry appeared, including a number of psalm translations and the first sonnet printed here; this was the only volume of Milton's work to be printed until the publication of *Paradise Lost* in 1667. Milton's other late works include the shorter epic *Paradise Regained*, the tragedy *Samson Agonistes*, and an unfinished theological manifesto *De doctrina christiana* (*On Christian Doctrine*), which remained undiscovered until the nineteenth century.

Sonnet 7—On His Being Arrived at the Age of 23.

How soon hath Time the suttle theef of youth,
Stoln on his wing my three and twentith yeer!
My hasting dayes flie on with full career,
But my late spring no bud or blossom shew'th.
Perhaps my semblance might deceive the truth,
That I to manhood am arriv'd so near,
And inward ripenes doth much less appear,
That som more timely-happy spirits indu'th.°   *endows*
Yet be it less or more, or soon or slow,
It shall be still in strictest measure eev'n,
To that same lot, however mean, or high,

Toward which Time leads me, and the will of Heav'n;
All is, if I have grace to use it so,
As ever in my great task Masters eye.[38]

Sonnet 18—On the late Massacher in Piemont[39]

Avenge O Lord thy slaughter'd Saints, whose bones
Lie scatter'd on the Alpine mountains cold,
Ev'n them who kept thy truth so pure of old
When all our Fathers worship't Stocks and Stones,[40]
Forget not: in thy book record their groanes
Who were thy Sheep and in their antient Fold
Slayn by the bloody Piemontese that roll'd
Mother with Infant down the Rocks. Their moans
The Vales redoubl'd to the Hills, and they
To Heav'n. Their martyr'd blood and ashes sow
O're all th' Italian fields where still doth sway
The triple Tyrant: that from these may grow
A hunder'd-fold, who having learnt thy way
Early may fly the Babylonian wo.

Sonnet 19—On His Blindness

When I consider how my light is spent,
E're half my days, in this dark world and wide,
And that one Talent which is death to hide,
Lodg'd with me useless, though my Soul more bent
To serve therewith my Maker, and present

---

38. For both Sonnet 7 and Sonnet 19, see the parable of the talents at Matthew 25.14–30.

39. The Waldensians, or Vaudois, were a Protestant group that had lived in the Piedmont region in Europe since the late twelfth century. Many Protestants viewed the sect as practicing a pure strain of early Christianity, removed from the corrupting influence of Rome. In 1655, the Catholic Duke of Savoy pushed the sect back into a circumscribed region of the mountains; encountering what they claimed was resistance, the Duke's army massacred all the Vaudois. Milton was tasked by Cromwell's government with expressing England's official shock at the actions of the French forces. The sonnet extends that outrage to the Pope himself, called in line 12 the "triple Tyrant" for the *triregnum*, or three-tiered miter, he wears upon his head.

40. Stocks: pieces of wood. See Jeremiah 3.9.

My true account, least he returning chide,
Doth God exact day labour, light deny'd,
I fondly ask;[41] But patience to prevent
That murmur, soon replies, God doth not need
Either man's work or his own gifts, who best
Bear his milde yoak,[42] they serve him best, his State
Is Kingly. Thousands at his bidding speed
And post o're Land and Ocean without rest:
They also serve who only stand and waite.

Upon the Circumcision

Ye flaming Powers, and winged Warriours bright,
That erst with Musick, and triumphant song
First heard by happy watchful Shepherds ear,
So sweetly sung your Joy the Clouds along
Through the soft silence of the list'ning night;
Now mourn, and if sad share with us to bear
Your fiery essence can distill no tear,
Burn in your sighs, and borrow
Seas wept from our deep sorrow,
He who with all Heav'ns heraldry whileare°   *long ago*
Enter'd the world, now bleeds to give us ease;
Alas, how soon our sin
      Sore doth begin
           His Infancy to sease!°   *seize*
O more exceeding love or law more just?
Just law indeed, but more exceeding love!
For we by rightfull doom remediles°   *helpless*
Were lost in death, till he that dwelt above
High thron'd in secret bliss, for us frail dust
Emptied his glory, ev'n to nakednes;
And that great Cov'nant which we still transgress
Intirely satisfi'd,
And the full wrath beside

---

41. See the parable of the day-laborers at Matthew 20.1–16. Here, "fondly" can be understood to mean "foolishly."
42. See Matthew 11.30.

Of vengeful Justice bore for our excess,
And seals obedience first with wounding smart
This day, but O ere long
      Huge pangs and strong
            Will pierce more neer his heart.

from *Paradise Lost*
BOOK 3, LINES 1–55

Hail holy light, ofspring of Heav'n first-born,
Or of th' Eternal Coeternal beam[43]
May I express thee unblam'd? since God is light,
And never but in unapproached light
Dwelt from Eternitie, dwelt then in thee,
Bright effluence of bright essence increate.
Or hear'st thou rather pure Ethereal stream,
Whose Fountain who shall tell? before the Sun,
Before the Heavens thou wert, and at the voice
Of God, as with a Mantle didst invest
The rising world of waters dark and deep,
Won from the void and formless infinite.
Thee I re-visit now with bolder wing,
Escap't the Stygian Pool,[44] though long detain'd
In that obscure sojourn, while in my flight
Through utter and through middle darkness borne
With other notes then to th' Orphean Lyre[45]
I sung of Chaos and Eternal Night,
Taught by the heav'nly Muse to venture down
The dark descent, and up to reascend,
Though hard and rare: thee I revisit safe,
And feel thy sovran vital Lamp; but thou
Revisit'st not these eyes, that rowle° in vain   *roll*

---

43. Milton alludes to the theological principle that the co-eternal Son of God expresses the substance of the eternal God, as a sunbeam expresses the substance of the sun.

44. The River Styx, in the Greek mythological underworld of Hades. Milton's narrator has left the Hell of Books 1 and 2 of his epic and turns now his descriptive eye toward heaven. He offers this invocation for divine guidance to assist in his poetic endeavors.

45. In Greek mythology, the poet Orpheus visits Hades to plead eloquently for the release of his wife, Eurydice.

To find thy piercing ray, and find no dawn;
So thick a drop serene hath quencht thir Orbs,[46]
Or dim suffusion veild. Yet not the more
Cease I to wander where the Muses haunt
Cleer Spring, or shadie Grove, or Sunnie Hill,
Smit° with the love of sacred Song; but chief   *smitten*
Thee Sion and the flowrie Brooks beneath
That wash thy hallowd feet, and warbling flow,
Nightly I visit: nor somtimes forget
Those other two equal'd with me in Fate,
So were I equal'd with them in renown,
Blind Thamyris and blind Mæonides,
And Tiresias and Phineus Prophets old.[47]
Then feed on thoughts, that voluntarie move
Harmonious numbers; as the wakeful Bird[48]
Sings darkling, and in shadiest Covert hid
Tunes her nocturnal Note. Thus with the Year
Seasons return, but not to me returns
Day, or the sweet approach of Ev'n or Morn,
Or sight of vernal bloom, or Summers Rose,
Or flocks, or heards, or human face divine;
But cloud in stead, and ever-during dark
Surrounds me, from the chearful wayes of men
Cut off, and for the Book of knowledg fair[49]
Presented with a Universal blanc
Of Nature's works to mee expung'd and ras'd,
And wisdome at one entrance quite shut out.
So much the rather thou Celestial light
Shine inward, and the mind through all her powers
Irradiate, there plant eyes, all mist from thence
Purge and disperse, that I may see and tell
Of things invisible to mortal sight.

---

46. The phrase "a drop serene" is a rough translation of the Latin term for cataracts, *Gutta serena,* which
    caused Milton's blindness.
47. Thamyris was a blind man of Thrace mentioned in Homer's *Iliad;* Maeonides is the blind poet Homer;
    Tiresias is the blind prophet of Sophocles' *Oedipus Tyrannos;* Phineus was a blind prophet-king of
    ancient Thrace.
48. The nightingale.
49. That is, creation itself.

William Cartwright
(1611–1643)

BEST KNOWN AS A DRAMATIST, Cartwright was born in Gloucestershire and educated at Oxford, where he studied metaphysics and became famous for his eloquent preaching. He became a cleric and served at Salisbury Cathedral. Cartwright associated with Ben Jonson and was among the poets who followed Jonson's comedic theatrical style. In addition to his plays, an edition of Cartwright's collected poems was published in 1651.

Confession

I do confess, O God, my wand'ring Fires
Are kindled not from Zeal, but loose desires;
   My ready Tears, shed from Instructed Eyes,
Have not been Pious Griefs, but Subtleties;
   And only sorry that Sins miss, I ow
To thwarted wishes al the Sighs I blow;
   My Fires thus merit Fire; my Tears the fall
Of Showers provoke; my Sighs for Blasts do call.
   O then Descend in Fire; but let it be
Such as snatch'd up the Prophet; such as We
Read of in Moses Bush, a Fire of Joy,
Sent to Enlighten, rather than Destroy.
   O then Descend in Showers; But let them be
Showers only and not Tempests; such as we
Feel from the Mornings Eye-lids; such as Feed,
Not Choak the sprouting of the Tender Seed.

   O then Descend in Blasts; But let them be
Blasts only, and not Whirlwinds; such as we
Take in for Health's sake, soft and easie Breaths,
Taught to Conveigh Refreshments, and not Deaths.
   So shall the Fury of my Fires asswage,
And that turn Fervour which was Brutish Rage;
   So shall my Tears be then untaught to feign,

And the diseased Waters Heal'd again;
   So shall my Sighs not be as Clouds t'invest
My Sins with Night, but Winds to purge my Breast.

Anne Bradstreet
(1612–1672)

ANNE DUDLEY WAS BORN TO a nonconforming (religiously dissenting from the Church of England) former soldier of Queen Elizabeth, Thomas Dudley, who managed the affairs of the Earl of Lincoln. In 1630 Dudley sailed with his family for America with John Winthrop and the Massachusetts Bay Company. Anne and her husband, Simon Bradstreet, who was her father's business associate, went as well. The family settled in Ipswich, Massachusetts, where Bradstreet and her husband raised eight children. During this period, Bradstreet wrote a number of poems, many of which were spirited off to England by her brother-in-law, purportedly without her knowledge, and published in 1650 under the title *The Tenth Muse, Lately Sprung Up in America*. It was the only volume of her work to appear during her lifetime; an expanded American edition was released in 1678. A sequence of religious poems, *Contemplations*, was not published until the middle of the nineteenth century.

Upon a Fit of Sickness, *Anno*. 1632.

Twice ten years old not fully told
      since nature gave me breath,
My race is run, my thread spun,
      lo, here is fatal Death.
All men must dye, and so must I
      this cannot be revok'd
For Adam's sake, this word God spake
      when he so high provok'd.
Yet live I shall, this life's but small,
      in place of highest bliss,
Where I shall have all I can crave,
      no life is like to this.

For what's this but care and strife?
      since first we came from womb,
Our strength doth waste, our time doth hast,
      and then we go to th' tomb.
O Bubble blast, how long can'st last?
      that always art a breaking,
No sooner blown, but dead and gone,
      ev'n as a word that's speaking.
O whilst I live this grace me give,
      I doing good may be
Then death's arrest I shall count best,
      because it's thy decree;
Bestow much cost there's nothing lost,
      to make Salvation sure,
O great's the gain, though got with pain,
      comes by profession pure.
The race is run, the field is won,
      the victory's mine I see,
For ever know, thou envious foe,
      the foyle belongs to thee.

Richard Crashaw
(1613–1649)

THE SON OF A PURITAN PREACHER, Crashaw converted to Catholicism in the 1640s. After being educated at Cambridge, he left England to avoid the rising animosity toward Catholics during the English Civil War; his friend Abraham Cowley found him living in poverty in Paris, and introduced him to the exiled Queen Henrietta Maria, wife of Charles I. She encouraged Crashaw to go to Rome, and sped his way with a recommendation to the Pope. Crashaw was ultimately given a position serving a cardinal. Crashaw's early verse is indebted to the classical tradition, and he composed many epigrams—or short, pithy poems—on biblical episodes during his time at Cambridge. Crashaw's major volume of poetry, published in 1646, combines two sequences, *Steps to the Temple* and *The Delights of the Muses,* the first with a devotional focus, the second secular. An expanded edition of his religious poems, *Carmen Deo Nostro,* was published posthumously, in 1652.

The Authors Motto

Live, Jesus, Live, and let it bee
My life to dye, for love of thee.

On the still surviving Marks of our Saviour's Wounds.

What ever story of their crueltie,
Or Naile, or Thorne, or Speare have writ in Thee,
       Are in another sense
          Still legible;
     Sweet is the difference:
         Once I did spell
         Every red letter
            A wound of thine;
         Now (what is better)
            Balsame° for mine.   *balm*

To our Lord, upon the Water made Wine.

Thou water turn'st to Wine (faire friend of Life)
       Thy foe to crosse the sweet Arts of thy Reigne,
Distils from thence the Teares of wrath and strife,
       And so turns wine to Water backe againe.

Our Lord in His Circumcision to His Father.[50]

To thee these first fruits of my growing death
(For what else is my life?) lo I bequeath.
Tast this, and as thou lik'st this lesser flood
Expect a Sea, my heart shall make it good.
Thy wrath that wades heere now, e're long shall swim,
The flood-gate shall be set wide ope for him.
Then let him drinke, and drinke, and doe his worst,

---

50. In keeping with Jewish tradition, Jesus would have been ritually circumcised eight days after his birth. For the biblical importance of sacrificing "first fruits," see Nehemiah 10.35, Ezekiel 44.30, 1 Corinthians 15.20.

To drowne the wantonnesse of his wild thirst.
Now's but the Nonage of my paines, my feares
Are yet both in their hopes, not come to yeares.
The day of my darke woes is yet but morne,
My teares but tender, and my death new-borne.
Yet may these unfledg'd griefes give fate some guesse,
These Cradle-torments have their towardnesse.° aptness
These purple buds of blooming death may bee,
Erst the full stature of a fatall tree.
And till my riper woes to age are come,
This knife may be the speares *Præludium*.° Prelude

On the wounds of our crucified Lord.

O These wakeful wounds of thine!
    Are they Mouthes? or are they eyes?
Be they Mouthes, or be they eyne,
    Each bleeding part some one supplies.

Lo! a mouth, whose full-bloom'd lips
    At too deare a rate are roses.
Lo! a blood-shot eye! that weeps
    And many a cruell teare discloses.

O thou that on this foot hast laid
    Many a kisse, and many a Teare,[51]
Now thou shal't have all repaid,
    What soe'er thy charges were.

This foot hath got a Mouth and lippes,
    To pay the sweet summe of thy kisses:
To pay thy Teares, an Eye that weeps
    In stead of Teares such Gems as this is.

The difference only this appears,
    (Nor can the change offend)
The debt is paid in *Ruby*-Teares,
    Which thou in Pearles did'st lend.

---

51. Crashaw identifies the figure who washes and kisses Jesus's feet at John 12.3 as Mary Magdalene.

Richard Crashaw   179

On our crucified Lord, naked and bloody.

Th' have left thee naked Lord, O that they had;
This Garment too I would they had deny'd.
Thee with thy selfe they have too richly clad,
Opening the purple wardrobe of Thy side.
      O never could bee found Garments too good
      For thee to weare, but these, of thine owne blood.

A Song of divine Love.

Lord when the sence of thy sweet grace,
Sends up my soule to seeke thy face,
Thy blessed eyes breed such desire,
I dye in love's delicious fire.
O love I am thy *sacrifice;*
Be still triumphant, blessed Eyes.
Still shine on me faire sunnes! that I
Still may behold, though still I dye.

The second part.
Though still I dye, I live againe,
Still longing so to be still slaine.
So gainfull is such losse of breath,
I dye even in desire of death.
Still live in me this longing strife
Of living *death,* and dying *life,*
For while thou sweetly slaiest *mee,*
Dead to my selfe, I live in *thee.*

Andrew Marvell
(1621–1678)

ENGLISH POET AND Parliamentarian Marvell was born in Yorkshire. After attending Cambridge, Marvell traveled on the European continent and served as a tutor for a succession of prominent families, including Lord General Thomas Fairfax, the anti-Royalist military leader, and Oliver Cromwell. He worked with Milton on Cromwell's Council of State and was elected to Parliament to represent his childhood home of Hull. After the restoration of the monarchy in 1660, Marvell helped Milton avoid execution for his role in arguing for the execution of Charles I. In addition to a substantial body of poetic work, much of it influenced by classical literature, Marvell wrote prose satires and at least one political tract. His work was published posthumously by his housekeeper.

The Coronet

When for the Thorns with which I long, too long,
With many a piercing wound,
My Saviours head have crown'd,
I seek with Garlands to redress that Wrong:
Through every Garden, every Mead,°   *meadow*
I gather flow'rs (my fruits are only flow'rs)
Dismantling all the fragrant Towers[52]
That once adorn'd my Shepherdesses head.
And now when I have summ'd up all my store,
Thinking (so I my self deceive)
So rich a Chaplet thence to weave
As never yet the king of Glory wore:
Alas I find the Serpent old
That, twining in his speckled breast,
About the flow'rs disguis'd does fold,
With wreaths of Fame and Interest.
Ah, foolish Man, that would'st debase with them,
And mortal Glory, Heavens Diadem!

---

52. "Fragrant Towers": woman's hair ornaments; metaphorically, praise-filled poetic rhetoric.

But thou who only could'st the Serpent tame,
Either his slipp'ry knots at once untie,
And disintangle all his winding Snare,
Or shatter too with him my curious frame:
And let these wither, so that he may die,
Though set with Skill and chosen out with Care.
That they, while Thou on both their Spoils dost tread,
May crown thy Feet, that could not crown thy Head.

Henry Vaughan
(1622–1695)

VAUGHAN WAS A PHYSICIAN and poet, twin brother to the philosopher and alchemist Thomas Vaughan. He was proudly Welsh, and called himself the "Silurist" in homage to the Silures, a group of Welsh Celts who had resisted Roman conquest. He published one collection of mostly secular poetry, *Olor Iscanus* (*The Swan of the Usk*, a river near Vaughan's hometown), before turning his energies fully to spiritual writing. His best-known book, *Silex Scintillans* (*The Fiery Flint*), brought him some literary acclaim, and it was republished within a few years in an expanded edition. As a supporter of Charles I, Vaughan was distressed by the events of the English Civil War, and many of his poems reflect his disappointment in what he saw as a general decline in both civic and religious life, and a nostalgia for a more innocent past.

Distraction

O Knit me, that am crumbled dust! the heape
    Is all dispers'd, and cheape;
  Give for a handfull, but a thought
      And it is bought;
      Hadst thou
Made me a starre, a pearle, or a rain-bow,
    The beames I then had shot
    My light had lessend not,
      But now

I find my selfe the lesse, the more I grow;
           The world
Is full of voices; Man is call'd, and hurl'd
        By each, he answers all,
        Knows ev'ry note, and call,
           Hence, still
Fresh dotage tempts, or old usurps his will.
Yet, hadst thou clipt my wings, when Coffin'd in
        This quicken'd masse of sinne,
  And saved that light, which freely thou
          Didst then bestow,
          I feare
I should have spurn'd, and said thou didst forbeare;
        Or that thy store was lesse,
        But now since thou didst blesse
          So much,
I grieve, my God! that thou hast made me such.
          I grieve?
O, yes! thou know'st I doe; come, and releive
        And tame, and keep downe with thy light
        Dust that would rise, and dimme my sight,
         Lest left alone too long
         Amidst the noise, and throng,
          Oppressed I
Striving to save the whole, by parcells dye.

The Pursuite

    Lord! what a busie, restles thing
        Hast thou made man!
Each day and houre he is on wing,
        Rests not a span;
Then having lost the Sunne, and light
        By clouds surpriz'd,
He keeps a Commerce in the night
        With aire disguis'd;
Hadst thou given to this active dust
        A state untir'd,

The lost Sonne had not left the huske,
    Nor home desir'd;
That was thy secret, and it is
    Thy mercy too,
For when all fails to bring to blisse,
    Then, this must doe.
Ah! Lord! and what a Purchase will that be,
To take us sick, that sound would not take thee?

Unprofitableness

How rich, O Lord! how fresh thy visits are!
'Twas but just now my bleak leaves hopeles hung
    Sullyed with dust and mud;
Each snarling blast shot through me, and did share
Their Youth, and beauty, Cold showres nipt, and wrung
    Their spiciness and bloud;
But since thou didst in one sweet glance survey
Their sad decays, I flourish, and once more
    Breath all perfumes, and spice;
I smell a dew like *Myrrh*, and all the day
Wear in my bosome a full Sun; such store
    Hath one beam from thy Eys.
But, ah, my God! what fruit hast thou of this?
What one poor leaf did ever I let fall
    To wait upon Thy wreath?
Thus thou all day a thankless weed doest dress,
And when th' hast done, a stench, or fog is all
    The odour I bequeath.

The Night
JOHN 3.2

    Through that pure *Virgin-shrine*,
That sacred veil drawn o'er thy glorious noon,
That men might look and live as glow-worms shine,
    And face the moon:
    Wise *Nicodemus* saw such light
    As made him know his God by night.

Most blest believer he!
Who in that land of darkness and blinde eyes
Thy long-expected healing wings could see,
    When thou didst rise,
  And, what can never more be done,
  Did at mid-night speak with the Sun!

    O who will tell me, where
He found thee at that dead and silent hour!
What hallow'd solitary ground did bear
    So rare a flower,
  Within whose sacred leafs did lie
  The fulness of the Deity.

    No mercy-seat of gold,
No dead and dusty *Cherub,* nor carv'd stone,
But his own living works did my Lord hold
    And lodge alone;
  Where *trees* and *herbs* did watch and peep
  And wonder, while the *Jews* did sleep.

    Dear night! this world's defeat;
The stop to busie fools; cares check and curb;
The day of Spirits; my soul's calm retreat
    Which none disturb!
  Christ's[53] progress, and His prayer time;
  The hours to which high Heaven doth chime.

    God's silent, searching flight:
When my Lord's head is fill'd with dew, and all
His locks are wet with the clear drops of night;
    His still, soft call;
  His knocking-time; the soul's dumb watch,
  When spirits their fair kindred catch.

    Were all my loud, evil days
Calm and unhaunted as is thy dark Tent,
Whose peace but by some *Angel's* wing or voice
    Is seldom rent;
  Then I in Heaven all the long year
  Would keep, and never wander here.

---

53. Mark, chap 1.35. S. Luke, chap. 21.37 [Vaughan's note].

But living where the Sun
Doth all things wake, and where all mix and tyre
Themselves and others, I consent and run
          To ev'ry myre;
     And by this worlds ill-guiding light,
     Erre more than I can do by night.

          There is in God (some say)
A deep, but dazling darkness; As men here
Say it is late and dusky, because they
          See not all clear;
     O for that Night! where I in him
     Might live invisible and dim!

The Book

Eternal God! Maker of all
That have lived here since the man's fall;
The Rock of ages! in whose shade
They live unseen, when here they fade;

Thou knew'st this *paper* when it was
Mere *seed,* and after that but *grass;*
Before 'twas *dressed* or *spun,* and when
Made *linen,* who did *wear* it then:
What were their lives, their thoughts, and deeds,
Whether good *corn* or fruitless *weeds.*

     Thou knew'st this *tree* when a green *shade*
Covered it, since a *cover* made,
And where it flourished, grew, and spread,
As if it never should be dead

     Thou knew'st this harmless *beast* when he
Did live and feed by Thy decree
On each green thing; then slept (well fed)
Clothed with this *skin* which now lies spread
A *covering* o'er this aged book;
Which makes me wisely weep, and look
On my own dust; mere dust it is,

But not so dry and clean as this.
Thou knew'st and saw'st them all, and though
Now scattered thus, dost know them so.

   O knowing, glorious Spirit! when
Thou shalt restore trees, beasts, and men,
When Thou shalt make all new again,
Destroying only death and pain,
Give him amongst Thy works a place
Who in them loved and sought Thy face!

Mary Carey
(c. 1609–c. 1681)

DAUGHTER OF A NOBLEMAN, Carey married in her youth a Royalist knight. After his death, she married an officer in the Parliamentary forces, on the opposing political side. Carey was the author of a memoir, in which she describes her life as a military wife during the English Civil War and the years following. As this poem suggests, she gave birth to many children, all but two dying in infancy.

Written by me at the death of my 4th son, and 5th Child, Peregrine Payler

I thought my All was given before
But Mercy order'd me one more.
A Peregrine,[54] my God me sent
Him back againe I doe present.
As a Love-Token, 'mongst my others
One Daughter, and her four deare Brothers;
To my Lord Christ, my only bliss
Is, he is mine, and I am his:
My dearest Lord, hast thou fulfill'd thy will,
Thy Hand-Maid's pleas'd, compleately happy still.

---

54. From the Latin for *Pilgrim*.

Lancelot Addison

(1632–1703)

ENGLISH CLERGYMAN ADDISON served seven years as chaplain of the army garrison at Tangiers, where he became fascinated by both Judaism and Islam. He wrote several studies of the customs and rites of foreign cultures, inflected by a sympathetic and liberal-minded perspective uncommon for his time. He was later appointed chaplain to King Charles II. Addison wrote a number of hymns and religious lyrics, and published a volume, *Devotional Poems, Festival and practical*, in 1699. He was the father of writer Joseph Addison.

The Penitential Declaration

Lord, I *love*, and I *adore;*
And I would do so more and more,
All along below, before
Thou op'st the *everlasting Door,*
And admittest me before
Thy self, where I shall *sin no more.*
Place not, Lord, upon my *score*
Those Guilts that do *offend* me sore,
Because they have *displeas'd thee* more
Than I can *pay* for, tho' I tore
This sinful Flesh to quite the score:
But *this thy Son* has done before.

A Sigh of Penitential Love; after any Fall
I

My Love, my Life, my Dear, my All,
Never let me once more *fall.*
My All, my Dear, my Life, my Love,
Grant me *Conquest* from above.

2

My Life, my Love, my All, my Dear,
Accept a Penitential *Tear*
Dropping from *Grief, Love* and *Fear,*
My panting Heart; O let it move
With no *Passion,* but thy *Love.*

3

Let it *throb,* and let it *beat*
Only with that *Holy Heat.*
Let its *Flames,* and let its *fires,*
Only be of *chast Desires;*
Just like the *Flames* of those above,
Who do nought else but *sing* and *love.*

4

When, when, my Soul, shall we enjoy
The *dear* and Rapturous *Imploy!*
For this we'll live, for this let's die;
'Tis worth it, for 'tis *Ecstacy.*

Good-Friday
1

Blest Lord, I *sigh* and *mourn,* and come away;
With thee I will be *crucify'd* to day:
I'll *bleed too* that from thee I've gone astray.

2

A *Bleeding Heart* I will present to thee,
Who to thy Father didst present for me,
This day, a *Bleeding Body* on the Tree.

3

My Heart shall *bleed*, that I deny to thee
The Fruit of all thy *Sufferings* there for me.
So I have done; but thus I'll do no more:
No more I'll put upon the dismal Score.

4

Ne'er wert thou *scorn'd* and *spit on;* and thou ne'er
Suffer'd'st one *Stripe*, didst *bleed*, or shed one *Tear*
For fallen Angels; but thou *didst for me:*
Oh what is't, Lord, that I have *done for thee.*

5

What have we *done*, my Soul, for all this *Love?*
How have we *labour'd*, and how have we *strove*
Our due Returns of Gratitude to prove?
Why this we've done: the Lamb that once was slain,
We wretchedly have *crucify'd* again.

6

For this how can we chuse but *sigh*, and say,
I with thee will *be crucify'd* to Day.

7

I'll *sigh* and *bleed*, and *groan*, and *weep*, and *mourn;*
I'll give you what you *dy'd* for: my *Return:*
My *Quick Return* from all known Mortal Sin
That has been chosen, voluntary been.

No more, dear Lord, by Avarice, Lust, or Pride,
By Envy, or by one known Sin beside,
I'll *pierce* (I hope) thy Hands, or Feet, or Side.
No more I'll *crucify* my Lord, no more.—
Let my Tears speak the rest, while I adore.

Katherine Philips
(1632–1664)

BORN TO A PRESBYTERIAN family in London, and married at a young age to a
Parliamentarian who signed Charles I's death warrant, Philips nevertheless seems to
have supported the King's political and church policies. Her friendship with members
of Charles II's circle may have saved her husband after the monarchy was restored. She
was precociously literary, and began in her adolescence to write verse and plays with a
coterie who shared an admiration for Cavalier plays and poetry and for French litera-
ture. The pet-name that grew from that society would become her literary pseudonym;
the volume of her work that appeared in 1664 was entitled *Poems by the most deservedly
admired Mrs Katherine Philips, the matchless Orinda*. Philips also published a translation
of a French play, Corneille's *La mort de Pompée*, which was staged in Dublin in 1663.

A Prayer

O God, enlarge my heart
To entertain what Thou wouldst fain impart.
Nor let that soul, by several titles thine,
And most capacious form'd for things divine,
(So nobly meant, that when it most doth miss,
'Tis is mistaken pantings after bliss,)
Degrade it self, in sordid things delight,
Or by prophaner mixtures lose its right.
Oh! that, with fixt unbroken thoughts, it may
Admire the light which does obscure the day.

And since 'tis angels' work it hath to do,
May its composure be like angels' too.
When shall these clogs of sense and fancy break,
That I may hear the God within me speak?
When, with a silent and retired art,
Shall I with all this empty hurry part?
To the still voice above, my soul advance;
My light and joy placed in his countenance?
By whose dispence my soul to such frame brought,
May tame each trecherous, fix each scattering thought;
With such distinctions all things here behold,
And so to separate each dross from gold,
That nought may satisfy my soul, set free
From earth, but to enjoy and study Thee.

An Collins
(fl. 1653)

ONE COPY OF *Divine Songs and Meditacions,* a volume of poetry published in Lon-
don in 1653, survives today, and is our only source for information about the life of its
author, An Collins. She seems to have been a Protestant, and some of her poems lean
toward the doctrines of a mild Puritanism. The introductory poem to her collection
indicates that she was of a sickly constitution and kept largely to her house, and sug-
gests that she may have lived in the country rather than in London itself. She reports
in her poem "The Discourse" that she experienced a personal religious conversion
at some point and turned her mind from the concerns of the world to holy con-
templation.

Another Song.

The Winter of my infancy being over-past
I then supposed, suddenly the Spring would hast°   *hasten*
Which useth every thing to cheare
With invitacion to recreacion
This time of yeare,

The Sun sends forth his radient beames to warm the ground
The drops distil, between the gleams delights abound,
Ver° brings her mate the flowery Queen,   *Spring*
The Groves shee dresses, her Art expresses
On every Green.

But in my Spring it was not so, but contrary.
For no delightfull flowers grew to please the eye.
No hopefull bud, nor fruitfull bough.
No moderat showers which causeth flowers
To spring and grow.

My Aprill was exceeding dry, therfore unkind;
Whence tis that small utility I look to find,
For when that Aprill is so dry,
(As hath been spoken) it doth betoken
Much scarcity.

Thus is my Spring now almost past in heavinesse
The Sky of pleasure's over-cast with sad distresse
For by a comfortlesse Eclips,
Disconsolacion and sore vexacion.
My blossom nips.

Yet as a garden is my mind enclosed fast[55]
Being to safety so confind from storm and blast
Apt to produce a fruit most rare.
That is not common with every woman
That fruitfull are.

A Love of goodnesse is the cheifest plant therin
The second is, (for to be briefe) Dislike to sin,
These grow in spight of misery.
Which Grace doth nourish and cause to flourish
Continually.

But evill mocions, currupt seeds, fall here also
whenc springs prophanesse as do weeds where flowers grow
Which must supplanted be with speed
These weeds of Error, Distrust and Terror,
Lest woe succeed.

---

55. See Song of Songs 4.12.

So shall they not molest, the plants before exprest
Which countervails these outward wants, & purchase rest
Which more commodious is for me
Then outward pleasures or earthly treasures
Enjoyd would be.

My little Hopes of worldly Gain I fret not at.
As yet I do this Hope retain; though Spring be lat°   *late*
Perhaps my Sommer-age may be.
Not prejudiciall, but benificiall
Enough for me.

Admit the worst it be not so, but stormy too,
He learn my selfe to undergo more then I doe
And still content my self with this
Sweet Meditacion and Contemplacion
Of heavenly blis,

Which for the Saints reserved is, who persevere
In Piety and Holynesse, and godly Feare,
The pleasures of which blis divine
Neither Logician nor Rhetorician
Can well define.

Eldred Revett
(fl. 1657)

VERY LITTLE IS KNOWN ABOUT Revett's life, but he did publish a volume of poetry in 1657. He was one of twelve children of a merchant-class family of Suffolk, in the southeast of England. He attended Cambridge, and later seems to have gone to law school in London. He associated with some Royalist poets, including Richard Lovelace. Beyond the poems *Humane and Divine* that appear in the 1657 collection, work by Revett shows up in a number of miscellaneous collections during the 1650s.

Prayer

1

A Fleece of Angell-downe that flyes
    In a golden cloud of Breath;
Still upward to the kindred skyes
    And above them hovereth
        A *Soule,*
In *Parcell* ushering the whole.

2

A most illustrious *break* of *Day,*
    From the *Night* of Death and *sin,*
A Bright and *Emissary* Ray
    Of a cheerfull *light within;*
        A *Spice!*
Smoaks from the Heart *in sacrifice:*

3

A *Spirit* hath got leave to *play*
    From its *Chains* of *Flesh* and *Blood.*
A soul *escap'd* to *learn* the way
    To its longed for abroad;
        A thought,
Then up *in the third Heavens caught.*

4

A *talking* with the *Holy One,*
    A Familiar conference:
A *wrestling* for a sparkling throne
    Got by *holy violence.*
        A *Plate.*
And *Clapper* to Saint *Peters* Gate.

Julia Palmer
(c. 1637–c. 1718)

JULIA PALMER WAS A nonconforming Calvinist who bequeathed her manuscript of two "centuries," or sets of a hundred poems each, to a pair of apothecaries in Westminster. Although biographical information is difficult to trace, she is probably the Julia Palmer whose son was apprenticed to an apothecary in the 1680s. Palmer composed her poetry between 1671 and 1673, a period during which the English throne enacted the Declaration of Indulgence, which licensed nonconformists with freedom to worship and to preach; Palmer's husband Nicholas was among those newly licensed preachers.

from *Centuries*
2.35—THE SOULL UNDER THE DISTEMPERS OF ITS BODY
RELEIVES IT SELF, BY EYEING ITS FUTURE GLORY, AND
FREEDOME.

How doth this mouldring tent of clay
retard the soull, whilst here
In its progressive, holy way
by breaches that appear

But when to heaven, it shall get
It then shall freely soare
the body, then shall be a let°   *impediment*
unto the soull no more

No pained head, or akeing hart
Shall indispose thee then
To sing his praise, or act thy part
among the sons of men

No malencholy, in thee there
Shall any more apear
To steall away, thy chousest° fare   *choicest*
and soull delighting chear

No painfull hectic, cold, or heat
Shall when there, take ther turns

And in the body, make their seat
love only, sweetly burns

In heaven, the body shall be
A clog to'th soull no more
But it shall be, agile, and free
ready, with it to soare

Then cease my soull, for to complain
of distempers unkind
When thy body, returns again
each dust, shall be calcyn'd.°   *calcined*

Thomas Traherne
(c. 1637–1674)

THE SON OF A SHOEMAKER, Traherne may have been orphaned as a young child and raised by a relative. After graduating from Oxford, Traherne was appointed rector of Credenhill, a parish near Hereford. In 1667, he became private chaplain to Sir Orlando Bridgeman, the Lord Keeper of the Great Seal to Charles II; he lived out his life in that nobleman's household. With the exception of a brace of theological tracts published around the time of his death, Traherne's work remained largely unknown during his lifetime. Manuscripts of his poems passed from hand to hand until they were discovered at a London bookstall in the late nineteenth century, and their authorship was later traced to Traherne. More of his poetry and prose continued to surface over the course of the twentieth century, including a manuscript of visionary, rhapsodic work in mixed genre called *Commentaries of Heaven*, which was rescued, half-burning and stinking, from a Lancashire trash heap in 1967.

The Rapture.

I

      Sweet Infancy!
O fire of Heaven! O Sacred Light!
      How Fair and Bright!
      How Great am I,
Whom all the World doth magnifie!

2

      O Heavenly Joy!
O Great and Sacred Blessedness,
        Which I possess!
        So great a Joy
Who did into my Armes convey!

3

      From GOD abov
Being sent, the Heavens me enflame,
        To prais his Name.
        The Stars do move!
The Burning Sun doth shew his Love.

4

      O how Divine
Am I! To all this Sacred Wealth,
        This Life and Health,
        Who raisd? Who mine
Did make the same? What Hand Divine?

The Person.

1

      Ye Sacred Lims,
A richer Blazon I will lay
        On you, then first I found:
        That like Celestial Kings,
    Ye might with Ornaments of Joy
        Be always Crownd.
A Deep Vermilion on a Red,
On that a Scarlet I will lay,
        With Gold Ile Crown your Head,
        Which like the Sun shall Ray.
With Robes of Glory and Delight
        Ile make you Bright.

Mistake me not, I do not mean to bring
    New Robes, but to Display the Thing:
Nor Paint, nor Cloath, nor Crown, nor add a Ray,
But Glorify by taking all away.

2

      The Naked Things
Are most Sublime, and Brightest shew,
    When they alone are seen:
    Mens Hands then Angels Wings
Are truer Wealth even here below:
      For those but seem.
Their Worth they then do best reveal,
When we all Metaphores remove,
    For Metaphores conceal,
    And only Vapours prove.
They best are Blazond when we see
      The Anatomie,
Survey the Skin, cut up the Flesh, the Veins
    Unfold: The Glory there remains.
The Muscles, Fibres, Arteries and Bones
Are better far then Crowns and precious Stones.

3

      Shall I not then
Delight in these most Sacred Treasures
    Which my Great Father gave,
    Far more then other Men
  Delight in Gold? Since these are Pleasures,
    That make us Brave!
  Far Braver then the Pearl and Gold
  That glitter on a Ladies Neck!
    The Rubies we behold,
    The Diamonds that Deck
  The Hands of Queens, compard unto
    The Hands we view;
The Softer Lillies, and the Roses are

Less Ornaments to those that Wear
The same, then are the Hands, and Lips, and Ey
Of those who those fals Ornaments so prize.

4

     Let Veritie
    Be thy Delight: let me Esteem
    True Wealth far more then Toys:
    Let Sacred Riches be,
While falser Treasures only seem,
    My real Joys.
For Golden Chains and Bracelets are
But Gilded Manicles, wherby
    Old Satan doth ensnare,
    Allure, Bewitch the Ey.
Thy Gifts O God alone Ile prize,
    My Tongue, my Eys,
My cheeks, my Lips, my Ears, my Hands, my Feet;
    Their Harmony is far more Sweet;
Their Beauty true. And these in all my Ways
Shall Themes becom, and Organs of thy Praise.

Love.

I

    O Nectar! O Delicious Stream!
O ravishing and only Pleasure! Where
    Shall such another Theme
Inspire my Tongue with Joys, or pleas mine Ear!
    Abridgement of Delights!
    And Queen of Sights!
O Mine of Rarities! O Kingdom Wide!
O more! O Caus of all! O Glorious Bride!
    O God! O Bride of God! O King!
    O Soul and Crown of evry Thing!

2

         Did not I covet to behold
Som Endless Monarch, that did always live
         In Palaces of Gold
Willing all Kingdoms Realms and Crowns to give
         Unto my Soul! Whose Lov
            A Spring might prov
Of Endless Glories, Honors, friendships, Pleasures,
Joys, Praises, Beauties and Celestial Treasures!
         Lo, now I see there's such a King,
         The fountain Head of evry Thing!

3

         Did my Ambition ever Dream
Of such a Lord, of such a Love! Did I
         Expect so Sweet a Stream
As this at any time! Could any Ey
         Believ it? Why all Power
            Is used here
Joys down from Heaven on my Head to shower
And Jove beyond the Fiction doth appear
         Once more in Golden Rain to come
         To Danae's Pleasing Fruitfull Womb.[56]

4

         His Ganimede![57] His Life! His Joy!
Or he comes down to me, or takes me up
         That I might be his Boy,
And fill, and taste, and give, and Drink the Cup.
         But these (tho great) are all
            Too short and small,
Too Weak and feeble Pictures to Express

---

56. In ancient myth, Danaë became pregnant with Perseus when Jove, spying her sunbathing on a rock, fell into her lap as a shower of gold.

57. Jove, smitten with the beauty of the bathing Ganymede, transformed himself into an eagle and snatched the young boy up to Mount Olympus, where he became cupbearer to the gods.

The true Mysterious Depths of Blessedness.
  I am his Image, and his Friend.
  His Son, Bride, Glory, Temple, End.

Desire.

1

      For giving me Desire,
An Eager Thirst, a burning Ardent fire,
    A virgin Infant Flame,
A Love with which into the World I came,
  An Inward Hidden Heavenly Love,
   Which in my Soul did Work and move,
    And ever ever me Enflame,
With restlesse longing Heavenly Avarice,
   That never could be satisfied,
That did incessantly a Paradice
Unknown suggest, and som thing undescried
    Discern, and bear me to it; be
    Thy Name for ever praisd by me.

2

     My Parchd and Witherd Bones
Burnt up did seem: My Soul was full of Groans:
    My Thoughts Extensions were:
Like Paces Reaches Steps they did appear:
  They somwhat hotly did persue,
   Knew that they had not all their due;
    Nor ever quiet were:
But made my flesh like Hungry Thirsty Ground,
   My Heart a deep profound Abyss,
And evry Joy and Pleasure but a Wound,
So long as I my Blessedness did miss.
    O Happiness! A Famine burns,
    And all my Life to Angwish turns!

3

            Where are the Silent Streams,
The Living Waters, and the Glorious Beams,
          The Sweet Reviving Bowers,
The Shady Groves, the Sweet and Curious Flowers,
     The Springs and Trees, the Heavenly Days,
     The Flowry Meads, and Glorious Rayes,
        The Gold and Silver Towers?
Alass, all these are poor and Empty Things,
     Trees Waters Days and Shining Beams
Fruits, Flowers, Bowers, Shady Groves and Springs,
No Joy will yeeld, no more then Silent Streams.
     These are but Dead Material Toys,
     And cannot make my Heavenly Joys.

4

           O Love! ye Amities,
And Friendships, that appear abov the Skies!
         Ye Feasts, and Living Pleasures!
Ye Senses, Honors, and Imperial Treasures!
    Ye Bridal Joys! Ye High Delights;
    That satisfy all Appetites!
      Ye Sweet Affections, and
Ye high Respects! What ever Joys there be
      In Triumphs, Whatsoever stand
In Amicable Sweet Societie
Whatever Pleasures are at his right Hand
       Ye must, before I am Divine,
      In full Proprietie be mine.

5

       This Soaring Sacred Thirst,
Ambassador of Bliss, approached first,
        Making a Place in me,
That made me apt to Prize, and Taste, and See,
      For not the Objects, but the Sence
      Of Things, doth Bliss to Souls dispence,

And make it Lord like Thee.
Sence, feeling, Taste, Complacency and Sight,
   These are the true and real Joys,
The Living Flowing Inward Melting, Bright
And Heavenly Pleasures; all the rest are Toys:
   All which are founded in Desire,
      As Light in Flame, and Heat in fire.

The Return.

To Infancy, O Lord, again I com,
   That I my Manhood may improv:
   My early Tutor is the Womb;
      I still my Cradle lov.
   'Tis strange that I should Wisest be,
   When least I could an Error see.

Till I gain strength against Temptation, I
   Perceiv it safest to abide
   An Infant still; and therfore fly
      (A lowly State may hide
   A man from Danger) to the Womb,
   That I may yet New-born becom.

My God, thy Bounty then did ravish me!
   Before I learned to be poor,
   I always did thy Riches see,
      And thankfully adore:
   Thy Glory and thy Goodness were
   My sweet Companions all the Year.

Edward Taylor
(1642–1729)

SON OF A NONCONFORMING Calvinist farmer, Taylor emigrated to the American colonies in 1668, on the heels of Charles II's Act of Uniformity, which prescribed the form that public worship was allowed to take in an effort to eliminate nonconformists from clerical positions. He attended Harvard and became the minister and physician in the small town of Westfield, far in the Massachusetts frontier. Taylor's major poetic works are *God's Determinations,* a sequence of dramatic verse debates about salvation, and the two series of *Preparatory Meditations,* lyric poems that Taylor composed as he prepared to administer the sacrament of the Lord's Supper to his small congregation. Taylor wrote in private, and left instructions that his poems never be published; his manuscript was found in the library at Yale University in 1937, having lain unknown for over two centuries.

from *Preparatory Meditations*
1.1

What Love is this of thine, that Cannot bee
      In thine Infinity, O Lord, Confinde,
Unless it in thy very Person see,
      Infinity, and Finity Conjoyn'd?
      What hath thy Godhead, as not satisfide
      Marri'de our Manhood, making it its Bride?

Oh, Matchless Love! filling Heaven to the brim!
      O're running it: all running o're beside
This World! Nay Overflowing Hell; wherein
      For thine Elect, there rose a mighty Tide!
      That there our Veans° might through thy Person bleed,   *veins*
      To quench those flames, that else would on us feed.

Oh! that thy Love might overflow my Heart!
      To fire the same with Love: for Love I would.
But oh! my streight'ned Breast! my Lifeless Sparke!
      My Fireless Flame! What Chilly Love, and Cold?
      In measure small! In Manner Chilly! See.
      Lord blow the Coal: Thy Love Enflame in mee.

1.8—JOH. 6.51. I AM THE LIVING BREAD.

I kening° through Astronomy Divine   *descrying*
  The Worlds bright Battlement, wherein I spy
A Golden Path my Pensill cannot line,
  From that bright Throne unto my Threshold ly.
  And while my puzzled thoughts about it pore
  I finde the Bread of Life in't at my doore.

When that this Bird of Paradise put in
  This Wicker Cage (my Corps) to tweedle praise
Had peckt the Fruite forbad: and so did fling
  Away its Food; and lost its golden dayes;
  It fell into Celestiall Famine sore:
  And never could attain a morsell more.

Alas! alas! Poore Bird, what wilt thou doe?
  The Creatures field no food for Souls e're gave.
And if thou knock at Angells dores they show
  An Empty Barrell: they no soul bread have.
  Alas! Poore Bird, the Worlds White Loafe is done.
  And cannot yield thee here the smallest Crumb.

In this sad state, Gods Tender Bowells run
  Out streams of Grace: And he to end all strife
The Purest Wheate in Heaven, his deare-dear Son
  Grinds, and kneads up into this Bread of Life.
  Which Bread of Life from Heaven down came and stands
  Disht on thy Table up by Angells Hands.

Did God mould up this Bread in Heaven, and bake,
  Which from his Table came, and to shine goeth?
Doth he bespeake thee thus, This Soule Bread take.
  Come Eate thy fill of this thy Gods White Loafe?
  Its Food too fine for Angells, yet come, take
  And Eate thy fill. Its Heavens Sugar Cake.

What Grace is this knead in this Loafe? This thing
  Souls are but petty things it to admire.
Yee Angells, help: This fill would to the brim
  Heav'n s whelm'd-down Chrystall meele Bowle, yea and higher.
  This Bread of Life drops in thy mouth, doth Cry.
  Eate, Eate me, Soul, and thou shalt never dy.

When thy Bright Beams, my Lord, do strike mine Eye,
    Methinkes I then could truely Chide out right
My Hide bound Soule that stands so niggardly
    That scarce a thought gets glorified by't.
    My Quaintest Metaphors are ragged Stuff,
    Making the Sun seem like a Mullipuff.°   *puffball*

Its my desire, thou shouldst be glorifi'de:
    But when thy Glory shines before mine eye,
I pardon Crave, lest my desire be Pride.
    Or bed thy Glory in a Cloudy Sky.
    The Sun grows wan; and Angells palefac'd shrinke,
    Before thy Shine, which I besmeere with Inke.

But shall the Bird sing forth thy Praise, and shall
    The little Bee present her thankfull Hum?
But I who see thy shining Glory fall
    Before mine Eyes, stand Blockish, Dull, and Dumb?
    Whether I speake, or speechless stand, I spy,
    I faile thy Glory: therefore pardon Cry.

But this I finde; My Rhymes do better suite
    Mine own Dispraise than tune forth praise to thee.
Yet being Chid, whether Consonant, or Mute,
    I force my Tongue to tattle, as you see.
    That I thy glorious Praise may Trumpet right,
    Be thou my Song, and make Lord, mee thy Pipe.

This shining Sky will fly away apace,
    When thy bright Glory splits the same to make
Thy Majesty a Pass, whose Fairest Face
    Too foule a Path is for thy Feet to take.
    What Glory then, shall tend thee through the Sky
    Draining the Heaven much of Angells dry?

What Light then flame will in thy Judgment Seate,
    'Fore which all men, and angells shall appeare?
How shall thy Glorious Righteousness them treate,
    Rend'ring to each after his Works done here?
    Then Saints With Angells thou wilt glorify:
    And burn Lewd Men, and Divells Gloriously.

Edward Taylor   207

One glimps, my Lord, of thy bright Judgment day,
      And Glory piercing through, like fiery Darts,
All Divells, doth me make for Grace to pray,
      For filling Grace had I ten thousand Hearts.
      I'de through ten Hells to see thy Judgment Day
      Wouldst thou but guild my Soule with thy bright Ray.

2.12—EZEK. 37.24. DAVID MY SERVANT SHALL BE THEIR KING.

Dull, Dull indeed! What shall it e're be thus?
      And why? Are not thy Promises, my Lord,
Rich, Quick'ning things? How should my full Cheeks blush
      To finde mee thus? And those a lifeless Word?
      My Heart is heedless: unconcernd hereat:
      I finde my Spirits Spiritless, and flat.

Thou Courtst mine Eyes in Sparkling Colours bright,
      Most bright indeed, and soul enamoring,
With the most Shining Sun, whose beames did smite
      Me with delightfull Smiles to make mee spring.
      Embellisht knots of Love assault my minde
      Which still is Dull, as if this Sun ne're shin'de.

David in all his gallantry now comes,
      Bringing to tende thy Shrine, his Royall Glory,
Rich Prowess, Prudence, Victories, Sweet Songs,
      And Piety to Pensill out thy Story;
      To draw my Heart to thee in this brave shine
      Of typick Beams, most warm. But still I pine.

Shall not this Lovely Beauty, Lord, set out
      In Dazzling Shining Flashes 'fore mine Eye,
Enchant my heart, Love's golden mine, till't spout
      Out Streames of Love refin'd that on thee lie?
      Thy Glory's great: Thou Davids Kingdom shalt
Enjoy for aye.° I want and thats my fault.   *always*

Spare me, my Lord, spare me, I greatly pray,
      Let me thy Gold pass through thy Fire untill
Thy Fire refine, and take my filth away.
      That I may shine like Gold, and have my fill

Of Love for thee; untill my Virginall[58]
Chime out in Changes sweet thy Praises shall.

Wipe off my Rust, Lord, with thy wisp° me scoure,   *brush*
    And make thy Beams pearch on my Strings their blaze.
My tunes Cloath with thy Shine, and Quavers° poure   *eighth notes*
    My Cursing Strings on, loaded with thy Praise.
    My Fervent Love with Musick in her hand,
    Shall then attend thyselfe, and thy Command.

2.144—CANT. 6.11.[59] I WENT DOWN INTO THE GARDEN OF NUTS
TO SE THE FRUITS OF THE VALLY, TO SE WHETHER THE VINE
FLOWERISHED AND THE POMEGRANATE BUDDED.

Eternal Majesty, my blessed Lord,
    Art thou into thy Nutty Garden come?
To se the Vallys fruits on thy accord:
    Whether thy Vines do flowrish and thick hange
    To se whether thy Pomegranates do bud,
    And that thy nuttree gardens fruit is good?

Am I a grafted Branch in th' true true Vine?
    Or planted Pomegranat thy Garden in
And do I flowerish as a note of Wine?
    And do my pomegranates now bud and spring?
    Oh let my blossoms and my Buds turn fruite
    Lest fruitless I suffer thy prooning Hook.

And with thy Spirituall Physick purge thou mee:
    My very Essence that much fruite't may beare,
Most joyous and delightfull unto thee.
    The Spirituall Grapes and Pomegranates most fare.
    If in thy Nut Tree Garden I am found
    Barren thy prooning knife will Cut and Wound.

If in thy nuttery, I should be found
    To beare no Nutmegs, Almonds, but a nut
All Wormeate, or in barrenness abound

---

58. A keyboard instrument, similar to a harpsichord.
59. Canticles is the Latin name for the Song of Songs, or Song of Solomon.

I well may feare thy prooning hook will Cut
And Cut me off as is the fruitless Vine:
That evermore doth fruitfulness decline.

But when thou in thy garden dost descend
And findst my branch clusterd with spirituall Grapes;
And my trees limbs with fruits downward to bend,
Each bows full reev'd° with Spirituall Pomegranates.   *wreathed*
My Vines and blossom and the Grapes thereon
Will smell indeed like Smell of Lebanon.

Shall this poore barren mould of mine e're bee
Planted with Spirituall Vines and pomegranates?
Whose Bud and Blossome flowrish shall to thee?
And with perfumed joys thee graciate?°   *favor*
Then Spirituall joyes flying on Spicy Wings
Shall entertain thee in thy Visitings.

And if thou makest mee to be thy mold
Though Clayey mould I bee, and run in mee
Thy Spirits Gold, thy Trumpet all of gold,
Though I be Clay Ist° thy Gold-Trumpet bee.   *I*
Then in Angelick melody I will
Trumpet thy Glory and with gracious Skill.

Huswifery

Make me, O Lord, thy Spinning Wheele compleat;
Thy Holy Worde my Distaff make for mee.[60]
Make mine Affections thy Swift Flyers neate,[61]
And make my Soule thy holy Spoole to bee.
My Conversation make to be thy Reele,
And reele the yarn thereon spun of thy Wheele.

Make me thy Loome then, knit therein this Twine:
And make thy Holy Spirit, Lord, winde quills:
Then weave the Web thyselfe. The yarn is fine.

---

60. Distaff: a staff with a split end for holding wool or cotton, from which the thread is drawn into the
    spinning wheel.
61. The flyer twists the yarn before winding it onto the spindle, and is powered by a treadle wheel.

Thine Ordinances make my Fulling Mills.[62]
Then dy the same in Heavenly Colours Choice,
All pinkt with Varnish't Flowers of Paradise.

Then cloath therewith mine Understanding, Will,
        Affections, Judgment, Conscience, Memory;
My Words and Actions, that their shine may fill
        My wayes with glory and thee glorify.
        Then mine apparell shall display before yee
        That I am Cloathd in Holy robes for glory.

---

62. Fulling mills are rollers for beating impurities out of cloth.

5

The Poetic Sublime

THE EIGHTEENTH AND NINETEENTH CENTURIES

AFTER NEARLY TWO CENTURIES of religious upheaval, redefinition, and contro-versy, which culminated in England in a civil war, Parliamentary approval of the Tol-eration Act of 1689 relaxed religious tensions by granting some freedom of worship to Dissenters—those whose beliefs departed from the tenets of the established state Church of England. Though these policies notably did not extend to Catholics or Jews, they nevertheless helped to forge a culture of increased religious moderation and im-proved theological tolerance in England. As a consequence, during this period the cul-tural position of religion generally moved away from the violent flashpoint of division that it had been during the English Renaissance.

This diffusing of religious tensions coincided with a growing consensus con-cerning the social good, even in the face of diverse philosophical ideas. Virtue came to be seen as a product of social impulses rather than divine law, and a general belief in the natural sympathies that draw people together prompted a custodial investment in the common good by individuals. This turn toward a sensibility of interconnectedness cor-responded to the development of enthusiastic religious communities within the larger nation, in England and in America. Under the influence of the Great Awakening, com-munal worship turned toward a more emotional spirituality, fueled both by powerful preaching and by the singing of hymns. In the works of such giants of hymnody as Charles Wesley and Isaac Watts, the gathered worshippers sing together: "Come, let us anew our journey pursue . . . His adorable will let us gladly fulfill"; the intense, pleading singular of the seventeenth-century devotional lyric becomes a resolutely corporate plural, "I" becomes "We." While lyric reveries like Thomas Gray's "Elegy Written in a Country Churchyard" and Edward Young's "Night Thoughts" were among the century's most beloved poems, the most popular poetic genres of the period tend toward communal genres: satires, ballads, didactic verse, and hymns, all capitalizing upon shared knowledge and common points of reference.

But even as the devotional lyric retreated in prominence behind these more communal genres, the influence of Romanticism capitalized upon many of the same interests that drove the Great Awakening to produce a new kind of lyric poetry. Just as that religious movement privileged an affective and experiential Christianity, Romanticism appealed to genuine and deep emotion. Romanticism relocated religion in the inner world of the human spirit, and the Romantic priority placed on sensibility—the affective response to experience as a phenomenon simultaneously mental and bodily—led to the elevation of first-person accounts of thoughts and feelings. Romanticism's new emphasis on emotional extremes such as terror and awe, particularly in confronting nature and the universe, made for an aesthetic that championed experiences of the sublime. But the sublime was felt very much as an aesthetic event: especially in the wake of the Enlightenment, with its focus on reason and scientific empiricism, for many writers of the eighteenth and nineteenth centuries religion was less relevant as a source for conventional piety and reverence than as an aesthetic field, a set of charged and culturally familiar symbols that might be put to use for literary ends.

FURTHER READING

Barth, Robert J. *Romanticism and Transcendence: Wordsworth, Coleridge, and the Religious Imagination.* Columbia: University of Missouri Press, 2003.

Canuel, Mark. "Romanticism, Religion, Secularization." *Eighteenth-Century Life,* 33, no. 3 (2009): 150–155.

Colville, Derek. *Victorian Poetry and the Romantic Religion.* Albany: State University of New York Press, 1970.

Davie, Donald. *The Eighteenth-Century Hymn in England.* Cambridge: Cambridge University Press, 1993.

Duffy, Cian. *Shelley and the Revolutionary Sublime.* Cambridge: Cambridge University Press, 2005.

Marshall, Madeline Forell, and Janet Todd. *English Congregational Hymns in the Eighteenth Century.* Lexington: University Press of Kentucky, 1982.

Roberts, Wendy Raphael. "Demand My Voice: Hearing God in Eighteenth-Century American Poetry." *Early American Literature,* 45, no. 1 (2010): 119–144.

Starzyk, Lawrence J. "'That Promised Land': Poetry and Religion in the Early Victorian Period." *Victorian Studies: A Journal of the Humanities, Arts and Sciences,* 16 (1973): 269–290.

Vickers, Brian, and Nancy S. Striever. *Rhetoric and the Pursuit of Truth: Language Change in the Seventeenth and Eighteenth Centuries.* Los Angeles: William Andrews Clark Memorial Library, UCLA, 1985.

Hymns of the Long Eighteenth Century

THE LONG EIGHTEENTH CENTURY witnessed a flourishing of hymn culture, both in England and the American colonies. In England, mainstream Anglican public worship limited its performances of song to musical versions of the psalms (in a translation by Nahum Tate and Nicholas Brady, which had supplanted the Sternhold and Hopkins psalter around the turn of the eighteenth century), but among dissenting congregations hymns began to play a central role in group worship. The Great Awakening, a movement that deemphasized ritual and ceremony in favor of an intensely personal Christianity, swept through Protestant Europe and British America beginning in the 1730s and 1740s. With its encouragement of introspection and a particularly affective piety, the Great Awakening prompted increased attention to the ways in which hymns might foster a profound emotional response. Many hymns of the period are inspired by both Greco-Roman hymn traditions and the ancient Hebrew poetry of the Bible. They often express spiritual struggle, and they appeal to experience in a way that manages to be both personal and impersonal enough to signify across confessional divides, involving individual singers in a communal story of conversion and commitment. The texts selected here represent a range of confessional allegiances, and many of these hymns continue to live today in the hymnals of various denominations.

Joseph Addison
(1672–1719)

FOUNDER OF THE WIDELY READ periodical *The Spectator*, Joseph Addison was the eldest son of writer and cleric Lancelot Addison. Joseph was raised in the cathedral close at Lichfield. After attending Oxford, where he became known for his Latin verse, Addison traveled to Europe, hoping to secure diplomatic employment. He returned to England in 1703, and attained the position of Under-Secretary of State; he later served in Parliament, first in Ireland and then representing his home county of Wiltshire. Though he is mostly remembered for his essays, he did produce some poetry and fiction, as well as a translation of Virgil's *Georgics*.

Divine Ode.

I

The spacious firmament on high,
With all the blue æthereal sky,
And spangled heavens, a shining frame,
Their great Original proclaim:
Th' unwearied sun from day to day,
Does his Creator's pow'r display,
And publishes to every land
The work of an Almighty hand.

2

Soon as the ev'ning shades prevail,
The moon takes up the wond'rous tale,
And nightly to the list'ning earth,
Repeats the story of her birth:
Whilst all the stars that round her burn,
And all the planets in their turn,
Confirm the tidings as they roll,
And spread the truth from pole to pole.

3

What though in solemn silence, all
Move round the dark terrestrial ball?
What though, nor real voice nor sound
Amid their radiant orbs be found?
In reason's ear they all rejoice,
And utter forth a glorious voice,
For ever singing as they shine,
The hand that made us is divine.

Elizabeth Singer Rowe
(1674–1737)

DAUGHTER OF A DISSENTING minister, Rowe was born in Somerset, England. She wrote poetry from an early age, and during her young adulthood she was the principal contributor of poetry to *The Athenian Mercury*, a biweekly London newspaper. Her volume *A Collection of Divine Hymns and Poems* was published in 1709.

An Hymn

In vain the dusky night retires,
And sullen shadows fly;
In vain the morn with purple light
Adorns the eastern sky.

In vain the gaudy rising sun
The wide horizon gilds;
Comes glitt'ring o'er the silver springs,
And chears the dewy fields.

In vain, dispensing vernal sweets,
The morning breezes play;
In vain the birds, with chearful songs,
Salute the new-born day.

In vain! unless my Saviour's face
These gloomy clouds control;
And dissipate the sullen shades,
That press my drooping soul.

Oh! visit then thy servant, Lord,
With favour from on high;
Arise, my bright immortal sun,
And all these shades will die.

When, when, shall I behold thy face,
All radiant and serene,
Without these envious dusky clouds,
That make a veil between?

When shall that long-expected day
Of sacred vision be?
When my impatient soul shall make
A near approach to thee!

Isaac Watts
(1674–1748)

A POPULAR AND PROLIFIC writer, Watts is credited with having written nearly
seven hundred and fifty hymns. He was raised in a nonconforming Calvinist home, and
therefore was prohibited from attending either Oxford or Cambridge. He worked for
some time training preachers, though his interest was more in education than in preach-
ing; in addition to hymns, Watts wrote many books and essays on theology and on logic.

Godly sorrow arising from the sufferings of Christ.

Alas! and did my Saviour bleed,
And did my Sovereign die?
Would he devote that sacred head
For such a worm as I?

Thy body slain, sweet Jesus, thine,
And bath'd in its own blood,
While all expos'd to wrath divine
The glorious Sufferer stood.

Was it for crimes that I had done
He groan'd upon the tree?
Amazing pity! grace unknown!
And love beyond degree!

Well might the sun in darkness hide,
And shut his glories in,
When God the mighty Maker dy'd
For man the creature's sin.

Thus might I hide my blushing face
While his dear cross appears,
Dissolve my heart in thankfulness,
And melt my eyes to tears.

But drops of grief can ne'er repay
The debt of love I owe;
Here, Lord, I give myself away,
'Tis all that I can do.

Charles Wesley
(1707–1788)

THE SON OF AN ANGLICAN clergyman, Wesley became a leader of the Methodist movement in England. He studied classical languages and literature, and then entered the church in 1735, serving as chaplain to the garrison of English soldiers stationed in the colony of Georgia. Over his career, more than six thousand hymns by Wesley were published, and an additional two thousand were written without being set to music.

Jesus, Lover of My Soul

Jesus, lover of my soul,
let me to thy bosom fly,
while the nearer waters roll,
while the tempest still is high.
Hide me, O my Savior, hide,
till the storm of life is past;
safe into the haven guide;
O receive my soul at last.

Other refuge have I none,
hangs my helpless soul on thee;
leave, ah! leave me not alone,
still support and comfort me.
All my trust on thee is stayed,
all my help from thee I bring;
cover my defenseless head
with the shadow of thy wing.

Wilt Thou not regard my call?
Wilt Thou not accept my prayer?
Lo! I sink, I faint, I fall—
Lo! on Thee I cast my care;
Reach me out Thy gracious hand!
While I of Thy strength receive,
Hoping against hope I stand,
dying, and behold, I live.

Thou, O Christ, art all I want,
more than all in thee I find;
raise the fallen, cheer the faint,
heal the sick, and lead the blind.
Just and holy is thy name,
I am all unrighteousness;
false and full of sin I am;
thou art full of truth and grace.

Plenteous grace with thee is found,
grace to cover all my sin;
let the healing streams abound,
make and keep me pure within.
Thou of life the fountain art,
freely let me take of thee;
spring thou up within my heart;
rise to all eternity.

Jupiter Hammon
(1711–c. 1806)

BORN INTO SLAVERY ON Long Island, New York, Hammon was never emancipated. However, the family that held him encouraged his education. He became the first African American writer to be published in the Americas, and his poems and sermons brought him some fame. His 1786 "Address to the Negroes of the State of New York" was printed and circulated by abolitionist groups.

from *A Poem for Children with Thoughts on Death*

Little children they may die,
    Turn to their native dust,
Their souls shall leap beyond the skies,
    And live among the just.

Like little worms they turn and crawl,
    And gasp for every breath.
The blessed Jesus sends his call,
    And takes them to his rest.

Thus the youth are born to die,
    The time is hastening on,
The Blessed Jesus rends the sky,
    And makes his power known.
        Psalm ciii. 15.

Then ye shall hear the angels sing
    The trumpet give a sound,
Glory, glory to our King,
    The Saviour's coming down.
                    Matth. xxvi. 64.

Start ye saints from dusty beds,
    And hear a Saviour call,
Twas a Jesus Christ that died and bled,
    And thus preserv'd thy soul.

Then shall you hear the trumpet sound,
    And rend the native sky,
Those bodies starting from the ground,
    In the twinkling of an eye.
                    I Cor. xv. 51, 52, 53, 54.

There to sing the praise of God,
    And join the angelic train,
And by the power of his word,
    Unite together again.

John Henry Newton
(1725–1807)

HAVING BEEN RAISED IN LONDON, the son of a shipmaster, John Newton became a sailor. Newton worked for a time on slave trader ships, and many years later he repented his involvement with that sordid profession. After some time at sea, Newton had a profound conversion experience and became an evangelical Christian. He studied biblical languages and eventually became ordained in the Church of England, in which capacity he became Curate of Olney. In 1767, poet William Cowper took up residence in Olney. Newton and Cowper collaborated on a volume of hymns, which was published under the title *Olney Hymns* in 1779. The collection included "Faith's Review and Expectation," now better known by its opening phrase.

Faith's Review and Expectation

Amazing grace! (how sweet the sound)
    That sav'd a wretch like me!
I once was lost, but now am found,
    Was blind, but now I see.

'Twas grace that taught my heart to fear,
    And grace my fears reliev'd,
How precious did that grace appear,
    The hour I first believ'd!

Thro' many dangers, toils and snares,
    I have already come;
'Tis grace has brought me safe thus far,
    And grace will lead me home.

The Lord had promis'd good to me,
    His word my hope secures;
He will my shield and portion be,
    As long as life endures.

Yes, when this flesh and heart shall fail,
    And mortal life shall cease;
I shall possess, within the vail,
    A life of joy and peace.

The earth shall soon dissolve like snow,
    The sun forbear to shine;
But God, who call'd me hear below,
    Will be for ever mine.

The happy debtor.

Ten thousand talents once I owed,
    And nothing had to pay;
But Jesus freed me from the load,
    And washed my debt away.
Yet since the Lord forgave my sin,
    And blotted out my score;
Much more indebted I have been
    Than ere I was before.

My guilt is canceled quite I know,
    And satisfaction made;
But the vast debt of love I owe,
    Can never be repaid.
The love I owe for sin forgiven,
    For power to believe,
For present peace, and promised heaven,
    No angel can conceive.
That love of thine! thou sinner's Friend
    Witness thy bleeding heart!
My little all can ne'er extend
    To pay a thousandth part.
Nay more, the poor returns I make
    I first from thee obtain;
And 'tis of grace, that thou wilt take
    Such poor returns again.
'Tis well—it shall my glory be
    (Let who will boast their store)
In time, and to eternity,
    To owe thee more and more.

William Cowper
(1731–1800)

COWPER'S FATHER WAS RECTOR of the Church of St. Peter in Hertfordshire when William was born. William was intended for a clerkship in Parliament, but seems to have experienced a nervous breakdown. After having attempted suicide several times, he settled with a retired clergyman and his family and moved with them to Olney, where he met John Henry Newton. The two men collaborated on the influential hymnal *Olney Hymns,* of which two of his contributions appear here. Cowper also left behind a large body of poetry, as well as translations of Homer's *Iliad* and *Odyssey*.

The contrite heart.

The Lord will happiness divine
     On contrite hearts bestow;
Then tell me, gracious God, is mine
     A contrite heart or no?

I hear, but seem to hear in vain,
     Insensible as steel;
If aught is felt, 'tis only pain,
     To find I cannot feel.

I sometimes think myself inclined
     To love Thee if I could;
But often feel another mind,
     Averse to all that's good.

My best desires are faint and few,
     I fain would strive for more;
But when I cry, "My strength renew!"
     Seem weaker than before.

Thy saints are comforted, I know,
     And love Thy house of prayer;
I therefore go where others go,
     But find no comfort there.

Oh make this heart rejoice or ache;
     Decide this doubt for me;
And if it be not broken, break—
     And heal it, if it be.

Submission.

O Lord, my best desire fulfill
     And help me to resign,
Life, health, and comfort to thy will,
     And make thy pleasure mine.

Why should I shrink at thy command,
     Whose love forbids my fears?
Or tremble at the gracious hand
     That wipes away my tears?

No, let me rather freely yield
      What most I prize to thee;
Who never hast a good withheld,
      Or wilt withhold from me.

Thy favor, all my journey through,
      Thou art engaged to grant;
What else I want, or think I do,
      'Tis better still to want.

Wisdom and mercy guide my way,
      Shall I resist them both?
A poor blind creature of a day,
      And crushed before the moth!

But ah! my inward spirit cries,
      Still bind me to thy sway;
Else the next cloud that veils my skies,
      Drives all these thoughts away.

Phillis Wheatley
(1753–1784)

BORN IN GAMBIA, SENEGAL, Wheatley was sold into slavery as a child, and purchased by the Wheatley family of Boston, who encouraged her education in literature and the classics, and she learned to read the Bible in Greek and Latin. She was emancipated upon her master's death. She was the first African American poet to publish her own work. The 1773 publication of her first volume, *Poems on Various Subjects, Religious and Moral,* won her praise both in the colonies and in England, and earned her the admiration of Voltaire and George Washington. After her husband was imprisoned for debt, Wheatley was left to care for her sick infant son, and took work as a scullery maid at a boardinghouse. She died at the age of thirty-one, followed in death three hours later by her son.

An Hymn to the Evening

Soon as the sun forsook the eastern main
The pealing thunder shook the heav'nly plain;
Majestic grandeur! From the zephyr's wing,
Exhales the incense of the blooming spring.
Soft purl the streams, the birds renew their notes,
And through the air their mingled music floats.
Through all the heav'ns what beauteous dies are spread!
But the west glories in the deepest red:
So may our breasts with ev'ry virtue glow,
The living temples of our God below!
Fill'd with the praise of him who gives the light,
And draws the sable curtains of the night,
Let placid slumbers sooth each weary mind,
At morn to wake more heav'nly, more refin'd;
So shall the labours of the day begin
More pure, more guarded from the snares of sin.
Night's leaden sceptre seals my drowsy eyes,
Then cease, my song, till fair Aurora rise.

Henry Francis Lyte
(1793–1847)

A CURATE OF THE CHURCH OF England in Cornwall and Devonshire, Henry Lyte was born in Scotland and educated in Ireland. He published a volume entitled *Poems, chiefly Religious* in 1833, followed the next year by a collection of psalms and hymns called *The Spirit of the Psalms*. This piece was published with its now-familiar tune after Lyte's death, in 1861.

Abide with Me

Abide with me; fast falls the eventide;
The darkness deepens; Lord with me abide.
When other helpers fail and comforts flee,
Help of the helpless, O abide with me.

Swift to its close ebbs out life's little day;
Earth's joys grow dim; its glories pass away;
Change and decay in all around I see;
O Thou who changest not, abide with me.

Not a brief glance I beg, a passing word,
But as Thou dwell'st with Thy disciples, Lord,
Familiar, condescending, patient, free.
Come not to sojourn, but abide with me.

Come not in terrors, as the King of kings,
But kind and good, with healing in Thy wings;
Tears for all woes, a heart for every plea.
Come, Friend of sinners, thus abide with me.

Thou on my head in early youth didst smile,
And though rebellious and perverse meanwhile,
Thou hast not left me, oft as I left Thee.
On to the close, O Lord, abide with me.

I need Thy presence ev'ry passing hour.
What but Thy grace can foil the tempter's power?
Who, like Thyself, my guide and stay can be?
Through cloud and sunshine, Lord, abide with me.

I fear no foe, with Thee at hand to bless;
Ills have no weight, and tears no bitterness.
Where is death's sting? Where, grave, thy victory?
I triumph still, if Thou abide with me.

Hold Thou Thy cross before my closing eyes;
Shine through the gloom and point me to the skies.
Heaven's morning breaks, and earth's vain shadows flee;
In life, in death, O Lord, abide with me.

Sarah Flower Adams

(1805–1848)

BORN IN ESSEX, ENGLAND, Sarah Adams was the daughter of an English radical journalist and political writer who served six months in jail for having criticized in print the political involvements of a prominent Anglican bishop. Sarah was a Unitarian, and wrote a number of hymns, as well as religious prose and verse.

Nearer, My God, to Thee

Nearer, my God, to thee,
Nearer to Thee!
E'en tho' it be a cross
That raiseth me,
Still all my song shall be,
Nearer, my God, to thee,
Nearer, my God, to thee,
Nearer to thee!

Tho' like a wanderer,
The sun gone down,
Darkness be over me,
My rest a stone,
Yet in my dreams I'd be
Nearer, my God, to thee,
Nearer, my God, to thee,
Nearer to thee.

There let the way appear
Steps unto heaven;
All that thou sendest me
In mercy given;
Angels to beckon me
Nearer, my God, to thee,
Nearer, my God, to thee,
Nearer to thee.

Then, with my waking thoughts
Bright with thy praise,
Out of my stony griefs
Bethel I'll raise;[1]
So by my woes to be
Nearer, my God, to thee,
Nearer, my God, to thee,
Nearer to thee.

Or if on joyful wing
Cleaving the sky,
Sun, moon, and stars forgot,
Upwards I fly,
Still all my song shall be,
Nearer, my God, to thee,
Nearer, my God, to thee,
Nearer to thee!

Alexander Pope
(1688–1744)

AT THE TIME OF HIS BIRTH, Pope's Catholic family would have been subject to the continuing anti-Catholic sentiment and legislation that marked Restoration England. Catholics were banned from attending university, teaching, serving in public office, and voting, but in addition to his self-directed studies Pope attended a clandestine Catholic school in London until his family was forced to move outside the city limits due to a law restricting Catholics from living within ten miles of the city. He developed a circle of literary friends, in which coterie he wrote pastoral poems, satires, plays, and essays in both prose and heroic couplets, as well as translating Homer. Pope's poem "The Universal Prayer" was attached to *An Essay on Man;* his contemporary Thomas Warton remarked of it, "When it was first published, many orthodox persons were, I remember, offended at it, and called it, The Deist's Prayer. It were to be wished the Deists would make use of so good an one."

---

1. See Genesis 28 and 35.

The Universal Prayer

Father of all! in every age,
    In every clime adored,
By saint, by savage, and by sage,
    Jehovah, Jove, or Lord!

Thou Great First Cause, least understood:
    Who all my sense confined
To know but this—that thou art good,
    And that myself am blind:

Yet gave me, in this dark estate,
    To see the good from ill;
And binding Nature fast in fate,
    Left free the human will.

What conscience dictates to be done,
    Or warns me not to do,
This, teach me more than Hell to shun,
    That, more than Heaven pursue.

What blessings thy free bounty gives,
    Let me not cast away;
For God is paid when man receives,
    To enjoy is to obey.

Yet not to earth's contracted span,
    Thy goodness let me bound,
Or think thee Lord alone of man,
    When thousand worlds are round:

Let not this weak, unknowing hand
    Presume thy bolts to throw,
And deal damnation round the land,
    On each I judge thy foe.

If I am right, thy grace impart,
    Still in the right to stay;
If I am wrong, oh teach my heart
    To find a better way.

Save me alike from foolish pride,
    Or impious discontent,

At aught thy wisdom has denied,
　　Or aught thy goodness lent.

Teach me to feel another's woe,
　　To hide the fault I see;
That mercy I to others show,
　　That mercy show to me.

Mean though I am, not wholly so
　　Since quickened by thy breath;
Oh lead me wheresoe'er I go,
　　Through this day's life or death.

This day, be bread and peace my lot:
　　All else beneath the sun,
Thou know'st if best bestowed or not,
　　And let thy will be done.

To thee, whose temple is all space,
　　Whose altar, earth, sea, skies!
One chorus let all being raise!
　　All Nature's incense rise!

Christopher Smart
(1722–1771)

CHRISTOPHER SMART WAS BORN on a nobleman's estate, his father the steward of the aristocratic house. He was educated early in the classics, and at university studied religion and literature and wrote poems in English and Latin. A refractory spendthrift at school, Smart wrote parodies, satires, and humorous essays for magazines while he was still a student. He relocated to London and continued to be active both in writing and in running up debts. Though some of Smart's friends helped him to secure a contract to produce a weekly newspaper, in an effort to provide him with some sustainable income, the strain of publishing was perhaps too much for Smart; he lapsed into some kind of "fit." In 1757, Smart was admitted to St. Luke's Hospital for Lunatics as a "Curable" patient. His obsessions with religion and with constant prayer date from around this same period, and the incident that provoked Smart's institutionalization may have been aggressive public prayer. During his confinement, Smart worked on his two most famous poems, "A Song to David" and *Jubilate Agno*. He was released in 1763, and "A Song for David" was published shortly thereafter. Both Smart's fits and his financial troubles continued, however, and he died in debtors' prison.

from *Jubilate Agno*[2]

Let Elizur rejoice with the Partridge, who is a prisoner of state and is proud of his keepers.

Let Shedeur rejoice with Pyrausta, who dwelleth in a medium of fire, which God hath adapted for him.

Let Shelumiel rejoice with Olor, who is of a goodly savour, and the very look of him harmonizes the mind.

Let Jael rejoice with the Plover, who whistles for his live, and foils the marksmen and their guns.

Let Raguel rejoice with the Cock of Portugal—God send good Angels to the allies of England!

***

Let Bohan rejoice with the Scythian Stag—he is beef and breeches against want and nakedness.

Let Achsah rejoice with the Pigeon who is an antidote to malignity and will carry a letter.

Let Tohu rejoice with the Grouse—the Lord further the cultivating of heaths and the peopling of deserts.

---

2. Latin: *Rejoice in the Lamb.* Smart's poem incorporates a remarkable body of heterogeneous knowledge, and is generously peppered with references to figures from the Bible and the Apocrypha, as well as historical and contemporary figures. Smart engages in enthusiastic and inventive wordplay, often creating submerged puns on any given word's meaning in Hebrew, Old English, or other languages. Given the short sample of *Jubilate Agno* included here, the editors feel it would be merely distracting to attempt to illuminate by footnote all of Smart's references over the following pages, and we have elected to let the text stand unannotated. For a fuller treatment of the poem's referential richness, curious readers should consult the following studies: W. Moelwyn Merchant, "Patterns of Reference in Smart's *Jubilate Agno*," *Harvard Library Bulletin*, 14, no. 1 (1960): 20–26; and Marcus Walsh, "'Community of Mind': Christopher Smart and the Poetics of Allusion," in *Christopher Smart and the Enlightenment*, ed. Clement Hawes (New York: St. Martin's, 1999): 29–46.

Let Hillel rejoice with Ammodytes, whose colour is deceitful and he plots against the pilgrim's feet.

Let Eli rejoice with Leucon—he is an honest fellow, which is a rarity.

Let Shaul rejoice with Circos, who hath clumsy legs, but he can wheel it the better with his wings.—

Let Hamul rejoice with the Crystal, who is pure and translucent.

Let Ziphion rejoice with the Tit-Lark who is a groundling, but he raises the spirits.

Let Mibzar rejoice with the Cadess, as is their number, so are their names, blessed be the Lord Jesus for them all.

Let Jubal rejoice with Cascilia, the woman and the slow-worm praise the name of the Lord.

***

Let Cherub rejoice with the Cherub who is a bird and a blessed Angel.

***

For I am not without authority in my jeopardy, which I derive inevitably from the glory of the name of the Lord.

For I bless God whose name is Jealous—and there is a zeal to deliver us from everlasting burnings.

For my existimation is good even amongst the slanderers and my memory shall arise for a sweet savour unto the Lord.

For I bless the PRINCE of PEACE and pray that all the guns may be nail'd up, save such are for the rejoicing days.

For I have abstained from the blood of the grape and that even at the Lord's table.

For I have glorified God in GREEK and LATIN, the consecrated languages spoken by the Lord on earth.

For I meditate the peace of Europe amongst family bickerings and domestic jars.

For the HOST is in the WEST—the Lord make us thankful unto salvation.

For I preach the very GOSPEL of CHRIST without comment and with this weapon shall I slay envy.

For I bless God in the rising generation, which is on my side.

For I have translated in the charity, which makes things better and I shall be translated myself at the last.

For he that walked upon the sea, hath prepared the floods with the Gospel of peace.

For the merciful man is merciful to his beast, and to the trees that give them shelter.

For he hath turned the shadow of death into the morning, the Lord is his name.

For I am come home again, but there is nobody to kill the calf or to pay the musick.

For the hour of my felicity, like the womb of Sarah, shall come at the latter end.

For I shou'd have avail'd myself of waggery, had not malice been multitudinous.

For there are still serpents that can speak—God bless my head, my heart and my heel.

For I bless God that I am of the same seed as Ehud, Mutius Scævola, and Colonel Draper.

For the word of God is a sword on my side—no matter what other weapon a stick or a straw.

For I have adventured myself in the name of the Lord, and he hath marked me for his own.

For I bless God for the Postmaster general and all conveyancers of letters under his care especially Allen and Shelvock.

For my grounds in New Canaan shall infinitely compensate for the flats and maynes of Staindrop Moor.

For the praise of God can give to a mute fish the notes of a nightingale.

For I have seen the White Raven and Thomas Hall of Willingham and am my self a greater curiosity than both.

For I look up to heaven which is my prospect to escape envy by surmounting it.

For if Pharaoh had known Joseph, he woud have blessed God and me for the illumination of the people.

For I pray God to bless improvements in gardening till London be a city of palm-trees.

For I pray to give his grace to the poor of England, that Charity be not offended and that benevolence may increase.

For in my nature I quested for beauty, but God, God hath sent me to sea for pearls.

***

For I pray God to give them the food which I cannot earn for them any otherwise than by prayer.

For I pray God bless the Chinese which are of ABRAHAM and the Gospel grew with them at the first.

For I bless God in the honey of the sugar-cane and the milk of the cocoa.

For I bless God in the libraries of the learned and for all the booksellers in the world.

For I bless God in the strength of my loins and for the voice which he hath made sonorous.

For tis no more a merit to provide for oneself, but to quit all for the sake of the Lord.

For there is no invention but the gift of God, and no grace like the grace of gratitude.

For grey hairs are honourable and tell every one of them to the glory of God.

For I bless the Lord Jesus for the memory of GAY, POPE and SWIFT.

For all good words are from GOD, and all others are cant.

***

For I pray the Lord JESUS that cured the LUNATICK to be merciful to all my brethren and sisters in these houses.

For they work me with their harping-irons, which is a barbarous instrument, because I am more unguarded than others.

For the blessing of God hath been on my epistles, which I have written for the benefit of others.

For I bless God that the CHURCH of ENGLAND is one of the SEVEN ev'n the candlestick of the Lord.

For the ENGLISH TONGUE shall be the language of the WEST.

For I pray Almighty CHRIST to bless the MAGDALEN HOUSE and to forward a National purification.

For I have the blessing of God in the three POINTS of manhood, of the pen, of the sword, and of chivalry.

For I am inquisitive in the Lord, and defend the philosophy of the scripture against vain deceit.

For the nets come down from the eyes of the Lord to fish up men to their salvation.

For I have a greater compass both of mirth and melancholy than another.

For I bless the Lord Jesus in the innumerables, and for ever and ever.

For I am redoubted, and redoubtable in the Lord, as is Thomas Becket my father.

***

For I am making to the shore day by day, the Lord Jesus take me.

For I bless the Lord Jesus upon Ramsgate Pier—the Lord forward the building of harbours.

For I bless the Lord Jesus for his very seed, which is in my body . . .

For I pray to God for Nore, for the Trinity house, for all light-houses, beacons and buoys.

For I bless God that I am not in a dungeon, but am allowed the light of the Sun.

For I pray God for the pygmies against their feathered adversaries, as a deed of charity.

For I pray God for all those, who have defiled themselves in matters inconvenient.

***

For Snow is the dew candied and cherishes.

For times and seasons are the Lord's—Man is no chronologer.

For there is a circulation of the sap in all vegetables.

For soot is the dross of Fire.

For the clapping of the hands is naught unless it be to the glory of God.

For God will descend in visible glory when men begin to applaud him.

***

For the letter ל which signifies God by himself is on the fibre of some leaf in every Tree.[3]

For ל is the grain of the human heart and on the network of the skin.

---

3. The Hebrew character *lamed*, which signifies the L sound.

For ל is in the veins of all stones both precious and common.

For ל is upon every hair both of man and beast.

For ל is in the grain of wood.

For ל is in the ore of all metals.

For ל is on the scales of all fish.

For ל is on the petals of all flowers.

For ל is upon on all shells.

For ל is in the constituent particles of air.

For ל is on the mite of the earth.

For ל is in the water yea in every drop.

For ל is in the incomprehensible ingredients of fire.

For ל is in the stars the sun and in the Moon.

For ל is upon the Sapphire Vault.

For the doubling of flowers is the improvement of the gardners talent.

For the flowers are great blessings.

For the Lord made a Nosegay in the meadow with his disciples and preached upon the lily.

***

For the angels of God took it out of his hand and carried it to the Height.

For a man cannot have publick spirit, who is void of private benevolence.

For there is no Height in which there are not flowers.

For flowers have great virtues for all the senses.

For the flower glorifies God and the root parries the adversary.

For the flowers have their angels even the words of God's Creation.

For the warp and woof of flowers are worked by perpetual moving spirits.

For flowers are good both for the living and the dead.

For there is a language of flowers.

For there is a sound reasoning upon all flowers.

For elegant phrases are nothing but flowers.

For flowers are peculiarly the poetry of Christ.

For flowers are medicinal.

For flowers are musical in ocular harmony.

For the right names of flowers are yet in heaven. God make gard'ners better
nomenclators.

***

For A is the beginning of learning and the door of heaven.

For B is a creature busy and bustling.

For C is a sense quick and penetrating.

For D is depth.

For E is eternity—such is the power of the English letters taken singly.

For F is faith.

For G is God—whom I pray to be gracious to Liveware my fellow prisoner.

For H is not a letter, but a spirit—Benedicatur Jesus Christus, sic spirem!

For I is identity. God be gracious to Henry Hatsell.

For K is king.

For L is love. God in every language.

For M is musick and Hebrew מ is the direct figure of God's harp.[4]

For N is new.

For O is open.

For P is power.

For Q is quick.

For R is right.

---

4. The Hebrew character *mem,* which signifies the M sound.

For S is soul.

For T is truth. God be gracious to Jermyn Pratt and to Harriote his Sister.

For U is unity, and his right name is Uve to work it double.

For W is word.

For X is hope—consisting of two check G—God be gracious to Anne Hope.[5]

For Y is yea. God be gracious to Eennet and his family!

For Z is zeal.

***

For God has given us a language of monosyllables to prevent our clipping.

For a toad enjoys a finer prospect than another creature to compensate his lack.

> Tho' toad I am the object of man's hate.
> Yet better am I than a reprobate.   who has the worst of prospects.

For there are stones, whose constituent particles are little toads.

William Blake
(1757–1827)

BLAKE WAS AN ENGLISH POET and artist born in London to a merchant family. He was educated at home by his mother, who had rejected the teachings of the Church of England for the Moravian Church. He was apprenticed to an engraver, during which time he copied images from the Gothic churches in London. He studied art at the Royal Academy, and continued to experiment with new methods of etching and engraving throughout his life. His first collection of poems, *Poetical Sketches*, was published in 1783. His poetry and art were intertwined throughout his career, as he illustrated his own poems. At his death, Blake was working determinedly on a series of illustrations for Dante's *Inferno*, of which only a few images were completed.

---

5. In Smart's manuscript, the X was drawn as two Gs back to back, attached at their back curves.

The Divine Image

To Mercy, Pity, Peace, and Love,
All pray in their distress:
And to these virtues of delight
Return their thankfulness.

For Mercy, Pity, Peace, and Love,
Is God, our father dear:
And Mercy, Pity, Peace, and Love,
Is Man, his child and care.

For Mercy has a human heart,
Pity, a human face:
And Love, the human form divine,
And Peace, the human dress.

Then every man of every clime,
That prays in his distress,
Prays to the human form divine,
Love, Mercy, Pity, Peace.

And all must love the human form,
In heathen, Turk, or Jew.
Where Mercy, Love, & Pity dwell,
There God is dwelling too.

from *Milton: A Poem*
PREFACE

And did those feet in ancient time,
Walk upon Englands mountains green:
And was the holy Lamb of God,
On Englands pleasant pastures seen!

And did the Countenance Divine,
Shine forth upon our clouded hills?
And was Jerusalem builded here,
Among these dark Satanic Mills?

Bring me my Bow of burning gold:
Bring me my Arrows of desire:

Bring me my Spear: O clouds unfold!
Bring me my Chariot of fire!

I will not cease from Mental Fight,
Nor shall my Sword sleep in my hand:
Till we have built Jerusalem,
In Englands green & pleasant Land.

Would to God that all the Lords people were Prophets.
          Numbers XI. Ch 29 v.[6]

from *The Gates of Paradise*
TO THE ACCUSER WHO IS THE GOD OF THIS WORLD

Truly My Satan thou art but a Dunce
And dost not know the Garment from the Man
Every Harlot was a Virgin once
Nor canst thou ever change Kate into Nan[7]

Tho thou art Worshipd by the Names Divine
Of Jesus & Jehovah; thou art still
The Son of Morn in weary Nights decline
The lost Travellers Dream under the Hill.

Samuel Taylor Coleridge
(1772–1834)

ROMANTIC POET, CRITIC, AND philosopher Coleridge was born the son of a vicar in Devon, England. At Cambridge, Coleridge befriended the future Poet Laureate Robert Southey, with whom he planned to establish a utopian community, but they became disillusioned and parted. Coleridge's first collection, *Poems on Various Subjects*, appeared in 1796, and was followed the next year by another book of poems. His friendship with William Wordsworth produced the collaborative work *Lyrical Ballads*.

---

6. Blake's postscript adapts Numbers 11.29.

7. That is, you cannot alter an individual's character.

Suffering from chronic pain, Coleridge became addicted to opium and was on the verge of suicide, and for many years rarely left his house. During this period, he produced his major prose work *Biographia Literaria* (1817), as well as a number of political and theological writings.

My Baptismal Birthday

God's child in Christ adopted,—Christ my all—
What that earth boasts were not lost cheaply rather
Than forfeit that blessed name, by which I call
The Holy One, the Almighty God, my Father?
Father! in Christ we live, and Christ in Thee,
Eternal Thou, and everlasting we.
The heir of heaven, henceforth I fear not death;
In Christ I live! in Christ I draw the breath
Of the true life! Let then earth, sea, and sky
Make war against me; on my front I show
Their mighty Master's seal. In vain they try
To end my life, that can but end its woe.
Is that a death-bed where a Christian lies?
Yes, but not his—'Tis Death itself there dies.

Ralph Waldo Emerson
(1802–1892)

BORN IN MASSACHUSETTS, Emerson spent his early adulthood as a teacher in the schoolroom he and his brother had established in their mother's house. He later attended divinity school at Harvard. Emerson's first essay, *On Nature,* was published anonymously in 1836; in that work, he begins to formulate the philosophy that would come to be known as Transcendentalism—that is, that truth could be intuited directly from nature itself rather than needing to be revealed by God. Emerson's essays on philosophical topics including individuality and freedom, most of which began as lectures, were published throughout his life. Following a lecture in which he claimed that Jesus was a great man but not a god, he was denounced as an atheist; but Emerson believed that all things are connected to God, and are therefore divine.

Grace

How much, Preventing° God! how much I owe   *foresighted, fore-acting*
To the defences thou hast round me set:
Example, custom, fear, occasional slow,—
These scorned bondmen were my parapet.
I dare not peep over this parapet
To gauge with glance the roaring gulf below,
The depths of sin to which I had descended,
Had not these me against myself defended.

The Rhodora
ON BEING ASKED, WHENCE IS THE FLOWER.

In May, when sea-winds pierced our solitudes,
I found the fresh Rhodora in the woods,
Spreading its leafless blooms in a damp nook,
To please the desert and the sluggish brook.
The purple petals fallen in the pool
Made the black water with their beauty gay;
Here might the red-bird come his plumes to cool,
And court the flower that cheapens his array.
Rhodora! if the sages ask thee why
This charm is wasted on the earth and sky,
Tell them, dear, that, if eyes were made for seeing,
Then beauty is its own excuse for Being;
Why thou wert there, O rival of the rose!
I never thought to ask; I never knew;
But in my simple ignorance suppose
The self-same power that brought me there, brought you.

Gerald Griffin
(1803–1840)

BORN AND RAISED IN LIMERICK, Ireland, son of a tradesman, Griffin completed much of his literary work in London, writing novels, plays, and essays for periodicals in addition to poetry. In 1837 he entered the Teaching Order of the Christian Brothers, and lived out his life in the North Monastery in Cork.

To the Blessed Virgin Mary

As the mute nightingale in closest groves
  Lies hid at noon, but when day's piercing eye
  Is locked in night, with full heart beating high,
Poureth her plain song o'er the light she loves,
So, Virgin, ever pure and ever blest,
  Moon of religion, from whose radiant face,
  Reflected, streams the light of heavenly grace
On broken hearts, by contrite thoughts oppressed—
So Mary, they who justly feel the weight
  Of Heaven's offended majesty, implore
  Thy reconciling aid, with suppliant knee.
Of sinful man, O sinless Advocate!
  To thee they turn, nor him the less adore;
'Tis still HIS light they love, less dreadful seen in thee.

Elizabeth Barrett Browning
(1806–1861)

VICTORIAN POET ELIZABETH Barrett Browning was one of the most popular writers of her age, widely read in both Britain and America. Born the eldest of twelve children, she was tutored at home, and showed great facility with language early on:

she studied Greek and Latin, and tried her hand at writing an epic at the age of ten. As her writing began to be published, she produced poetry, translations, and prose. She was an activist writer throughout her prolific career, and helped to rouse support for child labor reforms through her poetry. Her 1844 collection *Poems* inspired a fan in the poet Robert Browning, who wrote with his admiration for her work. They met in 1845, and when they were married, they moved to Italy, where they lived for the duration of their marriage. Her last book, *A Musical Instrument,* was published posthumously; her translations of early Greek Christian poets (including her rendering of Clement of Alexandria's "Ode to the Saviour Christ," which can be found in Part 2 of this anthology) appeared two years after her death.

A Child's Thought of God

1

They say that God lives very high!
But if you look above the pines,
You cannot see our God. And why?

2

And if you dig down in the mines,
You never see Him in the gold,
Though from Him all that's glory shines.

3

God is so good, He wears a fold
Of heaven and earth across His face—
Like secrets kept, for love, untold.

4

But still I feel that His embrace
Slides down, by thrills, through all things made,
Through sight and sound of every place:

5

As if my tender mother laid
On my shut lids, her kisses' pressure,
Half-waking me at night; and said,
"Who kissed you through the dark, dear guesser?"

Bereavement

When some Beloveds, 'neath whose eyelids lay
The sweet lights of my childhood, one by one
Did leave me dark before the natural sun,
And I astonied fell, and could not pray,
A thought within me to myself did say,
"Is God less God, that *thou* art left undone?
Rise, worship, bless Him! in this sackcloth spun
As in that purple!"—But I answer, nay!
What child his filial heart in words can loose,
If he behold his tender father raise
The hand that chastens sorely? Can he choose
But sob in silence with an upward gaze?—
And *my* great Father, thinking fit to bruise,
Discerns in speechless tears, both prayer and praise.

The Soul's Expression

With stammering lips and insufficient sound,
I strive and struggle to deliver right
That music of my nature, day and night
With dream and thought and feeling, interwound,
And inly answering all the senses round
With octaves of a mystic depth and height,
Which step out grandly to the infinite
From the dark edges of the sensual ground!
This song of soul I struggle to outbear
Through portals of the sense, sublime and whole,
And utter all myself into the air:
But if I did it,—as the thunder-roll
Breaks its own cloud,—my flesh would perish there,
Before that dread apocalypse of soul.

Comfort

Speak low to me, my Saviour, low and sweet
From out the hallelujahs, sweet and low,
Lest I should fear and fall, and miss Thee so
Who art not missed by any that entreat.
Speak to me as to Mary at Thy feet[8]—
And if no precious gums my hands bestow,
Let my tears drop like amber, while I go
In reach of Thy divinest voice complete
In humanest affection—thus, in sooth,°   *truth*
To lose the sense of losing! As a child,
Whose song-bird seeks the wood for evermore,
Is sung to in its stead by mother's mouth;
Till, sinking on her breast, love-reconciled,
He sleeps the faster that he wept before.

Henry Wadsworth Longfellow
(1807–1882)

AMERICAN POET LONGFELLOW was born in Portland, Maine. He attended what would later become Bowdoin College, and during his studies he was offered a post as a professor of modern languages. He took a Grand Tour of Europe and immersed himself in its literature and languages. He went on to teach at Harvard, though he retired in 1854 to concentrate on writing poetry. His output was prodigious: Longfellow published sixteen collections of poetry (one of these appeared posthumously and was incomplete). He also wrote a number of novels and translations, including a revered translation of Dante's *Divine Comedy*. Longfellow was embraced by both critics and the reading public, and upon his death he was the first United States citizen to be honored with a bust in the Poets' Corner of London's Westminster Abbey.

---

8. See Matthew 26.7–13.

My Cathedral

Like two cathedral towers these stately pines
    Uplift their fretted summits tipped with cones;
    The arch beneath them is not built with stones,
    Not Art but Nature traced these lovely lines,
And carved this graceful arabesque of vines;
    No organ but the wind here sighs and moans,
    No sepulchre conceals a martyr's bones.
    No marble bishop on his tomb reclines.
Enter! the pavement, carpeted with leaves,
    Gives back a softened echo to thy tread!
    Listen! the choir is singing; all the birds,
In leafy galleries beneath the eaves,
    Are singing! listen, ere the sound be fled,
    And learn there may be worship with out words.

Alfred, Lord Tennyson
(1809–1892)

ALFRED, FIRST BARON TENNYSON, was born a rector's son, and though he had some distant aristocratic ancestry, his title was a product of his poetry: Tennyson was the first writer to be elevated to a British peerage in honor of his art. He published his first collection of poems in 1830 and continued publishing throughout his life. His work met with popular and critical success. At Cambridge, Tennyson met Arthur Henry Hallam, who became his dearest friend; at Hallam's death, Tennyson wrote what would be his masterpiece, and he published *In Memoriam A.H.H.* in 1850. That same year he succeeded Wordsworth as Poet Laureate of England—a position he held until his death in 1892.

from *In Memoriam A.H.H.*

55

The wish, that of the living whole
No life may fail beyond the grave,
Derives it not from what we have
The likest God within the soul?

Are God and Nature then at strife,
That Nature lends such evil dreams?
So careful of the type she seems,
So careless of the single life;

That I, considering everywhere
Her secret meaning in her deeds,
And finding that of fifty seeds
She often brings but one to bear,

I falter where I firmly trod,
And falling with my weight of cares
Upon the great world's altar-stairs
That slope thro' darkness up to God,

I stretch lame hands of faith, and grope,
And gather dust and chaff, and call
To what I feel is Lord of all,
And faintly trust the larger hope.

Charles Harpur
(1813–1868)

BORN IN NEW SOUTH WALES, Australia, the son of emancipated convicts, Harpur
was encouraged in his education from a young age. After a drought in the 1820s threat-
ened the family livelihood, Harpur moved to Sydney to find work, and there began
to contribute poems to newspapers and periodicals. While working on a cattle ranch,
Harpur published *The Bushrangers*, a play in five acts, and a number of poems. He kept
writing poetry even as he continued to work in both ranging and mining, and was the

first Australian writer to treat local concerns and issues. In addition to long historical poems, Harpur also wrote classical satires as well as love lyrics indebted to the English sixteenth-century sonneteering tradition.

How Full of God

How full of God those evening skies,
Arrayed in calmest loveliness;
But ah! To think how many eyes
Are wet with weeping none the less.

Nay, hearts are aching, eyes are wet
The more that they so richly glow,
Since in the past some glory set,
To leave them in the dark of woe.

To leave them dark, and such a tinge
O'er every aftersunset throw,
That it should only seem to fringe
The pall of a dead long ago.

Ah well-a-day! But so it is,
Pale sorrow groaneth everywhere,
And pain and loss we cannot miss;
To think is almost to despair.

Walt Whitman
(1819–1892)

WHITMAN WAS BORN ON LONG Island to parents with vague Quaker leanings. He left school at the age of eleven and spent time working as a journalist, a civil servant, a schoolteacher, and a volunteer nurse on the Civil War battlefields. Whitman published his first and most influential collection, *Leaves of Grass,* in 1855, financing the publication of its nearly eight hundred copies himself. He continued to edit and revise this volume until his death. Though not formally religiously affiliated, Whitman was influenced by the principles of deism and saw the soul as a divine thing.

A Noiseless Patient Spider

A noiseless patient spider,
I mark'd where on a little promontory it stood isolated,
Mark'd how to explore the vacant vast surrounding,
It launch'd forth filament, filament, filament, out of itself,
Ever unreeling them, ever tirelessly speeding them.

And you O my soul where you stand,
Surrounded, detached, in measureless oceans of space,
Ceaselessly musing, venturing, throwing, seeking the spheres to connect them,
Till the bridge you will need be form'd, till the ductile anchor hold,
Till the gossamer thread you fling catch somewhere, O my soul.

Emily Dickinson
(1830–1886)

EMILY DICKINSON WAS BORN, lived her life, and died in the family home in Amherst, Massachusetts. The family belonged to the Congregational Church, though Emily was not herself a member. She attended college at South Hadley Female Seminary, later Mount Holyoke. The poet and her sister Lavinia cared for their parents until their deaths, neither woman marrying. Though she preferred to keep to her home, Emily kept up a lively correspondence with newspaper editor Samuel Bowles, who published some of her poems, albeit anonymously and heavily edited. She also corresponded with Thomas Wentworth Higginson, a literary critic who became the poet's supporter and oversaw the publication of her poems after her death. Dickinson left nearly eighteen hundred poems among her belongings, organized into volumes tied together with twine. Her work has been continuously in print since 1890.

49

I never lost as much but twice,
And that was in the sod.
Twice have I stood a beggar
Before the door of God!

Angels—twice descending
Reimbursed my store—
Burglar! Banker—Father!
I am poor once more!

193

I shall know why—when Time is over—
And I have ceased to wonder why—
Christ will explain each separate anguish
In the fair schoolroom of the sky—

He will tell me what "Peter" promised—
And I—for wonder at his woe—
I shall forget the drop of Anguish
That scalds me now—that scalds me now!

249

Wild Nights—Wild Nights!
Were I with thee
Wild Nights should be
Our luxury!

Futile—the Winds—
To a Heart in port—
Done with the Compass—
Done with the Chart!

Rowing in Eden—
Ah, the Sea!
Might I but moor—Tonight—
In Thee!

437

Prayer is the little implement
Through which Men reach
Where Presence—is denied them.
They fling their Speech

By means of it—in God's Ear—
If then He hear—
This sums the Apparatus
Comprised in Prayer—

487

You love the Lord—you cannot see—
You write Him—every day—
A little note—when you awake—
And further in the Day.

An Ample Letter—How you miss—
And would delight to see—
But then His House—is but a Step—
And Mine's—in Heaven—You see.

564

My period had come for Prayer—
No other Art—would do—
My Tactics missed a rudiment—
Creator—Was it you?

God grows above—so those who pray
Horizons—must ascend—
And so I stepped upon the North
To see this Curious Friend—

His House was not—no sign had He—
By Chimney—nor by Door
Could I infer his Residence—
Vast Prairies of Air

Unbroken by a Settler—
Were all that I could see—
Infinitude—Had'st Thou no Face
That I might look on Thee?

The Silence condescended—
Creation stopped—for Me—
But awed beyond my errand—
I worshipped—did not "pray"—

754

My Life had stood—a Loaded Gun—
In Corners—till a Day
The Owner passed—identified—
And carried Me away—

And now We roam in Sovreign Woods—
And now We hunt the Doe—
And every time I speak for Him
The Mountains straight reply—

And do I smile, such cordial light
Upon the Valley glow—
It is as a Vesuvian face
Had let its pleasure through—

And when at Night—Our good Day done—
I guard My Master's Head—
'Tis better than the Eider Duck's
Deep Pillow—to have shared—

To foe of His—I'm deadly foe—
None stir the second time—
On whom I lay a Yellow Eye—
Or an emphatic Thumb—

Though I than He—may longer live
He longer must—than I—
For I have but the power to kill,
Without—the power to die—

881

I've none to tell me to but Thee
So when Thou failest, nobody.
It was a little tie—

It just held Two, nor those it held
Since Somewhere thy sweet Face has spilled
Beyond my Boundary—

If things were opposite—and Me
And Me it were—that ebbed from Thee
On some unanswering Shore—
Would'st Thou seek so—just say
That I the Answer may pursue
Unto the lips it eddied through—
So—overtaking Thee—

1461

"Heavenly Father"—take to thee
The supreme iniquity
Fashioned by thy candid Hand
In a moment contraband—
Though to trust us—seems to us
More respectful—"We are Dust"—
We apologize to thee
For thine own Duplicity—

1594

Immured in Heaven!
What a Cell!
Let every Bondage be,
Thou sweetest of the Universe,
Like that which ravished thee!

1751

There comes an hour when begging stops,
When the long interceding lips
Perceive their prayer is vain.
"Thou shalt not" is a kinder sword
Than from a disappointing God
"Disciple, call again."

Christina Rossetti
(1830–1894)

CHRISTINA ROSSETTI WAS BORN into a literary environment; her father was Italian poet-in-exile Gabriele Rossetti, and her mother was the sister of Lord Byron's friend and physician John Polidori. Her siblings William and Maria both became writers, and her brother Dante became a well-known poet and artist. Rossetti was educated at home, where her mother taught her literature, classics, and religious works. She published her first poem at age eighteen, and her most famous work, *Goblin Market*, appeared in 1862. In addition to a number of other collections of poetry, Rossetti also published *The Face of the Deep*, a work of devotional prose. Her Christmas poems "In the Bleak Midwinter" and "Love Came Down at Christmas," set to music after her death, have become familiar carols.

A Better Resurrection

I have no wit, no words, no tears;
My heart within me like a stone
Is numbed too much for hopes or fears.
Look right, look left, I dwell alone;
I lift mine eyes, but dimmed with grief
No everlasting hills I see;
My life is in the falling leaf:
O Jesus, quicken me.

My life is like a faded leaf,
My harvest dwindled to a husk:
Truly my life is void and brief
And tedious in the barren dusk;
My life is like a frozen thing,
No bud nor greenness can I see:
Yet rise it shall—the sap of spring;
O Jesus, rise in me.

My life is like a broken bowl,
A broken bowl that cannot hold
One drop of water for my soul

Or cordial in the searching cold;
Cast in the fire the perished thing;
Melt and remould it, till it be
A royal cup for Him, my King:
O Jesus, drink of me.

[Lord, dost Thou look on me]

Lord, dost Thou look on me, and will not I
    Launch out my heart to Heaven to look on Thee?
    Here if one loved me I should turn to see,
And often think on him and often sigh,
And by a tender friendship make reply
    To love gratuitous poured forth on me,
    And nurse a hope of happy days to be,
And mean "until we meet" in each good-bye.
Lord, Thou dost look and love is in Thine Eyes,
    Thy Heart is set upon me day and night,
        Thou stoopest low to set me far above:
O Lord, that I may love Thee make me wise;
    That I may see and love Thee grant me sight;
        And give me love that I may give Thee love.

Thomas Hardy
(1840–1928)

ENGLISH NOVELIST AND POET Thomas Hardy was born in Dorchester, and was schooled at home by his mother through his early childhood. His family was indifferently Anglican, and Hardy's own religious perspective seems to have been a mixture of agnosticism and deism. His novels imagine the influence of a capricious supernatural force rather than hewing to any firm theology. Hardy was known during his lifetime as a novelist, finding success with *Far from the Madding Crowd* (1874), *Tess of the d'Urbervilles* (1891), and *Jude the Obscure* (1895), among other works. He published the first volume of his poetry, *Wessex Poems,* years after he gained fame as a novelist, in 1889.

ἈΓΝΩΣΤΩι ΘΕΩι[9]

Long have I framed weak phantasies of Thee,
      O Willer masked and dumb!
      Who makest Life become,—
As though by labouring all-unknowingly,
      Like one whom reveries numb.

How much of consciousness informs Thy will,
      Thy biddings, as if blind,
      Of death-inducing kind,
Nought shows to us ephemeral ones who fill
      But moments in Thy mind.

Perhaps Thy ancient rote-restricted ways
      Thy ripening rule transcends;
      That listless effort tends
To grow percipient with advance of days,
      And with percipience mends.

For, in unwonted purlieus, far and nigh,
      At whiles or short or long,
      May be discerned a wrong
Dying as of self-slaughter; whereat I
      Would raise my voice in song.

The Bedridden Peasant to an Unknowing God

Much wonder I—here long low-laid—
That this dead wall should be
Betwixt the Maker and the made,
Between Thyself and me!

For, say one puts a child to nurse,
He eyes it now and then
To know if better 'tis, or worse,
And if it mourn, and when.

But Thou, Lord, giv'st us men our clay
In helpless bondage thus

---

9. Greek: *To the Unknown God.*

To Time and Chance, and seem'st straightway
To think no more of us!

That some disaster cleft Thy scheme
And tore us wide apart,
So that no cry can cross, I deem;
For Thou art mild of heart,

And would'st not shape and shut us in
Where voice can not be heard:
'Tis plain Thou meant'st that we should win
Thy succour by a word.

Might but Thy sense flash down the skies
Like man's from clime to clime,
Thou would'st not let me agonize
Through my remaining time;

But, seeing how much Thy creatures bear—
Lame, starved, or maimed, or blind—
Thou'dst heal the ills with quickest care
Of me and all my kind.

Then, since Thou mak'st not these things be,
But these things dost not know,
I'll praise Thee as were shown to me
The mercies Thou would'st show!

Gerard Manley Hopkins
(1844–1889)

GERARD MANLEY HOPKINS was born in Stratford in Essex, east of London, the oldest of nine children. His parents were devout Anglicans, his father a businessman and civil servant who worked as a church warden for a time, and his mother deeply involved in music and literature. Hopkins studied classics at Oxford, where he became dissatisfied with what he perceived as his moral lapses. Pursuing an ever stricter course of self-control, in 1866, Hopkins burned all his poems and determined to convert to Catholicism, a decision that estranged him from his family. He became a Jesuit and continued his studies in classics, music, and theology. He later returned to poetry and kept up a correspondence with Robert Bridges, a friend from his college days who would go on to be England's long-standing Poet Laureate in the early twentieth century. Indeed, it is through the influence of Bridges that the few poems Hopkins published during his lifetime saw print. Hopkins spent his final years as professor of Greek at University College Dublin, and died leaving many unpublished poems, kept private in part by his conviction that he could write nothing of value.

God's Grandeur

The world is charged with the grandeur of God.
      It will flame out, like shining from shook foil;
      It gathers to a greatness, like the ooze of oil
Crushed. Why do men then now not reck his rod?
Generations have trod, have trod, have trod;
      And all is seared with trade; bleared, smeared with toil;
      And wears man's smudge and shares man's smell: the soil
Is bare now, nor can foot feel, being shod.

And for all this, nature is never spent;
      There lives the dearest freshness deep down things;
And though the last lights off the black West went
      Oh, morning, at the brown brink eastward, springs—
Because the Holy Ghost over the bent
      World broods with warm breast and with ah! bright wings.[10]

As Kingfishers Catch Fire

As kingfishers catch fire, dragonflies draw flame;
      As tumbled over rim in roundy wells
      Stones ring; like each tucked string tells, each hung bell's
Bow swung finds tongue to fling out broad its name;
Each mortal thing does one thing and the same:
      Deals out that being indoors each one dwells;
      Selves—goes itself; *myself* it speaks and spells,
Crying *Whát I dó is me: for that I came.*

---

10. See Genesis 1.2.

I say móre: the just man justices;
      Keeps grace: thát keeps all his goings graces;
Acts in God's eye what in God's eye he is—
      Chríst. For Christ plays in ten thousand places,
Lovely in limbs, and lovely in eyes not his
      To the Father through the features of men's faces.

Spring

Nothing is so beautiful as Spring—
      When weeds, in wheels, shoot long and lovely and lush;
      Thrush's eggs look little low heavens, and thrush
Through the echoing timber does so rinse and wring
The ear, it strikes like lightnings to hear him sing;
      The glassy peartree leaves and blooms, they brush
      The descending blue; that blue is all in a rush
With richness; the racing lambs too have fair their fling.

What is all this juice and all this joy?
      A strain of the earth's sweet being in the beginning
In Eden garden.—Have, get, before it cloy,
      Before it cloud, Christ, lord, and sour with sinning,
Innocent mind and Mayday in girl and boy,
      Most, O maid's child, thy choice and worthy the winning.

The Windhover
TO CHRIST OUR LORD

I caught this morning morning's minion, king-
      dom of daylight's dauphin, dapple-dawn-drawn Falcon, in his riding
      Of the rolling level underneath him steady air, and striding
High there, how he rung upon the rein of a wimpling wing
In his ecstasy! then off, off forth on swing,
      As a skate's heel sweeps smooth on a bow-bend the hurl and gliding
      Rebuffed the big wind. My heart in hiding
Stirred for a bird—the achieve of; the mastery of the thing!

Brute beauty and valour and act, oh, air, pride, plume, here
      Buckle! AND the fire that breaks from thee then, a billion
Times told lovelier, more dangerous, O my chevalier!

No wonder of it: shéer plód makes plough down sillion
Shine, and blue-bleak embers, ah my dear,
    Fall, gall themselves, and gash gold-vermillion.

Pied Beauty

Glory be to God for dappled things—
    For skies of couple-colour as a brinded cow;
        For rose-moles all in stipple upon trout that swim;
Fresh-firecoal chestnut-falls; finches' wings;
    Landscape plotted and pieced—fold, fallow, and plough;
        And áll trádes, their gear and tackle and trim.

All things counter, original, spáre, strange;
    Whatever is fickle, frecklèd (who knows how?)
        With swíft, slów; sweet, sóur; adázzle, dím;
He fathers-forth whose beauty is pást change:
        Praise him.

Hurrahing in Harvest

Summer ends now; now, barbarous in beauty, the stooks arise
        Around; up above, what wind-walks! what lovely behaviour
        Of silk-sack clouds! has wilder, wilful-wavier
Meal-drift moulded ever and melted across skies?

I wálk, I líft up, Í lift úp heart, éyes,
        Down all that glory in the heavens to glean our Saviour;
        And, éyes, héart, what looks, what lips yet gáve you a
Rapturous love's greeting of realer, of rounder replies?

And the azurous hung hills are his world-wielding shoulder
        Majestic—as a stallion stalwart, very-violet-sweet!—
These things, these things were here and but the beholder
        Wánting; which two whén they ónce méet,
The heart rears wings bold and bolder
        And hurls for him, O half hurls earth for him off under his feet.

The Lantern Out of Doors

Sometimes a lantern moves along the night
   That interests our eyes. And who goes there?
   I think; where from and bound, I wonder, where,
With, all down darkness wide, his wading light?

Men go by me whom either beauty bright
   In mould or mind or what not else makes rare:
   They rain against our much-thick and marsh air
Rich beams, till death or distance buys them quite.

Death or distance soon consumes them: wind
   What most I may eye after, be in at the end
I cannot, and out of sight is out of mind.

Christ minds: Christ's interest, what to avow or amend
   There, éyes them, heart wánts, care háunts, foot fóllows kínd,
Their ránsom, théir rescue, ánd first, fást, last fríend.

Thou Art Indeed Just, Lord

*Justus quidem tu es, Domine, si disputem tecum; verumtamen
justa loquar ad te: Quare via impiorum prosperatur? &c.*[11]

Thou art indeed just, Lord, if I contend
With thee; but, sir, so what I plead is just.
Why do sinners' ways prosper? and why must
Disappointment all I endeavour end?

   Wert thou my enemy, O thou my friend,
How wouldst thou worse, I wonder, than thou dost
Defeat, thwart me? Oh, the sots and thralls of lust
Do in spare hours more thrive than I that spend,
Sir, life upon thy cause. See, banks and brakes
Now, leavèd how thick! lacèd they are again
With fretty chervil, look, and fresh wind shakes
Them; birds build—but not I build; no, but strain,
Time's eunuch, and not breed one work that wakes.
Mine, O thou lord of life, send my roots rain.

---

11. The headnote to this poem is a Latin version of the first two and a half lines of the poem; it quotes from
  Jeremiah 12.1.

To what serves Mortal Beauty?

To what serves mortal beauty—| dangerous; does set danc-
Ing blood—the O-seal-that-so | feature, flung prouder form
Than Purcell tune lets tread to?[12] | See: it does this: keeps warm
Men's wits to the things that are; | what good means—where a glance
Master more may than gaze, | gaze out of countenance.
Those lovely lads once, wet-fresh | windfalls of war's storm,
How then should Gregory, a father, | have gleanèd else from swarm-
Èd Rome?[13] But God to a nation | dealt that day's dear chance.
To man, that needs would worship | block or barren stone,
Our law says: Love what are | love's worthiest, were all known;
World's loveliest—men's selves. Self | flashes off frame and face.
What do then? how meet beauty? | Merely meet it; own,
Home at heart, heaven's sweet gift; | then leave, let that alone.
Yea, wish that though, wish all, | God's better beauty, grace.

Carrion Comfort

Not, I'll not, carrion comfort, Despair, not feast on thee;
Not untwist—slack they may be—these last strands of man
In me ór, most weary, cry *I can no more*. I can;
Can something, hope, wish day come, not choose not to be.

But ah, but O thou terrible, why wouldst thou rude on me
Thy wring-world right foot rock? lay a lionlimb against me? scan
With darksome devouring eyes my bruisèd bones? and fan,
O in turns of tempest, me heaped there; me frantic to avoid thee and flee?

Why? That my chaff might fly; my grain lie, sheer and clear.
Nay in all that toil, that coil, since (seems) I kissed the rod,
Hand rather, my heart lo! lapped strength, stole joy, would laugh, cheer.

Cheer whóm though? The héro whose héaven-handling flúng me, fóot tród
Me? or mé that fóught him? O whích one? is it éach one? That níght, that year
Of now done darkness I wretch lay wrestling with (my God!) my God.

---

12. Henry Purcell (1659?–1695) was an English composer of the Baroque era.
13. In the sixth century, Pope Gregory saw a group of English boys for sale in the Roman market as slaves. Gregory reportedly compared them to angels because of their fair hair, and he determined to convert pagan England to Catholicism.

That Nature is a Heraclitean Fire and of the comfort of the Resurrection[14]

Cloud-puffball, torn tufts, tossed pillows | flaunt forth, then chevy on an air-
Built thoroughfare: heaven-roysterers, in gay-gangs | they throng; they glitter in
    marches.
Down roughcast, down dazzling whitewash, | wherever an elm arches,
Shivelights and shadowtackle in long | lashes lace, lance, and pair.
Delightfully the bright wind boisterous | ropes, wrestles, beats earth bare
Of yestertempest's creases; | in pool and rutpeel parches
Squandering ooze to squeezed | dough, crust, dust; stanches, starches
Squadroned masks and manmarks | treadmire toil there
Footfretted in it. Million-fuelèd, | nature's bonfire burns on.
But quench her bonniest, dearest | to her, her clearest-selvèd spark
Man, how fast his firedint, | his mark on mind, is gone!
Both are in an únfathomable, all is in an enormous dark
Drowned. O pity and indig | nation! Manshape, that shone
Sheer off, disseveral, a star, | death blots black out; nor mark
               Is any of him at all so stark
But vastness blurs and time | beats level. Enough! the Resurrection,
A heart's-clarion! Away grief's gasping, | joyless days, dejection.
               Across my foundering deck shone
A beacon, an eternal beam. | Flesh fade, and mortal trash
Fall to the residuary worm; | world's wildfire, leave but ash:
In a flash, at a trumpet crash,
I am all at once what Christ is, | since he was what I am, and
This Jack, joke, poor potsherd, | patch, matchwood, immortal diamond,
               Is immortal diamond.

---

14. Heraclitus (c. 535–c. 475 B.C.E.) was a Greek philosopher most famous for his assertion of constant
    change and flux of everything, as expressed in the maxim "No one can step in the same river twice."

Oscar Wilde
(1854–1900)

BORN IN DUBLIN TO IRISH intellectuals and educated at Trinity College and Oxford, Wilde achieved his greatest popularity as a playwright, for witty plays including *The Importance of Being Earnest* (1895) and *Lady Windermere's Fan* (1892); he also produced poems, essays, and one novel, *The Picture of Dorian Gray* (1890). Wilde gained notoriety for his unconventionality and spent two years in prison as a consequence of his involvement with Lord Alfred Douglas, the judgment of a celebrity trial featuring a scandalous parade of moral accusations. While in prison, Wilde's health suffered, and he wrote *De Profundis*, a long letter about his spiritual journey through his literal and figurative trials. Upon his release he sought and was refused a retreat among the Jesuits. He died penniless in Paris, having requested and received a Catholic baptism the day before his death.

E Tenebris[15]

Come down, O Christ, and help me! reach thy hand,
    For I am drowning in a stormier sea
    Than Simon on thy lake of Galilee:
The wine of life is spilt upon the sand,
My heart is as some famine-murdered land,
    Whence all good things have perished utterly,
    And well I know my soul in Hell must lie
If I this night before God's throne should stand.
"He sleeps perchance, or rideth to the chase,
    Like Baal,[16] when his prophets howled that name
        From morn to noon on Carmel's smitten height."
Nay, peace, I shall behold before the night,
    The feet of brass, the robe more white than flame,
        The wounded hands, the weary human face.

---

15. Latin: *Out of the darkness.*
16. Ancient Near Eastern god, identified in the Hebrew Bible as a competing deity to the God of Israel; see 1 Kings 18.21–40.

Francis Adams

(1862–1893)

BORN IN MALTA, FRANCIS ADAMS was the son of an army surgeon, and the family moved frequently with his assignments. Young Francis was sent to school in England, and, after failing to find a diplomatic position, became a schoolmaster on the Isle of Wight. He published his first volume of poetry, *Henry and Other Tales,* in 1884. That same year, Adams emigrated to what were then the Australian colonies in an effort to improve his health. He contributed briefly to a Melbourne newspaper before taking a position as a tutor on a sheep station. He continued to write and publish and draw an income from his journalistic work. Adams wrote verse, essays, and a novel, and his best-known work is a collection of political poems, *Songs of the Army of the Night* (1887).

Prayer

This is what I pray
In this horrible day,
In this terrible night—
I may still have light.
Such as I have had,
That I go not mad.

This is what I seek—
I may keep me meek
Till mine eyes behold,
Till my lips have told
All this hellish Crime.—
Then it's sleeping time!

6

The Devotional Lyric in the Modern Era

CONFRONTED ON THE ONE HAND by their need to replace what they saw as Romanticism's ornamentation, sentimentality, and abject navel-gazing with an art more relevant to an age characterized by rapid technological advances and radical socio-cultural, psychological, and intellectual redefinitions, and on the other hand by their need to make sense of the horrific violence of the first and second world wars, Modernist poets found themselves writing at a time when religious devotion seemed to many irrelevant if not completely impossible. This does not mean, however, that Modernist poets of the English-speaking world cast aside their previous pieties and proceeded clean into a new and secular age. The lyric tradition, so firmly rooted in religious devotion, was far too strong a force simply to be abandoned. Modernist poets had as much difficulty, and even less success, putting religion behind them as they did reining in the Romantic impulses the great majority of them professed to consider so cloying. As a result, one finds in the Modernist era the presence of the devotional impulse in the absence of the devotional object.

How this presence-in-absence manifested itself varied from poet to poet (many of them were personally devout, even if the age in which they found themselves was becoming increasing secular) and from -ism to -ism: Impressionism, Futurism, Objectivism, Imagism, Symbolism, Constructivism, Acmeism, and so on. For Symbolists like Eliot and Yeats, the figure of the Poet Priest was especially appealing; they and poets like them saw the artist as assuming the roles traditionally filled by the clergy and considered things like ecstasy, transcendence, and revelation as the end results of artistic, not religious experience. As Yeats would write in "William Blake and the Imagination" (1897): "In [Blake's] time educated people believed that they amused themselves with books of imagination but that they 'made their souls' by listening to sermons and by doing or by not doing certain things. . . . In our time we are agreed that we 'make our souls' out of . . . books . . . or out of pictures, while we amuse ourselves, or, at best, make a poorer sort of soul, by listening to sermons or by doing or by not doing certain things."

The Imagists went in the other direction. Whereas Yeats made plain his desire for "the essences of things," William Carlos Williams and his Imagist counterparts (poets such as Ezra Pound and Hilda Doolittle) wanted the things themselves. "Say it! No ideas but in things," Williams cried in his poem "Paterson" (1927). Scrupulously deployed poetic technique brought to bear on real things, faithfully observed and carefully selected—this was how the devotional impulse Imagistically manifested itself. As poet-makers, artisans not priests, the Imagists sought not to transcend the modern world, but rather to discover in it that which was significant and transformative and to record what they found as accurately and specifically as possible. For them, every Thing was potentially a sacred object, a devotional object; it was up to poets, with their skill and technique, with the quality of their attention, to make the world's things shine.

Other poets, like Wallace Stevens, substituted poetry itself for the devotional object. Poets such as Countee Cullen and Langston Hughes substituted politics; in fact, Hughes made this political substitution explicit in his poem "Goodbye Christ," when he directed his divine addressee to yield place to "A real guy named / Marx Communist Lenin Peasant Stalin Worker ME— / I said, ME!" Whatever the proposed alternative, Modernism's approach to the devotional lyric was just that, an approach; it was a journey, not a destination. Try as they might, the Modernist poets of the English-speaking world could neither locate the devotional object nor find an adequate substitute for that object. The devotional impulse, though, part of the lyric sensibility for almost three thousand years, never let them rest. It kept them searching always, if not for God as their ancestors understood that entity, then at least for something that would suffice.

FURTHER READING

Hobson, Suzanne. *Angels of Modernism: Religion, Culture, Aesthetics 1910–1960*. Basingstoke, Hampshire: Palgrave Macmillan, 2011.

Hodgkins, Hope Howell. "Rhetoric versus Poetic: High Modernist Literature and the Cult of Belief." *Rhetorica: A Journal of the History of Rhetoric*, 16, no. 2 (Spring 1998): 201–225.

Martz, Louis L. *Many Gods and Many Voices: The Role of the Prophet in English and American Modernism*. Columbia: University of Missouri Press, 1998.

Materer, Timothy. *Modernist Alchemy: Poetry and the Occult*. Ithaca: Cornell University Press, 1996.

Quinones, Ricardo J. *Mapping Literary Modernism: Time and Development*. Princeton: Princeton University Press, 1985.

Vetter, Lara. *Modernist Writings and Religio-Scientific Discourse: H.D., Loy, and Toomer*. Basingstoke, Hampshire: Palgrave Macmillan, 2010.

William Butler Yeats
(1865–1939)

BORN IN DUBLIN, W. B. YEATS was the son of the Irish painter John Butler Yeats, who is best known for his portraits of the young poet and of the Irish separatist John O'Leary, a man who would encourage Yeats in 1885 to address more Irish themes and subjects in his work. Clearly, this was advice Yeats took to heart; but while he would turn from the more romantic subjects of his youth, he never lost his interest in spiritualism and the occult. Shortly after meeting O'Leary, Yeats abandoned Theosophy and joined a secret society called the Golden Dawn. Yeats would practice ritual magic with that society for more than three decades, eventually attaining the highest possible level of membership. Yeats published many books over the course of his lifetime—poetry, fiction, nonfiction, and drama—though he is perhaps best known for his poetry collections *The Wild Swans at Coole* (1919), *The Tower* (1928), and *The Winding Stair and Other Poems* (1933). He was awarded the Nobel Prize for Literature in 1923.

A Prayer on Going into My House

God grant a blessing on this tower and cottage
And on my heirs, if all remain unspoiled,
No table or chair or stool not simple enough
For shepherd lads in Galilee; and grant
That I myself for portions of the year

May handle nothing and set eyes on nothing
But what the great and passionate have used
Throughout so many varying centuries
We take it for the norm; yet should I dream
Sinbad the sailor's brought a painted chest,
Or image, from beyond the Loadstone Mountain,
That dream is a norm; and should some limb of the devil
Destroy the view by cutting down an ash
That shades the road, or setting up a cottage
Planned in a government office, shorten his life,
Manacle his soul upon the Red Sea bottom.

A Prayer for Old Age

God guard me from those thoughts men think
In the mind alone;
He that sings a lasting song
Thinks in a marrow-bone;

From all that makes a wise old man
That can be praised of all;
O what am I that I should not seem
For the song's sake a fool?
I pray—for fashion's word is out
And prayer comes round again—
That I may seem, though I die old,
A foolish, passionate man.

Robert Frost
(1874–1963)

THOUGH MOST OFTEN ASSOCIATED with the people, culture, and landscapes of
New England, Robert Frost was born in San Francisco. He moved to Massachusetts
when he was eleven years old, eventually studying both at Dartmouth and at Harvard,
though he never graduated from either institution. Frost moved to England in 1912,

where he met and befriended Ezra Pound, who became an early champion of his work. By the time Frost returned to America in 1915, he had published two books, *A Boy's Will* (1913) and *North of Boston* (1915), and had managed to establish himself on both continents. He would go on to win the Pulitzer Prize for Poetry four times for his collections *New Hampshire* (1924), *Collected Poems* (1931), *A Further Range* (1937), and *A Witness Tree* (1943).

A Prayer in Spring

Oh, give us pleasure in the flowers today;
And give us not to think so far away
As the uncertain harvest; keep us here
All simply in the springing of the year.

Oh, give us pleasure in the orchard white,
Like nothing else by day, like ghosts by night;
And make us happy in the happy bees,
The swarm dilating round the perfect trees.

And make us happy in the darting bird
That suddenly above the bees is heard,
The meteor that thrusts in with needle bill,
And off a blossom in mid air stands still.

For this is love and nothing else is love,
The which it is reserved for God above
To sanctify to what far ends He will,
But which it only needs that we fulfill.

Bereft

Where had I heard this wind before
Change like this to a deeper roar?
What would it take my standing there for,
Holding open a restive door,
Looking down hill to a frothy shore?
Summer was past and the day was past.
Sombre clouds in the west were massed.
Out on the porch's sagging floor,
Leaves got up in a coil and hissed,

Blindly striking at my knee and missed.
Something sinister in the tone
Told me my secret must be known:
Word I was in the house alone
Somehow must have gotten abroad,
Word I was in my life alone,
Word I had no one left but God.

[Forgive, O Lord]

Forgive, O Lord, my little jokes on Thee
And I'll forgive Thy great big one on me.

William Carlos Williams
(1883–1963)

WILLIAM CARLOS WILLIAMS was born in Rutherford, New Jersey, earned a medical degree from the University of Pennsylvania, and spent his life working as a country doctor in the town of his birth. While studying at the University of Pennsylvania, Williams met and befriended Ezra Pound and would become, with Pound, Hilda Doolittle, F. S. Flint, and others, an important member of the Imagist movement. In the aftermath of the publication in 1922 of Eliot's *The Waste Land*—a poem that would have a profound impact on Williams, both positively and negatively—Williams published *Spring and All* in 1923. Over the course of his lifetime, Williams produced numerous volumes of poetry, prose, and translations. His last volume, *Pictures from Brueghel and Other Poems* (1962), earned him a posthumous Pulitzer.

Sunday

Small barking sounds
Clatter of metal in a pan
A high fretting voice
and a low voice musical
as a string twanged—

The tempo is evenly drawn
give and take
A splash of water, the
ting a ring
of small pieces of metal
dropped, the clap of a door
A tune nameless as Time—

Then the voices—
Sound of feet barely moving
Slowly
And the bark, "What?"
"The same, the same, the—"
scrape of a chair
clickaty tee—

"Over Labor Day they'll
be gone"
"Jersey City, he's the
engineer—" "Ya"
"Being on the Erie R.R.
is quite convenient"

"No, I think they're—"
"I think she is. I think—"
"German-American"
"Of course the Govern—"
. . . .
A distant door slammed.
Amen.

Ezra Pound
(1885–1972)

EZRA WESTON LOOMIS POUND was born in what is now Idaho. At the University of
Pennsylvania he befriended poet Hilda Doolittle, who would publish under the name
H.D. Throughout his early education, Pound traveled extensively in Europe, and after

receiving an M.A. in Romance languages and a brief stint teaching in Indiana, he relocated to Europe permanently. In addition to writing his own poetry, he was a prolific literary critic and editor who helped to shape the careers of contemporaries including T. S. Eliot, Robert Frost, and James Joyce. Outraged by World War I, Pound moved in 1924 to Italy, where he later expressed support for both Mussolini and Hitler. He was arrested for treason at the conclusion of World War II for having delivered radio broadcasts critical of the United States and of Jews, and he spent months in a military prison in Pisa. That episode triggered a psychological breakdown in Pound, who was deemed unfit to stand trial and was incarcerated in psychiatric hospitals for fourteen years. His wartime politics haunted him until his death; in 1972, the American Academy of Arts and Sciences proposed to honor him with a literary medal but the plan was shouted down by a tempest of opposition. The author of an extensive roster of poetry, essays, speeches, and translations, Pound is best known for *The Cantos* (1948) and for his translations of Chinese poetry.

The Lake Isle

O God, O Venus, O Mercury, patron of thieves,
Give me in due time, I beseech you, a little tobacco-shop,
With the little bright boxes
            piled up neatly upon the shelves
And the loose fragrant cavendish
            and the shag,
And the bright Virginia
            loose under the bright glass cases,
And a pair of scales
            not too greasy,
And the *volailles*° dropping in for a word or two in passing,   *chicks, slang for "whores"*
For a flip word, and to tidy their hair a bit.

O God, O Venus, O Mercury, patron of thieves,
Lend me a little tobacco-shop,
            or install me in any profession
Save this damn'd profession of writing,
            where one needs one's brains all the time.

Marianne Moore
(1887–1972)

BORN IN KIRKWOOD, MISSOURI, Marianne Moore was raised in the home of her maternal grandfather, who served as the pastor of the local Presbyterian church. Following her grandfather's death, Moore and her family moved to Pennsylvania, where she attended Bryn Mawr College. She worked as a teacher before making her way, with her mother, to New York City, where she would live out the rest of her life. Moore secured a position at the New York Public Library and became the editor, in 1925, of *Dial* literary magazine. She edited that publication until it published its final issue in 1929, after which time she supported herself exclusively by writing poetry and prose pieces. Among her many books in publication, Moore was most recognized for her *Collected Poems* (1951), which received the National Book Award for Poetry (1952), the Pulitzer Prize for Poetry (1952), and the Bollingen Prize for Poetry from Yale University (1953).

By Disposition of Angels

Messengers much like ourselves? Explain it.
Steadfastness the darkness makes explicit?
Something heard most clearly when not near it?
      Above particularities,
these unparticularities praise cannot violate.
   One has seen, in such steadiness never deflected,
   how by darkness a star is perfected.

Star that does not ask me if I see it?
Fir that would not wish me to uproot it?
Speech that does not ask me if I hear it?
      Mysteries expound mysteries.
Steadier than steady, star dazzling me, live and elate
   no need to say, how like some we have known; too like her,
   too like him, and a-quiver forever.

T. S. Eliot

(1888–1965)

THOMAS STEARNS ELIOT WAS born in St. Louis and attended Harvard (both as an undergraduate and as a graduate student), the Sorbonne, and Oxford. In 1914, he moved to England, where he came under the influence, as did so many of his contemporaries, of Ezra Pound, whose effect on Eliot's work cannot be overstated. Working first as a schoolteacher and then as a bank clerk, Eliot eventually turned to literary editing, founding the literary journal *Criterion* (1922–1939). He became the director of Faber & Faber in 1925. In 1927, Eliot became a British citizen and joined the Church of England. "Ash Wednesday" is the first long poem Eliot wrote after his conversion; it was published at Easter 1930. Roundly considered one of the most important and influential poets of the twentieth century, he was awarded the Nobel Prize in Literature in 1948. His books include *Prufrock and Other Observations* (1917), *The Waste Land* (1922), and *Four Quartets* (1943).

Ash Wednesday

I

Because I do not hope to turn again
Because I do not hope
Because I do not hope to turn
Desiring this man's gift and that man's scope
I no longer strive to strive towards such things
(Why should the agèd eagle stretch its wings?)
Why should I mourn
The vanished power of the usual reign?

Because I do not hope to know
The infirm glory of the positive hour
Because I do not think
Because I know I shall not know
The one veritable transitory power
Because I cannot drink
There, where trees flower, and springs flow, for there is nothing again

Because I know that time is always time
And place is always and only place
And what is actual is actual only for one time
And only for one place
I rejoice that things are as they are and
I renounce the blessèd face
And renounce the voice
Because I cannot hope to turn again
Consequently I rejoice, having to construct something
Upon which to rejoice

And pray to God to have mercy upon us
And pray that I may forget
These matters that with myself I too much discuss
Too much explain
Because I do not hope to turn again
Let these words answer
For what is done, not to be done again
May the judgement not be too heavy upon us

Because these wings are no longer wings to fly
But merely vans to beat the air
The air which is now thoroughly small and dry
Smaller and dryer than the will
Teach us to care and not to care
Teach us to sit still.

Pray for us sinners now and at the hour of our death
Pray for us now and at the hour of our death.

2

Lady, three white leopards sat under a juniper-tree
In the cool of the day, having fed to satiety
On my legs my heart my liver and that which had been contained
In the hollow round of my skull. And God said
Shall these bones live? shall these
Bones live?[1] And that which had been contained

---

1. See Ezekiel 37.1–3.

T. S. Eliot   283

In the bones (which were already dry) said chirping:
Because of the goodness of this Lady
And because of her loveliness, and because
She honours the Virgin in meditation,
We shine with brightness. And I who am here dissembled
Proffer my deeds to oblivion, and my love
To the posterity of the desert and the fruit of the gourd.
It is this which recovers
My guts the strings of my eyes and the indigestible portions
Which the leopards reject. The Lady is withdrawn
In a white gown, to contemplation, in a white gown.
Let the whiteness of bones atone to forgetfulness.
There is no life in them. As I am forgotten
And would be forgotten, so I would forget
Thus devoted, concentrated in purpose. And God said
Prophesy to the wind, to the wind only for only
The wind will listen. And the bones sang chirping
With the burden of the grasshopper, saying

Lady of silences
Calm and distressed
Torn and most whole
Rose of memory
Rose of forgetfulness
Exhausted and life-giving
Worried reposeful
The single Rose
Is now the Garden
Where all loves end
Terminate torment
Of love unsatisfied
The greater torment
Of love satisfied
End of the endless
Journey to no end
Conclusion of all that
Is inconclusible
Speech without word and
Word of no speech
Grace to the Mother

For the Garden
Where all love ends.

Under a juniper-tree the bones sang, scattered and shining
We are glad to be scattered, we did little good to each other,
Under a tree in the cool of day, with the blessing of sand,
Forgetting themselves and each other, united
In the quiet of the desert. This is the land which ye
Shall divide by lot. And neither division nor unity
Matters. This is the land. We have our inheritance.

3

At the first turning of the second stair
I turned and saw below
The same shape twisted on the banister
Under the vapour in the fetid air
Struggling with the devil of the stairs who wears
The deceitful face of hope and of despair.

At the second turning of the second stair
I left them twisting, turning below;
There were no more faces and the stair was dark,
Damp, jaggèd, like an old man's mouth drivelling, beyond repair,
Or the toothed gullet of an agèd shark.

At the first turning of the third stair
Was a slotted window bellied like the figs's fruit
And beyond the hawthorn blossom and a pasture scene
The broadbacked figure drest in blue and green
Enchanted the maytime with an antique flute.
Blown hair is sweet, brown hair over the mouth blown,
Lilac and brown hair;
Distraction, music of the flute, stops and steps of the mind over the third
    stair,
Fading, fading; strength beyond hope and despair
Climbing the third stair.

Lord, I am not worthy
Lord, I am not worthy

        but speak the word only.

4

Who walked between the violet and the violet
Who walked between
The various ranks of varied green
Going in white and blue, in Mary's colour,
Talking of trivial things
In ignorance and knowledge of eternal dolour
Who moved among the others as they walked,
Who then made strong the fountains and made fresh the springs

Made cool the dry rock and made firm the sand
In blue of larkspur, blue of Mary's colour,
Sovegna vos[2]

Here are the years that walk between, bearing
Away the fiddles and the flutes, restoring
One who moves in the time between sleep and waking, wearing

White light folded, sheathing about her, folded.
The new years walk, restoring
Through a bright cloud of tears, the years, restoring
With a new verse the ancient rhyme. Redeem
The time. Redeem
The unread vision in the higher dream
While jewelled unicorns draw by the gilded hearse.

The silent sister veiled in white and blue
Between the yews, behind the garden god,
Whose flute is breathless, bent her head and signed but spoke no word

But the fountain sprang up and the bird sang down
Redeem the time, redeem the dream
The token of the word unheard, unspoken

Till the wind shake a thousand whispers from the yew

And after this our exile

---

2. Italian: *Be mindful*. Eliot alludes to Dante's *Purgatorio*, Canto 26.147: "sovenha vos a temps de ma dolor!" ("Be mindful in due time of my sorrows").

5

If the lost word is lost, if the spent word is spent
If the unheard, unspoken
Word is unspoken, unheard;
Still is the unspoken word, the Word unheard,
The Word without a word, the Word within
The world and for the world;
And the light shone in darkness and
Against the Word the unstilled world still whirled
About the centre of the silent Word.

   O my people, what have I done unto thee.

Where shall the word be found, where will the word
Resound? Not here, there is not enough silence
Not on the sea or on the islands, not
On the mainland, in the desert or the rain land,
For those who walk in darkness
Both in the day time and in the night time
The right time and the right place are not here
No place of grace for those who avoid the face
No time to rejoice for those who walk among noise and deny the voice

Will the veiled sister pray for
Those who walk in darkness, who chose thee and oppose thee,
Those who are torn on the horn between season and season, time and time,
  between
Hour and hour, word and word, power and power, those who wait
In darkness? Will the veiled sister pray
For children at the gate
Who will not go away and cannot pray:
Pray for those who chose and oppose

   O my people, what have I done unto thee.

Will the veiled sister between the slender
Yew trees pray for those who offend her
And are terrified and cannot surrender
And affirm before the world and deny between the rocks
In the last desert before the last blue rocks

The desert in the garden the garden in the desert
Of drouth, spitting from the mouth the withered apple-seed.

    O my people.

6

Although I do not hope to turn again
Although I do not hope
Although I do not hope to turn

Wavering between the profit and the loss
In this brief transit where the dreams cross
The dreamcrossed twilight between birth and dying
(Bless me father) though I do not wish to wish these things
From the wide window towards the granite shore
The white sails still fly seaward, seaward flying
Unbroken wings

And the lost heart stiffens and rejoices
In the lost lilac and the lost sea voices
And the weak spirit quickens to rebel
For the bent golden-rod and the lost sea smell
Quickens to recover
The cry of quail and the whirling plover
And the blind eye creates
The empty forms between the ivory gates
And smell renews the salt savour of the sandy earth

This is the time of tension between dying and birth
The place of solitude where three dreams cross
Between blue rocks
But when the voices shaken from the yew-tree drift away
Let the other yew be shaken and reply.

Blessèd sister, holy mother, spirit of the fountain, spirit of the
    garden,
Suffer us not to mock ourselves with falsehood
Teach us to care and not to care
Teach us to sit still
Even among these rocks,

Our peace in His will
And even among these rocks
Sister, mother
And spirit of the river, spirit of the sea,
Suffer me not to be separated

And let my cry come unto Thee.

e. e. cummings
(1894–1962)

IN ADDITION TO WRITING POETRY, Edward Estlin Cummings was a painter, es-
sayist, and playwright. Born into a Unitarian family in Massachusetts, Cummings at-
tended Harvard and worked in the book industry upon graduating. He enlisted in the
Ambulance Corps in France during World War I, but was vocal in his opposition to the
war and his lack of enmity toward the Germans; in consequence, he was arrested by
the French military on suspicion of spying. Upon his release, he was drafted into the
U.S. Army. He traveled widely throughout his life, particularly in Europe, settling fi-
nally in New Hampshire. He wrote more than a dozen books in which he experimented
with the expressive capacities of punctuation and orthography. His many awards in-
clude the Bollingen Prize in 1958.

i thank You God for most this amazing

i thank You God for most this amazing
day:for the leaping greenly spirits of trees
and a blue true dream of sky; and for everything
which is natural which is infinite which is yes
(i who have died am alive again today,
and this is the sun's birthday; this is the birth
day of life and love and wings; and of the gay
great happening illimitably earth)
how should tasting touching hearing seeing
breathing any—lifted from the no

of all nothing—human merely being
doubt imaginable You?
(now the ears of my ears awake
and now the eyes of my eyes are opened)

Jean Toomer
(1894–1967)

NATHAN EUGENE PINCHBACK Toomer was born in Washington, D.C., the descendant of both European and African American ancestors (his grandfather was P. B. S. Pinchback, Louisiana's first African American governor). As his skin was extremely light, he lived both in all-white and all-black segregated communities at various times of his life. Eventually, he would refuse racial classification altogether, preferring to think of himself, and to live as much as was possible, only as an American. Around the time of the publication of his book of prose poetry, *Cane* (1923), Toomer became interested in the spiritual teachings of George Ivanovich Gurdjieff, the founder of Unitism, and preached the gospel of that spiritual system until the mid-1930s. In 1940, he became a Quaker. Toomer wrote a great deal, but published relatively few books, *Cane* and *Essentials* (1931) being the most remarkable. *The Collected Poems of Jean Toomer* was published by the University of North Carolina Press twenty-one years after his death.

Georgia Dusk

The sky, lazily disdaining to pursue
The setting sun, too indolent to hold
A lengthened tournament for flashing gold,
Passively darkens for night's barbecue,

A feast of moon and men and barking hounds,
An orgy for some genius of the South
With blood-hot eyes and cane-lipped scented mouth,
Surprised in making folk-songs from soul sounds.

The sawmill blows its whistle, buzz-saws stop,
And silence breaks the bud of knoll and hill,

Soft settling pollen where plowed lands fulfill
Their early promise of a bumper crop.

Smoke from the pyramidal sawdust pile
Curls up, blue ghosts of trees, tarrying low
Where only chips and stumps are left to show
The solid proof of former domicile.

Meanwhile, the men, with vestiges of pomp,
Race memories of king and caravan,
High-priests, an ostrich, and a juju-man,
Go singing through the footpaths of the swamp.

Their voices rise . . . the pine trees are guitars,
Strumming, pine-needles fall like sheets of rain . . .
Their voices rise . . . the chorus of the cane
Is caroling a vesper to the stars . . .

O singers, resinous and soft your songs
Above the sacred whisper of the pines,
Give virgin lips to cornfield concubines,
Bring dreams of Christ to dusky cane-lipped throngs.

Hart Crane
(1899–1932)

HART CRANE WAS BORN IN Garrettsville, Ohio, the son of candy-maker Clarence
Crane (inventor of Life Savers). He dropped out of high school and left home for New
York City, where he took temporary work as a copywriter and began to publish poems
in literary magazines. Crane would eventually publish two books of poetry, *White
Buildings* (1926) and *The Bridge* (1930). Crane's short life was characterized by alco-
holism, family discord, self-destructive behavior, manic depression, and, though his
poetic skill was great and his artistic ambition epic, a sense of his own failure. He com-
mitted suicide by throwing himself into the Gulf of Mexico from the deck of the ocean
liner on which he was traveling back to America after a year spent in Mexico on a Gug-
genheim Fellowship.

Lachrymae Christi[3]

Whitely, while benzene
Rinsings from the moon
Dissolve all but the windows of the mills
(Inside the sure machinery
Is still
And curdled only where a sill
Sluices its one unyielding smile)

Immaculate venom binds
The fox's teeth, and swart
Thorns freshen on the year's
First blood. From flanks unfended,
Twanged red perfidies of spring
Are trillion on the hill.

And the nights opening
Chant pyramids,—
Anoint with innocence,—recall
To music and retrieve what perjuries
Had galvanized the eyes.

While chime
Beneath and all around
Distilling clemencies,—worms'
Inaudible whistle, tunneling
Not penitence
But song, as these
Perpetual fountains, vines,—

Thy Nazarene[4] and tinder eyes.

(Let sphinxes from the ripe
Borage of death have cleared my tongue
Once and again; vermin and rod
No longer bind. Some sentient cloud
Of tears flocks through the tendoned loam:
Betrayed stones slowly speak.)

---

3. Latin: *Tears of Christ*.
4. A title applied to Jesus of Nazareth.

Names peeling from Thine eyes
And their undimming lattices of flame,
Spell out in palm and pain
Compulsion of the year, O Nazarene.

Lean long from sable, slender boughs,
Unstanched and luminous. And as the nights
Strike from Thee perfect spheres,
Life up in lilac-emerald breath the grail
Of earth again—

                Thy face
From charred and riven stakes, O
Dionysus, Thy
Unmangled target smile.

The Hurricane

Lo, Lord, Thou ridest!
Lord, Lord, Thy swifting heart

Naught stayeth, naught now bideth
But's smithereened apart!

Ay! Scripture flee'th stone!
Milk-bright, They chisel wind

Rescindeth flesh from bone
To quivering whittlings thinned—

Swept—whistling straw! Battered,
Lord, e'en boulders now out-leap

Rock sockets, levin-lathered!
Nor, Lord, may worm out-creep

Thy drum's gambade, its plunge abscond!
Lord God, while summits crashing

Whip sea-kelp screaming on blond
Sky-seethe, high heaven dashing—

Thou ridest to the door, Lord!
Thou bidest wall nor floor, Lord!

Kenneth Slessor
(1901–1971)

BORN IN ORANGE, NEW SOUTH Wales, Kenneth Adolphe Schloesser (the family's ancestors were German-Jewish; Slessor's father changed the family name in 1914) was a poet and journalist and remains one of Australia's most revered literary figures. He began his career as a journalist in 1920 as a reporter for the *Sydney Sun;* he would become the editor of that publication in 1944, near the end of his tenure as official war correspondent for the Australian Army. Over his career, he worked for a variety of Australian newspapers and magazines. His poetic endeavors began somewhat earlier, in 1917, and he is today known more for his poetic accomplishments—he is credited with introducing a classical European sensibility to the Australian tradition of bush balladry—than he is for his journalistic success. His books include *Thief of the Moon* (1924), *Earth-Visitors* (1926), *Cuckooz Contrey* (1932), and *Five Bells* (1939).

Vesper-Song of the Reverend Samuel Marsden[5]

My cure of souls, my cage of brutes,
Go lick and learn at these my boots!
When tainted highways tear a hole,
I bid my cobbler welt the sole.
O, ye that wear the boots of Hell,
Shall I not welt a soul as well?
    O, souls that leak with holes of sin,
    Shall I not let God's leather in,
    Or hit with sacramental knout
    Your twice-convicted vileness out?

Lord, I have sung with ceaseless lips
A tinker's litany of whips,
Have graved another Testament
On backs bowed down and bodies bent.
My stripes of jeweled blood repeat

---

5. Marsden (1764–1838), was an English-born cleric and missionary, believed to have introduced Christianity to New Zealand. He was appointed to the position of magistrate in Australia, in which position, notorious for assigning severe corporal punishments, he became known as the "flogging parson."

A scarlet Grace for holy meat.
  Not mine, the Hand that writes the weal
  On this, my vellum of puffed veal,
  Not mine, the glory that endures,
  But Yours, dear God, entirely Yours.

Are there not Saints in holier skies
Who have been scourged to Paradise?
O, Lord when I have come to that,
Grant there may be a Heavenly Cat
With twice as many tails as here—
  And make me, God, Your Overseer.
  But if the veins of Saints be dead,
  Grant me a whip in Hell instead,
  Where blood is not so hard to fetch.

But I, Lord, am Your humble wretch.

George Oppen
(1908–1984)

GEORGE OPPEN WAS BORN IN New Rochelle, New York, the son of a wealthy diamond merchant. After a childhood and early adulthood plagued by trauma and instability (his mother committed suicide, his father remarried a woman George despised, he was expelled from high school following a car accident in which his passenger was killed, he left Oregon State University after being suspended for engaging in inappropriate behavior with the woman who would eventually become his wife), he founded the Objectivist Press with Louis Zukofsky and Charles Reznikoff in 1932. His first book of poetry, *Discrete Series*, was published by that press a year later. Oppen became increasingly politically active over the course of the Great Depression, and he stopped writing poetry altogether shortly after the publication of *Discrete Series*. He would not write poetry again until 1958, when he and his wife returned to the United States from Mexico where, as communists, they had been living in order to avoid Senator Joseph McCarthy and the House Un-American Activities Committee. Oppen's other books include *The Materials* (1962), *Of Being Numerous* (1968), for which he was awarded the Pulitzer Prize, and *Myth of the Blaze* (1975).

Psalm
VERITAS SEQUITUR . . .[6]

In the small beauty of the forest
The wild deer bedding down—
That they are there!

Their eyes
Effortless, the soft lips
Nuzzle and the alien small teeth
Tear at the grass

The roots of it
Dangle from their mouths
Scattering earth in the strange woods.
They who are there.

Their paths
Nibbled thru the fields, the leaves that shade them
Hang in the distances
Of sun

The small nouns
Crying faith
In this in which the wild deer
Startle, and stare out.

---

6. Latin: *Truth follows* . . . , a shortened quote from Thomas Aquinas: *veritas sequitur esse rei* ("truth fol-
lows the essence of things"—that is, understanding is the result of the truth that is within things).

7

The Twentieth-Century Devotional
Lyric After Modernism

THE POETS WHO WROTE AND published during the fifty-five-year period between the end of World War II and the beginning of the twenty-first century were remarkable not just for the strength and beauty of the work they produced, but also for the number of movements and schools into which they fragmented. From the ashes of Modernism arose the post-Modernist poetries of the New York School, the Beats, the Objectivists, the New Formalists, the Martian Poets, the Black Mountain Poets, the Deep Imagists, the L=A=N=G=U=A=G=E Poets, the Confessionals, and the poets of the San Francisco Renaissance, among others. With these groups emerged a new interest in the poetries of identity and the voices of those previously relegated to the margins because of their race, class, gender, and/or sexual orientation. Indeed, the nearer the twentieth century drew to its conclusion, the more difficult it became to speak of postwar Anglophone poetry in terms of a single, unified phenomenon.

The vast majority of post–World War II poets, regardless of what group they belonged to, were able to recover and re-place the devotional object that went missing during the Modernist period. However, though the devotional object transitioned successfully from pre- to post-Modernism, it did not emerge from that period unchanged. The poets writing after World War II viewed the devotional object with the same skepticism with which they viewed much of the devotional—indeed, the poetic—tradition. In the same way that they embraced Modernist technical experimentation but rejected what they saw as the movement's elitism, so they welcomed the return of the devotional object but rejected the hierarchized distance that had traditionally separated that object from those who would devote themselves to it.

Consequently, in the poetries of the last half of the twentieth century, the intimate replaced the infinite, and though God's will remained as unknowable as it had ever been, God became something familiar, something of which it was possible to conceive on an almost human scale. By the end of the twentieth century, the devotional object was rarely conceived of, or addressed, unironically by poets as some kind of Super-Being; rather, the figure of God-as-Boss or simply God-as-Other came to define the discourse, along with a lowering of diction and tone. Post–World War II devotional writing tends to approach its devotional object with an irony and irreverence that foregrounds those features that were always present in the devotional lyric, albeit tempered with reverence: petulance, accusation, and reproof.

FURTHER READING

Altieri, Charles. *The Art of Twentieth-Century American Poetry: Modernism and After.* Hoboken, N.J.: Wiley-Blackwell, 2006.

Barfoot, C. C., ed. *In Black and Gold: Contiguous Traditions in Post-War British and Irish Poetry.* Amsterdam: Rodopi, 1994.

Finkelstein, Norman. *On Mount Vision: Forms of the Sacred in Contemporary American Poetry.* Iowa City: University of Iowa Press, 2010.

Glicksberg, Charles I. *Literature and Religion: A Study in Conflict.* Dallas: Southern Methodist University Press, 1960.

Gregory, Horace. "Rediscovery of Religious Poetry." *Commonweal,* 65 (1957): 361–363.

Huk, Romana, ed. *Assembling Alternatives: Reading Postmodern Poetries Transnationally.* Middletown, Conn.: Wesleyan University Press, 2003.

Hungerford, Amy. *Postmodern Belief: American Literature and Religion Since 1960.* Princeton: Princeton University Press, 2010.

Kee, James M. "'Postmodern' Thinking and the Status of the Religious." *Religion and Literature,* 22, nos. 2–3 (1990): 47–60.

Elizabeth Bishop
(1911–1979)

BORN IN WORCESTER, MASSACHUSETTS, Bishop went to live with her grandparents on a farm in Nova Scotia as a child after her mother was institutionalized, her father having died shortly after her birth. Later in childhood, she returned to live with her father's family in Massachusetts. She studied music and planned to become a composer before majoring in English. Bishop's father had left her an inheritance that allowed her to live independently, and over the course of her life, Bishop lived in France, Key West, and Brazil, where she remained for fifteen years. In her later life she taught courses at Harvard, New York University, and MIT. Her much-celebrated collections of poetry include the volumes *North & South* (1946), *Questions of Travel* (1965), and *Geography III* (1976).

Anaphora

Each day with so much ceremony
begins, with birds, with bells,
with whistles from a factory;
such white-gold skies our eyes
first open on, such brilliant walls
that for a moment we wonder
"Where is the music coming from, the energy?

The day was meant for what ineffable creature
we must have missed?" Oh promptly he
appears and takes his earthly nature
    instantly, instantly falls
    victim of long intrigue,
    assuming memory and mortal
    mortal fatigue.

More slowly falling into sight
and showering into stippled faces,
darkening, condensing all his light;
in spite of all the dreaming
squandered upon him with that look,
suffers our uses and abuses,
sinks through the drift of bodies,
sinks through the drift of classes
to evening to the beggar in the park
who, weary, without lamp or book
    prepares stupendous studies:
    the fiery event
    of every day in endless
    endless assent.

R. S. Thomas
(1913–2000)

RONALD STUART THOMAS WAS born in Cardiff, Wales, and spent forty-two years ministering to the people of rural Wales as an Anglican clergyman, though he left the church in 1978. Thomas's first three poetry collections—*The Stones of the Field* (1946), *An Acre of Land* (1952), and *The Minister* (a play in verse, 1953)—were published with very little fanfare. His fourth book, however, *Song at the Year's Turning: Poems, 1942–1954* (1955), proved to be his breakout volume and earned him significant critical praise and a new national audience. His reputation has increased significantly since that volume's publication, and he is now considered by many to be one of the most important Welsh poets of the twentieth century. He was nominated for the Nobel Prize in Literature in 1996.

Kneeling

Moments of great calm,
Kneeling before an altar
Of wood in a stone church
In summer, waiting for the God
To speak; the air a staircase
For silence; the sun's light
Ringing me, as though I acted
A great role. And the audiences
Still; all that close throng
Of spirits waiting, as I,
For the message.
        Prompt me, God;
But not yet. When I speak,
Though it be you who speak
Through me, something is lost.
The meaning is in the waiting.

Praise

I praise you because
you are artist and scientist
in one. When I am somewhat
fearful of your power,
your ability to work miracles
with a set-square, I hear
you murmuring to yourself
in a notation Beethoven
dreamed of but never achieved.
You run off your scales of
rain water and sea water, play
the chords of the morning
and evening light, sculpture
with shadow, join together leaf
by leaf, when spring
comes, the stanzas of
an immense poem. You speak
all languages and none,

answering our most complex
prayers with the simplicity
of a flower, confronting
us, when we would domesticate you
to our uses, with the rioting
viruses under our lens.

Via Negativa[1]

Why no! I never thought other than
That God is that great absence
In our lives, the empty silence
Within, the place where we go
Seeking, not in hope to
Arrive or find.
He keeps the interstices
In our knowledge, the darkness
Between stars. His are the echoes
We follow, the footprints he has just
Left. We put our hands in
His side hoping to find
It warm. We look at people
And places as though he had looked
At them, too; but miss the reflection.

John Berryman
(1914–1972)

JOHN BERRYMAN WAS BORN John Allyn Smith, Jr., in McAlester, Oklahoma, and attended Columbia University. Berryman's first published poems appeared in a volume called *Five Young American Poets*. His poetic reputation was firmly established in 1956 with *Homage to Mistress Bradstreet*. In 1964, Berryman published *77 Dream Songs*, and

---

1. Latin for the *negative way*, also called *negative theology*, which attempts to describe God only in terms
of what God is not.

four years later published *His Toy, His Dream, His Rest*, a collection of over three hundred additional Dream Songs, for which he was awarded both the National Book Award for Poetry and the Bollingen Prize in 1969. The series "Eleven Addresses to the Lord" appears in the last book he published during his lifetime, *Love and Fame* (1970). Berryman was plagued throughout his life by alcoholism and depression and ultimately committed suicide by leaping from Minneapolis's Washington Avenue Bridge.

Dream Song 28: Snow Line

It was wet & white & swift and where I am
we don't know. It was dark and then
it isn't.
I wish the barker would come. There seems to be eat
nothing. I am usually tired.
I'm alone too.

If only the strange one with so few legs would come,
I'd say my prayers out of my mouth, as usual.
Where are his note I loved?
There may be horribles; it's hard to tell.
The barker nips me but somehow I feel
he too is on my side.

I'm too alone. I see no end. If we could all
run, even that would be better. I am hungry.
The sun is not hot.
It's not a good position I am in.
If I had to do the whole thing over again
I wouldn't.

Eleven Addresses to the Lord
I

Master of beauty, craftsman of the snowflake,
inimitable contriver,
endower of Earth so gorgeous & different from the boring Moon,
thank you for such as it is my gift.

I have made up a morning prayer to you
containing with precision everything that most matters.

"According to Thy will" the thing begins.
It took me off & on two days. It does not aim at eloquence.

You have come to my rescue again & again
in my impassable, sometimes despairing years.
You have allowed my brilliant friends to destroy themselves
and I am still here, severely damaged, but functioning.

Unknowable, as I am unknown to my guinea pigs:
how can I "love" you?
I only as far as gratitude & awe
confidently & absolutely go.

I have no idea whether we live again.
It doesn't seem likely
from either the scientific or the philosophical point of view
but certainly all things are possible to you,

and I believe as fixedly in the Resurrection-appearances to Peter & to Paul
as I believe I sit in this blue chair.
Only that may have been a special case
to establish their initiatory faith.

Whatever your end may be, accept my amazement.
May I stand until death forever at attention
for any your least instruction or enlightenment.
I even feel sure you will assist me again, Master of insight & beauty.

2

Holy, as I suppose I dare to call you
without pretending to know anything about you
but infinite capacity everywhere & always
& in particular certain goodness to me.

Yours is the crumpling, to my sister-in-law terrifying thunder,
yours the candelabra buds sticky in Spring,
Christ's mercy,
the gloomy wisdom of godless Freud:

yours the lost souls in ill-attended wards,
those agonized thro' the world

at this instant of time, all evil men,
Belsen, Omaha Beach,—[2]

incomprehensible to man your ways.
May be the Devil after all exists.
"I don't try to reconcile anything" said the poet at eighty,
"This is a damned strange world."

Man is ruining the pleasant earth & man.
What at last, my Lord, will you allow?
Postpone till after my children's deaths your doom
if it be thy ineffable, inevitable will.

I say "Thy kingdom come," it means nothing to me.
Hast Thou prepared astonishments for man?
One sudden Coming? Many so believe.
So not, without knowing anything, do I.

3

Sole watchman of the flying stars, guard me
against my flicker of impulse lust: teach me
to see them as sisters & daughters. Sustain
my grand endeavours: husbandship & crafting.

Forsake me not when my wild hours come;
grant me sleep nightly, grace soften my dreams;
achieve in me patience till the thing be done,
a careful view of my achievement come.

Make me from time to time the gift of the shoulder.
When all hurt nerves whine shut away the whiskey.
Empty my heart toward Thee.
Let me pace without fear the common path of death.

Cross am I sometimes with my little daughter:
fill her eyes with tears. Forgive me, Lord.
Unite my various soul,
sole watchman of the wide & single stars.

---

2. World War II sites of atrocity and carnage: Belsen was a Nazi concentration camp; Omaha Beach
   where U.S. forces battled, with heavy casualties, to secure a beachhead in Normandy, France.

4

If I say Thy name, art Thou there? It may be so.
Thou art not absent-minded, as I am.
I am so much so I had to give up driving.
You attend, I feel, to the matters of man.

Across the ages certain blessings swarm,
horrors accumulate, the best men fail:
Socrates, Lincoln, Christ mysterious.
Who can search Thee out?

except Isaiah & Pascal, who saw.
I dare not ask that vision, though a piece of it
at last in crisis was vouchsafèd me.
I altered then for good, to become yours.

Caretaker! take care, for we run in straits.
Daily, by night, we walk naked to storm,
some threat of wholesale loss, to ruinous fear.
Gift us with long cloaks & adrenalin.

Who haunt the avenues of Angkor Wat
recalling all that prayer, that glory dispersed,
haunt me at the corner of Fifth & Hennepin.
Shield & fresh fountain! Manifester! Even mine.

5

Holy, & holy. The damned are said to say
"We never thought we would come into this place."
I'm fairly clear, my Friend, there's no such place
ordained for inappropriate & evil man.

Surely they fall dull, & forget. We too,
the more or less just, I feel fall asleep
dreamless forever while the worlds hurl out.
Rest may be your ultimate gift.

Rest or transfiguration! come & come
whenever Thou wilt. My daughter & my son
fend will without me, when my work is done
in Your opinion.

Strengthen my widow, let her dream on me
thro' tranquil hours less & down to less.
Abrupt elsewhere her heart, I sharply hope.
I leave her in wise Hands.

6

Under new management, Your Majesty:
Thine. I have solo'd mine since childhood, since
my father's suicide when I was twelve
blew out my most bright candle faith, and look at me.

I served at Mass six dawns a week from five,
adoring Father Boniface & you,
memorizing the Latin he explained.
Mostly we worked alone. One or two women.

Then my poor father frantic. Confusions & afflictions
followed my days. Wives left me.
Bankrupt I closed my doors. You pierced the roof
twice & again. Finally you opened my eyes.

My double nature fused in that point of time
three weeks ago day before yesterday.
Now, brooding thro' a history of the early Church,
I identify with everybody, even the heresiarchs.

7

After a Stoic, a Peripatetic, a Pythagorean,
Justin Martyr[3] studied the words of the Saviour,
finding them short, precise, terrible, & full of refreshment.
I am tickled to learn this.

Let one day desolate Sherry, fair, thin, tall,
at 29 today her life the Sahara Desert,
who has never once enjoyed a significant relation,
so find His lightning words.

---

3. Second-century Christian theologian.

John Berryman   307

A Prayer for the Self

Who am I worthless that You spent such pains
and take my pains again?
I do not understand; but I believe.
Jonquils respond with wit to the teasing breeze.

Induct me down my secrets. Stiffen this heart
to stand their horrifying cries, O cushion
the first the second shocks, will to a halt
in mid-air there demons who would be at me.

May fade before, sweet morning on sweet morning,
I wake my dreams, my fan-mail go astray,
and do me little goods I have not thought of,
ingenious & beneficial Father.

Ease in their passing my beloved friends,
all others too I have cared for in a travelling life,
anyone anywhere indeed. Lift up
sober toward truth a scared self-estimate.

9

Surprise me on some ordinary day
with a blessing gratuitous. Even I've done good
beyond their expectations. What count we then
upon Your bounty?

Interminable: an old theologian
asserts that even to say You exist is misleading.
Uh-huh. I buy that Second-century fellow.
I press his withered glorifying hand.

You certainly do not as I exist,
impersonating as well the meteorite
& flaring in your sun your waterfall
or blind in caves pallid fishes.

Bear in mind me, Who have forgotten nothing,
& Who continues. I may not foreknow
& fail much to remember. You sustain
imperial desuetudes, at the kerb a widow.

10

Fearful I peer upon the mountain path
where once Your shadow passed, Limner of the clouds
up their phantastic guesses. I am afraid,
I never until now confessed.

I fell back in love with you, Father, for two reasons:
You were good to me, & a delicious author,
rational & passionate. Come on me again,
as twice you came to Azarias & Misael.[4]

President of the brethren, our mild assemblies
inspire, & bother the priest not to be dull;
keep us week-long in order; love my children,
my mother far & ill, far brother, my spouse.

Oil all my turbulence as at Thy dictation
I sweat out my wayward works.
Father Hopkins said the only true literary critic is Christ.
Let me lie down exhausted, content with that.

11

Germanicus leapt upon the wild lion in Smyrna,
wishing to pass quickly from a lawless life.[5]
The crowd shook the stadium.
The proconsul marvelled.

"Eighty & six years have I been his servant,
and he has done me no harm.
How can I blaspheme my King who saved me?"
Polycarp, John's pupil, facing the fire.[6]

Make too me acceptable at the end of time
in my degree, which then Thou wilt award.
Cancer, senility, mania,
I pray I may be ready with my witness.

---

4. See the Book of Daniel, chapters 1–3.

5. Germanicus was a martyr of Smyrna, thrown to wild animals in a local amphitheater. When the beasts
   did not attack, Germanicus provoked them into attacking, gaining the admiration of the arena.

6. A second-century Bishop of Smyrna who died a martyr. Sent to be burned at the stake, he was finally
   stabbed to death when the fire failed to harm him.

Dylan Thomas
(1914–1953)

DYLAN MARLAIS THOMAS WAS born in Swansea, Glamorgan, Wales, and began writing poetry at a very early age. He dropped out of school when he was sixteen and worked for a short period of time as a reporter for the *South Wales Daily Post,* quitting that job after only a year and a half to focus entirely on his verse. Of all the poems that Thomas wrote over the course of his short and turbulent life (he was known as much for his public misbehavior and drunkenness as he was for his art), more than half of them were composed before his twentieth birthday. His first book of poems, *18 Poems,* appeared in 1934 and included many of the poems he wrote as a teenager. Seven more collections of poetry, three collections of prose, and one volume of scripts would appear before his death. More volumes of Thomas's work have been published since his death than during his lifetime.

from Vision and Prayer
2

Forever   falling   night   is   a   known
Star   and   country   to   the   legion
Of sleepers whose tongue I toll
To   mourn   his   deluging
Light through sea and soil
And we have come
To   know   all
P l a c e s
Ways
M a z e s
P a s s a g e s
Quarters and graves
Of   the   endless   fall.
Now   common   lazarus
Of the charting sleepers prays
Never   to   awake   and   arise
For the country of death is the heart's size.

And the star of the lost the shape of the eyes
In the name of the fatherless
In the name of the unborn
And the undesirers
Of midwiving morning's
Hands or instruments
O in the name
Of no one
Now or
No
One to
Be I pray
May the crimson
Sun spin a grave grey
And the colour of clay
Stream upon his martyrdom
In the interpreted evening
And the known dark of the earth amen.

I turn the corner of prayer and burn
In a blessing of the sudden
Sun. In the name of the damned
I would turn back and run
To the hidden land
But the loud sun
Christens down
The sky.
I
Am found.
O let him
Scald me and drown
Me in his world's wound.
His lightning answers my
Cry. My voice burns in his hand.
Now I am lost in the blinding
One. The sun roars at the prayer's end.

Thomas Merton
(1915–1968)

THOMAS JAMES MERTON WAS born in Prades, France, and following the death of his parents spent time in Italy, France, and England before beginning his studies at Columbia University in 1934. He remained at Columbia until 1939, having written his graduate thesis on William Blake. After his education, Merton converted to Catholicism, and in 1941 he entered the Abbey of Our Lady of Gethsemani, in Kentucky, where he spent the rest of his life as a Trappist monk. A prolific author, Merton published his first book of poetry, *Thirty Poems,* three years after he entered the abbey. Other books would follow at the rate of at least one a year—sometimes as many as four appeared in a single year—until his death by accidental electrocution in Thailand.

Trappists, Working

Now all our saws sing holy sonnets in this world of timber
Where oaks go off like guns, and fall like cataracts,
Pouring their roar into the wood's green well.

Walk to us, Jesus, through the wall of trees,
And find us still adorers in these airy churches,
Singing our other Office with our saws and axes.
Still teach Your children in the busy forest,
And let some little sunlight reach us, in our mental shades, and leafy studies.

When time has turned the country white with grain
And filled our regions with the thrashing sun,
Walk to us, Jesus, through the walls of wheat
When our two tractors come to cut them down:
Sow some light winds upon the acres of our spirit,
And cool the regions where our prayers are reapers,
And slake us, Heaven, with Your living rivers.

Robert Lowell

(1917–1977)

BORN IN BOSTON, ROBERT Lowell was the product of two of New England's oldest and most prominent families. He attended Harvard from 1935 to 1937, dropped out, attached himself to the poet Allen Tate, enrolled in Kenyon College, and graduated in 1940 with a degree in classics. That same year, Lowell converted to Catholicism. His first book, *Land of Unlikeness,* was hailed as an achievement upon its publication in 1944; however, it was not until his second book, *Lord Weary's Castle* (1946), was awarded the Pulitzer Prize that his reputation as a major American literary figure was established. Lowell published many volumes of poetry, prose, and translation, including *Life Studies* (1959), the volume often credited with helping to pioneer Confessional poetry.

On the Eve of the Feast of the Immaculate Conception, 1942

Mother of God, whose burly love
Turns swords to plowshares, come, improve
      On the big wars
And make this holiday with Mars
Your Feast Day, while Bellona's[7] bluff
Courage or call it what you please
      Plays blindman's buff
      Through virtue's knees.

Freedom and Eisenhower have won
Significant laurels where the Hun
      And Roman kneel
To lick the dust from Mars' bootheel
Like foppish bloodhounds; yet you sleep
Out our distemper's evil day
      And hear no sheep
      Or hangdog bay!

---

7. Ancient Roman goddess of war.

Bring me tonight no axe to grind
On wheels of the Utopian mind:
      Six thousand years
Cain's blood has drummed into my ears,
Shall I wring plums from Plato's bush[8]
When Burma's and Bizerte's dead[9]
      Must puff and push
      Blood into bread?

Oh, if soldiers mind you well
They shall find you are their belle
      And belly too;
Christ's bread and beauty came by you,
Celestial Hoyden, when our Lord
Gave up the weary Ghost and died,
      You shook a sword
      From his torn side.

Over the seas and far away
They feast the fair and bloody day
      When mankind's Mother,
Jesus' Mother, like another
Nimrod danced on Satan's head.[10]
The old Snake lopes to his shelled hole;
      Man eats the Dead
      From pole to pole.

Helltime

Our God; he walks with us, he talks with us,
in sleep, in thunder, and in wind and weather;
he strips the wind and gravel from our words,
and speeds us naked on the single way.

---

8. The *Republic* explains Plato's theory of Forms, which holds that the visible world is populated by objects (for example, a tree), while the intelligible world is populated by Forms (for example, the ideal concept of a tree), which is more real than its visible cognate.

9. Bizerte, or Benzert, is a city in Tunisia, a key offensive target for the Allied forces during World War II.

10. Nimrod: a king of Babylon; see Genesis 10.

Is he wind, or is he revelation,
the time-bomb buried in this ton of trash?
In some Bolivian tin mine we, the servants,
drop-outs and hoop-spines sway the cart together;
God finds no profit in descending here,
finds only smear, expendables of love,
nothing and helltime borne by faithful servants,
you have your place . . . if you are put
in your place enough times, you become your place . . .
the flatterer's all-forgiving, wounded smile.

Denise Levertov
(1923–1997)

LEVERTOV'S FATHER CONVERTED from Russian Hasidic Judaism to Anglicanism
after emigrating to the United Kingdom, and her mother was proudly Welsh. She was
educated at home in Essex. When she was twelve, she sent a few of her poems to T. S.
Eliot, and received an encouraging reply. In 1947, she married an American man
and moved to New York, becoming an American citizen. Her teaching career took her
to Brandeis University, MIT, Stanford University, and the University of Washington,
where she converted to Roman Catholicism. She served as poetry editor for *The Nation*
in the 1960s, and published over twenty books of poetry, as well as translations and
essays.

Mass for the Day of St. Thomas Didymus[11]
I. KYRIE

O deep unknown, guttering candle,
beloved nugget lodged
in the obscure heart's
last recess,
have mercy upon us.

---

11. See John 20.24–29. Levertov's section titles refer to prayers of the Catholic liturgy.

We choose from the past, tearing morsels to feed
pride or grievance.
We live in terror
of what we know:

death, death, and the world's
death we imagine
            and cannot imagine,
we who may be
the first and the last witness.

We live in terror
of what we do not know,
in terror of not knowing,
of the limitless, through which freefalling
forever, our dread
sinks and sinks,
                or
            of the violent closure of all.

Yet our hope lies
in the unknown,
in the unknowing.

O deep, remote unknown,
O deep unknown,
Have mercy upon us.

2. GLORIA

Praise the wet snow
            falling early.
Praise the shadow
            my neighbor's chimney casts on the tile roof
even this gray October day that should, they say,
have been golden.
                        Praise
the invisible sun burning beyond
            the white cold sky, giving us
light and the chimney's shadow.
Praise

god or the gods, the unknown,
that which imagined us, which stays
our hand,
our murderous hand,
                              and gives us
still,
in the shadow of death,
        our daily life,
        and the dream still
of goodwill, of peace on earth.
Praise
flow and change, night and
the pulse of day.

3. CREDO

I believe the earth
exists, and
in each minim mote
of its dust the holy
glow of thy candle.
Thou
unknown I know,
thou spirit,
giver,
lover of making, of the
wrought letter,
wrought flower,
iron, deed, dream.
Dust of the earth,
help thou my
unbelief. Drift,
gray become gold, in the beam of
vision. I believe and
interrupt my belief with
doubt. I doubt and
interrupt my doubt with belief. Be,
belovéd, threatened world.
                    Each minim
mote.

          Not the poisonous
luminescence forced
out of its privacy,
the sacred lock of its cell
broken. No,
the ordinary glow
of common dust in ancient sunlight.
Be, that I may believe. Amen.

4. SANCTUS

Powers and principalities—all the gods,
angels and demigods, eloquent animals, oracles,
storms of blessing and wrath—

        all that Imagination
        has wrought, has rendered,
        striving, in throes of epiphany—

        naming, forming—to give
        to the Vast Loneliness
        a hearth, a locus—

send forth their song towards
the harboring silence, uttering
the ecstasy of their names, the multiform
name of the Other, the known
Unknown, unknowable:

sanctus, hosanna, sanctus.

5. BENEDICTUS

Blesséd is that which comes in the name of the spirit,
that which bears
the spirit within it.

The name of the spirit is written
in woodgrain, windripple, crystal,

in crystals of snow, in petal, leaf,
moss and moon, fossil and feather,

blood, bone, song, silence,
very word of
very word,
flesh and
vision.

> (But what of the deft infliction
> upon the earth, upon the innocent,
> of hell by human hands?
>
> Is the word
> audible under or over the gross
> cacophony of malevolence?
> Yet to be felt
>   on the palm, in the breast,
> by deafmute dreamers,
>   a vibration
>   known in the fibers of
>   the tree of nerves, or witnessed
>   by the third eye to which
>   sight and sound are one?
>
> What of the emptiness,
> the destructive vortex that whirls
> no word with it?)

In the lion's indolence,
      there spirit is,
in the tiger's fierceness,
      that does not provide in advance
but springs
      only as hunger prompts,
      and the hunger
      of its young.

Blesséd is that which utters
its being,
the stone of stone,
the straw of straw,
      for there
spirit is.
      But can the name

utter itself
                        in the downspin of time?
Can it enter
                    the void?
                                        Blesséd
be the dust. From dust the world
utters itself. We have no other
hope, no knowledge.
                        The word
chose to become
flesh. In the blur of flesh
we bow, baffled.

6. AGNUS DEI

Given that lambs
are infant sheep, that sheep
are afraid and foolish, and lack
the means of self-protection, having
neither rage nor claws,
venom nor cunning,
what then
is this "Lamb of God"?

This pretty creature, vigorous
to nuzzle at milky dugs,
woolbearer, bleater
leaper in air for delight of being, who finds in astonishment
four legs to stand on, the grass
all it knows of the world?
            With whom we would like to play,
whom we'd lead with ribbons, but may not bring
into our houses because
it would soil the floor with its droppings?
What terror lies concealed
in strangest words, *O lamb*
of God that taketh away
the Sins of the World: an innocence
                smelling of ignorance,
                born in bloody snowdrifts,

licked by forebearing
dogs more intelligent than its entire flock put together?

God then,
encompassing all things, is
defenseless? Omnipotence
has been tossed away, reduced
to a wisp of damp wool?

And we,
frightened, bored, wanting
only to sleep till catastrophe
has raged, clashed, seethed and gone by without us, wanting then
to awaken in quietude without remembrance of agony,

we who in shamefaced private hope
had looked to be plucked from fire and given
a bliss we deserved for having imagined it,

is it implied that we
must protect this perversely weak
animal, whose muzzle's nudgings
suppose there is milk to be found in us?
Must hold to our icy hearts
a shivering God?

*

So be it.
Come, rag of pungent
quiverings,
dim star.
Let's try
if something human
still can shield you,
spark
of remote light.

Donald Justice

(1925–2004)

BORN IN MIAMI, DONALD RODNEY Justice was educated at the University of Miami, the University of North Carolina, and the University of Iowa. He is remembered at least as much for his teaching (at the Universities of Iowa and Florida) as for his writing; many of Justice's students have gone on to become prominent poets themselves. Justice's first collection of poems, *The Old Bachelor and Other Poems*, was published in 1951. His next book, *The Summer Anniversaries* (1960), won the Lamont Poetry Prize from the Academy of American Poets. Twelve collections followed—along with scripts, memoirs, essays, short stories, and libretti—each volume reinforcing and extending his reputation as a master craftsman and technical virtuoso. His many awards include the Bollingen Prize and the Pulitzer Prize.

To Satan in Heaven

Forgive, Satan, virtue's pedants, all such
As have broken our habits, or had none,
The keepers of promises, prizewinners,
Meek as leaves in the wind's circus, evenings;
Our simple wish to be elsewhere forgive,
Shy touchers of library atlases,
Envious of bird-flight, the whale's submersion;
And us forgive who have forgotten how,
The melancholy who, lacing a shoe,
Choose not to continue, the merely bored,
Who have modeled our lives after cloud-shapes;
For which confessing, have mercy on us,
The different and the indifferent,
In inverse proportion to our merit,
For we have affirmed thee secretly, by
Candle-glint in the polish of silver,
Between courses, murmured amenities,
See thee in mirrors by morning, shaving,
Or head in loose curls on the next pillow,
Reduced thee to our own scope and purpose,

Satan, who, though in heaven, downward yearned,
As the butterfly, weary of flowers,
Longs for the cocoon or the looping net.

A. R. Ammons
(1926–2001)

ARCHIE RANDOLPH AMMONS was born on a farm in rural North Carolina, near Whiteville, and began writing poetry while serving aboard the destroyer escort U.S.S. *Gunason* during World War II. After the war, he earned a degree in biology from Wake Forest University and a master's degree in English from the University of California, Berkeley. He taught at Cornell University from 1964 until his retirement in 1998. His first collection of poems, *Ommateum: With Doxology*, appeared in 1955. Over the course of a career that spanned nearly half a century, Ammons received many honors, including two National Book Awards, for *Collected Poems, 1951–1971* (1973) and *Garbage* (1993).

Hymn

I know if I find you I will have to leave the earth
and go on out
      over the sea marshes and the brant in bays
and over the hills of tall hickory
and over the crater lakes and canyons
and on up through the spheres of diminishing air
past the blackset noctilucent clouds
      where one wants to stop and look
way past all the light diffusions and bombardments
up farther than the loss of sight
      into the unseasonal undifferentiated empty stark

And I know if I find you I will have to stay with the earth
inspecting with thin tools and ground eyes
trusting the microvilli sporangia and simplest
      coelenterates

and praying for a nerve cell
with all the soul of my chemical reactions
and going right on down where the eye sees only traces

You are everywhere partial and entire
You are on the inside of everything and on the outside

I walk down the path down the hill where the sweetgum
has begun to ooze spring sap at the cut
and I see how the bark cracks and winds like no other bark
chasmal to my ant-soul running up and down
and if I find you I must go out deep into your
            far resolutions
and if I find you I must stay here with the separate leaves

Hymn IV

I hold you responsible for
every womb's neck
clogged with
killing growth

and for ducks on the bay
barking like hounds
all night
their wintering dreams

responsible for every action of
the brain that gives
me mind
and for all light

for the fishroe's
birth spawning forage to
night eels
nosing the tidal banks

I keep you existent at least as
a ghost crab
moon-extinguished his crisp
walk silenced on broken shells

answering at least as
the squiggling copepod
for the birthing and aging of
life's all-clustered grief

You have enriched us with
fear and contrariety
providing the searcher
confusion for his search

teaching by your snickering
wisdom and autonomy
for man
Bear it all

and keep me from my enemies'
wafered concision and zeal
I give you back to yourself
whole and undivided

James K. Baxter
(1926–1972)

BORN IN DUNEDIN, NEW ZEALAND, James K. Baxter was one of that country's most popular, outspoken, and celebrated poets. Having begun writing poetry seriously at the age of seven, he published his first collection of verse, *Beyond the Palisade*, in 1944, when he was just eighteen years old. His reputation grew considerably with the appearance of each subsequent volume, reaching its apex in 1957 with the international publication of his collection *In Fires of No Return*. That same year, Baxter broke with Anglicanism and was baptized into the Catholic Church. Eleven years later, Baxter had a dream vision that directed him to go to "Jerusalem." He interpreted the vision to mean that he should move not to the Jerusalem of the Middle East, but to the Maori settlement of Jerusalem located on the Whanganui River. He took with him only a Bible. Unfortunately, his new rugged existence was more than his body could bear and his health soon deteriorated; he died of a heart attack at the age of forty-six.

from *Jerusalem Sonnets*

1

The small grey cloudy louse that nests in my beard
Is not, as some would call it, "a pearl of God"—

No, it is a fiery tormentor
Waking me at 2 a.m.

Or thereabouts, when the lights are still on
In the houses in the pa,[12] to go across thick grass

Wet with rain, feet cold, to kneel
For an hour or two in front of the red flickering

Tabernacle light—what He sees inside
My meandering mind I can only guess—

A madman, a nobody, a raconteur
Whom he can joke with—"Lord," I ask Him,

"Do You or don't You expect me to put up with lice?"
His silent laugh still shakes the hills at dawn.

36

Brother Ass, Brother Ass, you are full of fancies,
You want this and that—a woman, a thistle,

A poem, a coffeebreak, a white bed, no crabs;
And now you complain of the weight of the Rider

Who will set you free to gallop in the light of the sun!
Ah well, kick Him off then, and see how you go

Lame-footed in the brambles; your disconsolate bray
Is ugly in my ears—long ago, long ago,

The battle was fought and the issue decided
As to who would be King—go on, little donkey

---

12. Maori: a fortified village or settlement.

Saddled and bridled by the Master of the world,
Be glad you can distinguish not an inch of the track,

That the stones are sharp, that your hide can itch,
That His true weight is heavy on your back.

from *Autumn Testament*
22

To pray for an easy heart is no prayer at all
Because the heart itself is the creaking bridge

On which we cross these Himalayan gorges
From bluff to bluff. To sweat out the soul's blood

Midnight after midnight is the ministry of Jacob,
And Jacob will be healed. This body that shivers

In the foggy cold, tasting the sour fat,
Was made to hang like a sack on its thief's cross,

Counting it better than bread to say the words of Christ,
"*Eli! Eli!*"[13] The Church will be shaken like a

Blanket in the wind, and we are the fleas that fall
To the ground for the dirt to cover. Brother thief,

You who are lodged in my ribcage, do not rail at
The only gate we have to paradise.

Allen Ginsberg
(1926–1997)

ALLEN GINSBERG WAS BORN in Newark, New Jersey, and was one of the leading voices of the Beat Generation, a literary movement that effectively began in San Francisco on the evening of October 7, 1955, when Ginsberg gave the first public performance of his ground-breaking poem "Howl." *Howl and Other Poems* was published a

---

13. See Mark 15.34.

year later by Lawrence Ferlinghetti and City Lights Books. The book was banned for obscenity: copies were seized by United States customs officials and both Ferlinghetti and the manager of City Lights Bookstore were arrested for publishing and selling obscene material. After a trial, *Howl* was found not to be obscene, though the poem stirs controversy even to this day. Many discrete collections of Ginsberg's poems, as well as several selected/collected editions of his work, followed the publication of *Howl and Other Poems*, *Kaddish and Other Poems* (1961) being perhaps the best known.

Psalm III

To God: to illuminate all men. Beginning with Skid Road.
Let Occidental and Washington be transformed into a higher place, the plaza of
     eternity.
Illuminate the welders in shipyards with the brilliance of their torches.
Let the crane operator lift up his arm for joy.
Let elevators creak and speak, ascending and descending in awe.
Let the mercy of the flower's direction beckon in the eye.
Let the straight flower bespeak its purpose in straightness—to seek the light.
Let the crooked flower bespeak its purpose in crookedness—to seek the light.
Let the crookedness and straightness bespeak the light.
Let Puget Sound be a blast of light.
I feed on your Name like a cockroach on a crumb—this cockroach is holy.

Seattle, June 1956

Galway Kinnell
(1927–)

AUTHOR OF NEARLY TWO DOZEN books of poetry, translation, and fiction, Galway Kinnell was born in Providence, Rhode Island. He studied at Princeton University, where he roomed with W. S. Merwin. He did field work for the Congress of Racial Equality (CORE) in the 1960s, helping to register southern black voters. Twice a Fulbright Fellow, Kinnell has taught in universities from France to Iran, and for many years he directed the creative writing program at New York University. He received both the Pulitzer Prize and the National Book Award in 1982 for his *Selected Poems*.

Prayer

Whatever happens. Whatever
what is is is what
I want. Only that. But that.

First Communion

The church is way over in the next county,
The same trip that last year we trekked
Carrying a sackful of ears to collect
The nickel-an-ear porcupine bounty.
Pictured on the wall over dark Jerusalem
Jesus is shining—in the dark he is a lamp.
On the tray he is a pastry wafer.
On the way home, there is regular talk
Of the fine preaching, before the regular jokes
Are allowed. The last time over
The same trail we brought two dollars homeward.
Now we carry the aftertaste of the Lord.
Soon a funny story about Uncle Abraham:
How, being liquored up, he got locked out
By his woman; how she must have taken blankets out
Later, for Sam says he found them, in the morning,
Asleep in each other's arms in the haybarn.

The sunlight streams through the afternoon
Another parable over the sloughs
And yellowing grass of the prairies.
Cold wind stirs, and the last green
Climbs to all the tips of the season, like
The last flame brightening on a wick.
Embers drop and break in sparks. Across the earth
Sleep is the overlapping of enough shadows.
In the wind outside a twig snaps
Like a tiny lid shutting somewhere in the ear.
Jesus, a boy thinks as his room goes out,
Jesus, it is a disappointing shed
Where they hang your picture
And drink juice, and conjure

Your person into inferior bread—
I would speak of injustice,
I would not go again into that place.

Anne Sexton
(1928–1974)

ANNE SEXTON WAS BORN Anne Gray Harvey in Newton, Massachusetts, and began writing poetry, on the advice of her doctor, following her first suicide attempt in 1955. Two years later, she enrolled in a creative writing workshop at the Boston Center for Adult Education, where she befriended poet Maxine Kumin. Encouraged by the success she enjoyed in that class, she enrolled in a graduate creative writing course Robert Lowell taught at Boston University. It was in Lowell's class that she met poets Sylvia Plath and George Starbuck. *To Bedlam and Part Way Back*, Sexton's first collection of poems, was published in 1960 and dealt explicitly with her struggles with mental illness. Six years later, her most acclaimed volume, *Live or Die*, appeared and was awarded the Pulitzer Prize for Poetry. In 1974, after a manuscript conference with Kumin to discuss her last book, *The Awful Rowing Toward God* (1975), Sexton ended her own life.

In the Deep Museum

My God, my God, what queer corner am I in?
Didn't I die, blood running down the post,
lungs gagging for air, die there for the sin
of anyone, my sour mouth giving up the ghost?
Surely my body is done? Surely I died?
And yet, I know, I'm here. What place is this?
Cold and queer, I sting with life. I lied.
Yes, I lied. Or else in some damned cowardice
my body would not give me up. I touch
fine cloth with my hand and my cheeks are cold.
If this is hell, then hell could not be much,
neither as special nor as ugly as I was told.

What's that I hear, snuffling and pawing its way
toward me? Its tongue knocks a pebble out of place
as it slides in, a sovereign. How can I pray?
It is panting; it is an odor with a face
like the skin of a donkey. It laps my sores.
It is hurt, I think, as I touch its little head.
It bleeds. I have forgiven murderers and whores
and now I must wait like old Jonah, not dead
nor alive, stroking a clumsy animal. A rat.
His teeth test me; he waits like a good cook,
knowing his own ground. I forgive him that,
as I forgave my Judas the money he took.

Now I hold his soft red sore to my lips
as his brothers crowd in, hairy angels who take
my gift. My ankles are a flute. I lose hips
and wrists. For three days, for love's sake,
I bless this other death. Oh, not in air—
in dirt. Under the rotting veins of its roots,
under the markets, under the sheep bed where
the hill is food, under the slippery fruits
of the vineyard, I go. Unto the bellies and jaws
of rats I commit my prophecy and fear.
Far below The Cross, I correct its flaws.
We have kept the miracle. I will not be here.

Praying to Big Jack
for Ruthie, my God-child

God, Jack of all trades,
I've got Ruthie's life to trade for today.
She's six. She's got her union card
and a brain tumor, that apple gone sick.
Take in mind, Jack, that her dimple
would erase a daisy. She's one of yours,
small walker of dogs and ice cream.
And she being one of yours
hears the saw lift off her skull
like a baseball cap. Cap off

and then what? The brains as
helpless as oysters in a pint container,
the nerves like phone wires.
God, take care, take infinite care
with the tumor lest it spread like grease.
Ruthie, somewhere in Toledo, has a twin,
mirror girl who plays marbles
and wonders: Where is the other me?
The girl of the same dress and my smile?
Today they sing together, they sing for alms.
God have you lapsed?
Are you so bitter with the world
you would put us down the drainpipe at six?

You of the top hat,
Mr. God,
you of the Cross made of lamb bones,
you of the camps, sacking the rejoice out of Germany,
I tell you this . . .
it will not do.
I will run up into the sky and chop wood.
I will run to sea and find a thousand-year servant.
I will run to the cave and bring home a Captain
if you will only, will only,
dear inquisitor.

Banish Ruth, plump Jack,
and you banish all the world.[14]

---

14. See William Shakespeare, *Henry IV Part 1*, Act 2, Scene 4, especially lines 1457–1463.

Geoffrey Hill
(1932–)

ENGLISH POET GEOFFREY HILL was born in Worcestershire. He was educated at Oxford and began teaching in Leeds. He spent the 1980s as a teaching Fellow at Cambridge, and then moved to the United States, where he was for many years professor of literature and religion at Boston University. His many collections of poetry include his first book, *For the Unfallen* (1959), a volume of *Selected Poems* (2006), and *Broken Hierarchies: Poems 1952–2012* (2013). His *Collected Critical Writings* won the 2009 Truman Capote Award for Literary Criticism. A fellow of both the Royal Society of Literature and the American Academy of Arts and Sciences, Hill was knighted in 2012 for "Services to Literature."

from Lachrimae: Or Seven Tears Figured in Seven Passionate Pavans[15]

> Passions I allow, and loves I approve, onely
> I would wishe that men would alter their
> object and better their intent.
>
> —St. Robert Southwell, *Marie Magdalens
> Funeral Teares,* 1591

I LACHRIMAE VERAE[16]

Crucified Lord, you swim upon your cross
and never move. Sometimes in dreams of hell
the body moves but moves to no avail
and is at one with that eternal loss.

You are the castaway of drowned remorse,
you are the world's atonement on the hill.
This is your body twisted by our skill
into a patience proper for redress.

---

15. *Lachrimae, or Seaven Teares, Figured in Seaven Passionate Pavans* was the title of a series of musical pieces by English composer John Dowland (1563–1628). *Lachrimae* is Latin for *tears;* a *pavane* is a slow, dignified dance.
16. Latin: *True tears.*

I cannot turn aside from what I do;
you cannot turn away from what I am.
You do not dwell in me nor I in you

however much I pander to your name
or answer to your lords of revenue,
surrendering the joys that they condemn.

4 LACHRIMAE COACTAE[17]

Crucified Lord, however much I burn
to be enamoured of your paradise,
knowing what ceases and what will not cease,
frightened of hell, not knowing where to turn,

I fall between harsh grace and hurtful scorn.
You are the crucified who crucifies,
self-withdrawn even from your own device,
your trim-plugged body, wreath of rakish thorn.

What grips me then, or what does my soul grasp?
If I grasp nothing what is there to break?
You are beyond me, innermost true light,

uttermost exile for no exile's sake,
king of our earth not caring to unclasp
its void embrace, the semblance of your quiet.

6 LACHRIMAE ANTIQUAE NOVAE[18]

Crucified Lord, so naked to the world,
you live unseen within that nakedness,
consigned by proxy to the judas-kiss
of our devotion, bowed beneath the gold,

with re-enactments, penances foretold:
scentings of love across a wilderness
of retrospection, wild and objectless
longings incarnate in the carnal child.

---

17. Latin: *Forced tears.*
18. Latin: *Old tears renewed.*

Beautiful for themselves the icons fade;
the lions and the hermits disappear.
Triumphalism feasts on empty dread,

fulfilling triumphs of the festal year.
We find you wounded by the token spear.
Dominion is swallowed with your blood.

7 LACHRIMAE AMANTIS[19]

What is there in my heart that you should sue
so fiercely for its love? What kind of care
brings you as though a stranger to my door
through the long night and in the icy dew

seeking the heart that will not harbour you,
that keeps itself religiously secure?
At this dark solstice filled with frost and fire
your passion's ancient wounds must bleed anew.

So many nights the angel of my house
had fed such urgent comfort through a dream,
whispered "your lord is coming, he is close"

that I have drowsed half-faithful for a time
bathed in pure tones of promise and remorse:
"tomorrow I shall wake to welcome him."

Mark Strand
(1934–)

BORN ON CANADA'S PRINCE Edward Island, Mark Strand lived throughout the
United States during his childhood and spent a good portion of his youth in South and
Central America, following the movements of his father's career in sales. He graduated
from Antioch College in Ohio, and then studied painting at Yale University with Josef

---

19. Latin: *Tears of a lover.*

Albers, earning a bachelor of fine arts degree. He studied nineteenth-century poetry in Italy before completing a master's degree at the Iowa Writers' Workshop. Strand's first collections of poetry, *Sleeping with One Eye Open* (1964) and *Reasons for Moving* (1968), established his dark, slightly surreal style. Recipient of the Pulitzer Prize, for *Blizzard of One* (1999), the Bollingen Prize, and a MacArthur Fellowship, Strand has published over fourteen collections of poetry, as well as several works of poetry in translation, three books for children, essays on literature, and critical studies on artists William Bailey and Edward Hopper. His collection of prose poems, *Almost Invisible,* appeared in 2012. He continues to work as a writer and collage artist from his home in Spain.

Poem After the Seven Last Words[20]

I

The story of the end, of the last word
of the end, when told, is a story that never ends.
We tell it and retell it—one word, then another
until it seems that no last word is possible,
that none would be bearable. Thus, when the hero
of the story says to himself, as to someone far away,
"Forgive them, for they know not what they do,"
we may feel that he is pleading for us, that we are
the secret life of the story and, as long as his plea
is not answered, we shall be spared. So the story
continues. So we continue. And the end, once more,
becomes the next, and the next after that.

2

There is an island in the dark, a dreamt-of place
where the muttering wind shifts over the white lawns
and riffles the leaves of trees, the high trees
that are streaked with gold and line the walkways there;
and those already arrived are happy to be the silken
remains of something they were but cannot recall;

---

20. Seven expressions attributed to Jesus during his crucifixion, drawn from the Gospels of Matthew, Mark, Luke, and John, though these writings separately record different utterances. Since the sixteenth century these sayings have been widely used in Good Friday services.

they move to the sound of stars, which is also imagined,
but who cares about that; the polished columns they see
may be no more than shafts of sunlight, but for those
who live on and on in the radiance of their remains
this is of little importance. There is an island
in the dark and you will be there, I promise you, you
shall be with me in paradise, in the single season of being,
in the place of forever, you shall find yourself. And there
the leaves will turn and never fall, there the wind
will sing and be your voice as if for the first time.

3

Someday someone will write a story telling
among other things of a parting between mother
and son, of how she wandered off, of how he vanished
in air. But before that happens, it will describe
how their faces shone with a feeble light and how
the son was moved to say, "Woman, look at your son,"
then to a friend nearby, "Son, look at your mother."
At which point the writer will put down his pen
and imagine that while those words were spoken
something else happened, something unusual like
a purpose revealed, a secret exchanged, a truth
to which they, the mother and son, would be bound,
but what it was no one would know. Not even the writer.

4

These are the days of spring when the sky is filled
with the odor of lilac, when darkness becomes desire,
and there is nothing that does not wish to be born;
days when the fate of the present is a breezy fullness,
when the world's great gift for fiction gilds even
the dirt we walk on, and we feel we could live forever
while knowing of course that we can't. Such is our plight.
The master of weather and everything else, if he wants,
can bring forth a dark of a different kind, one hidden
by darkness so deep it cannot be seen. No one escapes.

Not even the man who believed he was chosen to do so,
for when the dark came down he cried out, "Father, Father,
why have you forsaken me?" To which no answer came.

5

To be thirsty. To say, "I thirst."
To close one's eyes and see the giant world
that is born each time the eyes are closed.
To see one's death. To see the darkening clouds
as the tragic cloth of a day of mourning. To be the one
mourned. To open the dictionary of the Beyond and discover
what one suspected, that the only word in it
is nothing. To try to open one's eyes, but not to be
able to. To feel the mouth burn. To feel the sudden
presence of what, again and again, was not said.
To translate it and have it remain unsaid. To know
at last that nothing is more real than nothing.

6

"It is finished," he said. You could hear him say it,
the words almost a whisper, then not even that,
but an echo so faint it seemed no longer to come
from him, but from elsewhere. This was his moment,
his final moment. "It is finished," he said into a vastness
that led to an even greater vastness, and yet all of it
within him. He contained it all. That was the miracle,
to be both large and small in the same instant, to be
like us, but more so, then finally to give up the ghost,
which is what happened. And from the storm that swirled
in his wake a formal nakedness took shape, the truth
of disguise and the mask of belief were joined forever.

7

Back down these stairs to the same scene,
to the moon, the stars, the night wind. Hours pass
and only the harp off in the distance and the wind

moving through it. And soon the sun's gray disk,
darkened by clouds, sailing above. And beyond,
as always, the sea of endless transparence, of utmost
calm, a place of constant beginning that has within it
what no eye has seen, what no ear has heard, what no hand
has touched, what has not arisen in the human heart.
To that place, to the keeper of that place, I commit myself.

Charles Wright
(1935–)

BORN IN PICKWICK DAM, Tennessee, Charles Wright was educated at Davidson
College and the University of Iowa Writers' Workshop. He began to read and write
poetry while stationed in Italy during his four years of service in the U.S. Army, and
published his first collection of poems, *The Grave of the Right Hand,* in 1970. His sec-
ond and third collections, *Hard Freight* (1973) and *Country Music: Selected Early Poems*
(1983), were both nominated for the National Book Award; the latter received the
prize. Wright has published numerous collections of poems, including *Sestets: Poems*
(2009); *Scar Tissue* (2007), which won the International Griffin Poetry Prize; *Black
Zodiac* (1997), which won the Pulitzer Prize; and *Chickamauga* (1995), which won the
Lenore Marshall Prize from the Academy of American Poets. He has also written vol-
umes of criticism, and poetry in translation. His many honors include the American
Academy of Arts and Letters Award of Merit Medal and the Ruth Lilly Poetry Prize.

Stone Canyon Nocturne

Ancient of Days, old friend, no one believes you'll come back.
No one believes in his own life anymore.

The moon, like a dead heart, cold and unstartable, hangs by a thread
At the earth's edge,
Unfaithful at last, splotching the ferns and the pink shrubs.

In the other world, children undo the knots in their tally strings.
They sing songs, and their fingers blear.

And here, where the swan hums in his socket, where the bloodroot
And the belladonna insist on our comforting,
Where the fox in the canyon wall empties our hands, ecstatic for more,

Like a bead of clear oil the Healer revolves through the night wind,
Part eye, part tear, unwilling to recognize us.

As the Trains Roll Through, I Remember an Old Poem

Well, here we are again, old friend, Ancient of Days,
Eyeball to eyeball.
I blink, of course,
                        I blink more than ten thousand times.

Dear ghost, I picture you thus, eventually like
St. Francis in his hair shirt,
                        naked , walking in the winter woods,
Singing his own song in the tongue of the troubadours.

Terrestrial Music

What's up, grand architect of the universe?
                                    The stars are falling,
The moon is failing behind your vaporous laundry,
Planets are losing their names,
                        and darkness is dropping inches beneath the earth.

Down here, we take it in stride.
The horses go on with their chomp and snatch in the long grasses,
The dogs cringe,
                        and coyotes sing in the still woods, back out of sight.

The Gospel According to Yours Truly

Tell me again, Lord, how easy it all is—
                                    renounce this,
Renounce that, and all is a shining—
Tell me again, I'm still here,
                        your quick-lipped and malleable boy.

(Strange how the clouds bump and grind, and the underthings roll,
Strange how the grasses finger and fondle each other—
I renounce them, I renounce them, I renounce them.
                        Gnarly and thin, the nothings don't change . . .)

Hasta la Vista Buckaroo

So many have come and gone, undone
                        like a rhinestone cowboy,
Dazzle and snuff, Lord, dazzle and snuff,
In a two-bit rodeo.

The entrance to hell is just a tiny hole in the ground,
the size of an old pecan, soul-sized, horizon-sized.
Thousands go through it each day before the mist clears
                        thousands one by one you're next.

The Gospel According to Somebody Else

Comfort them all, Lord, comfort their odd shapes
                        and their stranded hair.
They seem so hand-haunted, so hymn-hewn,
In their slow drift toward received form.
Comfort them standing there,
                        then comfort them sitting down—

God knows his own, the old have no tears,
The thickness of winter clouds is the thickness of what's to come.

The Gospel According to St. Someone

Reflected radiance, moon envy, we hang outside
Ourselves like bats,
                        clothed in our flash dreams.
Sunset soaks down to the last leaves of the autumn trees.
Under our heads, the world is a long drop and an ache.
Above us, the sky forks,
                        great road to the left, great road to the right.

Someone will come and walk on his hands
                    through the dry grass to the altar.
Someone will take the wafer, someone will take the wine
And walk back through the gravestones.
Succor us, someone,
Let us drink from your mouth and let us eat from your tongue.

Eternal penny, counterfeit truth, score us and pay us off.
Buried November, read us our rites.
Salvation, worry our sins.
Awake, we all share the same world,
                    asleep, we're each in our own.
Lay me down, Lord, let me sleep.

Charles Simic
(1938–)

DUŠAN "CHARLES" SIMIĆ WAS born in Belgrade, Yugoslavia, and survived World War II to emigrate with his mother and brother to America, where they joined his father in Chicago. He was drafted into the U.S. Army in 1961, shortly after publishing his first poems at the age of twenty-one. His first collection, *What the Grass Says,* was published in 1967. Since then, he has published more than sixty books of poetry and prose in English and in translation, including *The World Doesn't End: Prose Poems,* for which he won the 1990 Pulitzer Prize. His *Selected Poems: 1963–2003* won the 2005 International Griffin Poetry Prize. His other honors and awards include a MacArthur Fellowship and the Wallace Stevens Award from the Academy of American Poets.

Prayer

You who know only the present moment,
O Lord,
You who remember nothing
Of what came before,
Who admire the beauty
Of a dead child,

The lovers embraced
In a field of flowers.

The game of chess
And the cracks on the poorhouse wall
Are equally interesting
And incomprehensible to You
Who know what it's like to be a tiger,
A mouse in the instant of danger,
And know nothing of my regrets,
My solitudes,
And my infinite horror of You.

Psalm

You've been a long time making up your mind,
O Lord, about these madmen
Running the world. Their reach is long
And their claws must have frightened you.

One of them found me with his shadow.
The day turned chill. I dangled
Between terror and valor
In the darkest corner of my son's bedroom.

I sought with my eyes, You in whom I do not believe.
You've been busy making the flowers pretty,
The lambs run after their mother,
Or perhaps you haven't been doing even that?

It was spring. The killers were full of sport
And merriment, and your divines
Were right at their side, to make sure
Our final goodbyes were said properly.

To the One Upstairs

Boss of all bosses of the universe.
Mr. know-it-all, wheeler-dealer, wire-puller,
And whatever else you're good at.
Go ahead, shuffle your zeros tonight.

Dip in ink the comets' tails.
Staple the night with starlight.

You'd be better off reading coffee dregs,
Thumbing the pages of the Farmer's Almanac.
But no! You love to put on airs,
And cultivate your famous serenity
While you sit behind your big desk
With zilch in your in-tray, zilch
In your out-tray,
And all of eternity spread around you.

Doesn't it give you the creeps
To hear them begging you on their knees,
Sputtering endearments,
As if you were an inflatable, life-size doll?
Tell them to button up and go to bed.
Stop pretending you're too busy to take notice.

Your hands are empty and so are your eyes.
There's nothing to put your signature to,
Even if you knew your own name,
Or believed the ones I keep inventing,
As I scribble this note to you in the dark.

Peter Cooley
(1940–)

PETER COOLEY WAS BORN IN Detroit, Michigan, into a family with no religious persuasion. He attended Cranbrook School for Boys but left after his junior year to attend Shimer College. While on his senior year in Paris he visited the Russian Orthodox Church with his White Russian émigré landlady and, after dabbling with Roman Catholicism, was baptized and confirmed in the Episcopal Church. He received his M.A. in art and literature from the University of Chicago, and his Ph.D. in English from the University of Iowa, where he was a student in the Writers' Workshop. He has published nine books of poetry, most recently *Night Bus to the Afterlife* (2013). Cooley has taught at Tulane University since 1975.

Poem Choosing to Remain Unfinished

Wilder, wilder, and wilder all my thoughts
looking out to dawn, not risen yet!
Possibility! Out of this darkness
something will come in which I'll throw myself,
mantle of new, unending life in him
and some small favor I'll perform today
by which I'll be the lame man who can walk,
the blind seeing again, the dumb guy
speaking in a tongue never known till now.
Darkness is the first miracle, oh God.

Louise Glück
(1943–)

LOUISE GLÜCK WAS BORN IN New York City and grew up on Long Island. The author of eleven books of poems, including *The Wild Iris* (1992), *Meadowlands* (1996), *Averno* (2006), *A Village Life* (2009), and *Poems, 1962–2012* (2012), and a collection of essays, *Proofs and Theories: Essays on Poetry* (1994), Glück was named the twelfth Poet Laureate of the United States in 2003. Glück's many awards include the Pulitzer Prize, the National Book Critics Circle Award, the Bollingen Prize for Poetry, and the Wallace Stevens Award from the Academy of American Poets. She teaches at Yale University and lives in Cambridge, Massachusetts.

Matins

Forgive me if I say I love you: the powerful
are always lied to since the weak are always
driven by panic. I cannot love
what I can't conceive, and you disclose
virtually nothing: are you like the hawthorn tree,
always the same thing in the same place,
or are you more the foxglove, inconsistent, first springing up
a pink spike on the slope behind the daisies,

and the next year, purple in the rose garden? You must see
it is useless to us, this silence that promotes belief
you must be all things, the foxglove and the hawthorn tree,
the vulnerable rose and tough daisy—we are left to think
you couldn't possibly exist. Is this
what you mean us to think, does this explain
the silence of the morning,
the crickets not yet rubbing their wings, the cats
not fighting in the yard?

Matins

I see it is with you as with the birches:
I am not to speak to you
in the personal way. Much
has passed between us. Or
was it always only
on the one side? I am
at fault, at fault, I asked you
to be human—I am no needier
than other people. But the absence
of all feeling, of the least
concern for me—I might as well go on
addressing the birches,
as in my former life: let them
do their worst, let them
bury me with the Romantics,
their pointed yellow leaves
falling and covering me.

Matins

You want to know how I spend my time?
I walk the front lawn, pretending
to be weeding. You ought to know
I'm never weeding, on my knees, pulling
clumps of clover from the flower beds: in fact
I'm looking for courage, for some evidence

my life will change, though
it takes forever, checking
each clump for the symbolic
leaf, and soon the summer is ending, already
the leaves turning, always the sick trees
going first, the dying turning
brilliant yellow, while a few dark birds perform
their curfew of music. You want to see my hands?
As empty now as at the first note.
Or was the point always
to continue without a sign?

Vespers

More than you love me, very possibly
you love the beasts of the field, even,
possibly, the field itself, in August dotted
with wild chicory and aster:
I know. I have compared myself
to those flowers, their range of feeling
so much smaller and without issue; also to white sheep,
actually gray: I am uniquely
suited to praise you. Then why
torment me? I study the hawkweed,
the buttercup protected from the grazing herd
by being poisonous: is pain
your gift to make me
conscious in my need of you, as though
I must need you to worship you,
or have you abandoned me
in favor of the field, the stoic lambs turning
silver in twilight; waves of wild aster and chicory shining
pale blue and deep blue, since you already know
how like your raiment it is.

Vespers

I know what you planned, what you meant to do, teaching me
to love the world, making it impossible
to turn away completely, to shut it out completely ever again—
it is everywhere; when I close my eyes,
birdsong, scent of lilac in early spring, scent of summer roses:
you mean to take it away, each flower, each connection with earth—
why would you wound me, why would you want me
desolate in the end, unless you wanted me so starved for hope
I would refuse to see that finally
nothing was left to me, and would believe instead
in the end you were left to me.

Ira Sadoff
(1945–)

IRA SADOFF WAS BORN IN Brooklyn and grew up in New York City, the son of
Russian Jewish immigrants. Intending to become a lawyer, he graduated from Cornell
as a sociology and psychology major, but then received an M.F.A. from the University
of Oregon. "Orphans" is part of a metaphysical sequence in his collection *True Faith*
(2012). He has published seven collections of poems, a novel, and a critical book, *History Matters: Contemporary Poetry on the Margins of Culture* (2009). *An Ira Sadoff Reader:
Selected Poetry and Prose* was published in 1992. Former poetry editor of the *Antioch
Review* and co-founder of *Seneca Review,* Sadoff has received fellowships from the National Endowment for the Arts and the Guggenheim Foundation.

Orphans

I cannot fawn
Dear Lord—oh I see
You tinker

With temperatures,
Bringing loves
For some to bury.

My friends
The diasporas
Shake a few fists

At your favored clouds
About to storm.
I won't deny

Parishioners' joys—
With faces both
Coming and going.

I too want a bliss
Like theirs:
Blankened or beautied.

Jorie Graham
(1950–)

JORIE GRAHAM WAS BORN IN New York City, daughter of a journalist and a sculptor. She was raised in Rome, Italy, and studied philosophy at the Sorbonne in Paris before attending New York University in filmmaking. She is the author of a number of collections of poetry, including *Place* (2012), *Sea Change* (2009), *Overlord* (2005), and *Never* (2003). Her volume of selected poems, *The Dream of the Unified Field*, won the 1996 Pulitzer Prize. Recipient of a MacArthur Fellowship, Graham teaches at Harvard University.

Praying *(Attempt of May 9 '03)*

I don't know where to start. I don't think my face
in my hands is right. Please don't let us destroy
Your world. No *the* world. I know I know nothing. I know I
can't use you like this. It feels better if I'm on
my knees, if my eyes are pressed shut as I can see
the other things, the tiniest ones. Which can still escape
us. Am I human. Please show me mercy. No please show

a way. If I look up all the possibility that you
might be there goes away. I need to be curled up this
way, face pressed, knees pulled up tight. I know
there are other ways, less protected, more expressive of
surrender. But here I can feel the whole crushing
emptiness on my back. Especially on my shoulders.
I thought just now how that emptiness could be my wings.
That you were there, maybe, laughing. That is the room above me,
here, before dawn, its two windows black, this
pillow pressed down hard against me, how it, how all of it,
made up the wings. There is a reason I
have to go fast. Have to try to slide into
something I can feel the beginning of. Right
here in my pushed-down face. Right
where eyes are pressed
so sleep doesn't go there anymore.
And the mirror—well that is another way if you wish. If you
look in for a very long time. But here, I did this other thing
again. (Here) (I write the open parenthesis, press my face,
try again, then lift, close) (then this clause to explain)
(to whom?) (always wanting to be forgiven) (not seen) (no)—See,
it is already being lost here, the channel is filling
in, these words—ah—these, these—
how I don't want *them* to be the problem too, there are
so many other obstacles, can't these be just a part of
my body, look (put my head down again) (am
working in total dark) (maybe this will not be
legible)—my ears covered to go further—maybe
if I had begun otherwise, maybe if I had
been taught to believe in You, I needed evidence,
others seem not to need it, they do not seem to me
graced, but yesterday when I asked Don he said yes, he
                              was sure, yes, yes,
everything was His plan, so it is a lapse of faith
to worry, you will have noted I cannot say "Your
plan," and now, as if dawn were creeping in, the
feeling of the reader is coming in, the one towards which
this tilts, like the plant I watched a long time yesterday the
head of, and then the stem itself,
to see if it turned towards the light as the light arrived,

I would say it did, very slightly, and I
                              could not *see it,*
though I never lifted my gaze, and tried very hard to blink only
when physically impossible not to, and yes, yes, in the end it
was in a different direction, I had marked where we started
so I knew for sure, although of course I know nothing, I could
begin this story anywhere, maybe I will open my
eyes now, although I have gotten nowhere and will
                              find myself
still just here, in the middle of my exactly given years, on
my knees naked in my room before dawn, the pillow
wet of course but what of it, nothing nothing comes of it,
                              out there where the
garbage truck will begin any second now, where I
can feel the whitening reefs (which
I have only read about) (if that means anything) (yes/no) under there where
                                                       they are,

the waters filtering through them, the pH wrong, the
terrible bleaching occurring, the temperature, what
is a few degrees, how fine are we supposed
to be, I am your instrument if only you would use me, a
degree a fraction of a degree in the beautiful thin
water, flowing through, finding as it is meant to *every*
hollow, and going in, carrying its devastation in, but looking so
simple, and a blue I have never seen, with light still in its
body as light is in mine here I believe, yes,
light a chemical analysis would reveal,
something partaking of the same photons
in this pillow, this paint on the wall, this wall,
which if I open my eyes will be five inches from my face,
which (the coral reefs having caverns) I try to go into—
because I can make myself very small is that a gift from you,
I think it might be one of the great gifts, that I can *make*
myself very small and go in, in from this room, down into the
fibrous crenellations of the reef, which if you look close are formed
by one node clipping onto an other, and then
the rounding-up as the damage occurs, as the weight is lost, now the coral
                              in with the
trucks, pipeknock kicking in, it is beginning
again—oh—when I open my eyes I see two white lines,

vertical, incandescent, I will keep all the knowledge
away I think, I try to think, I will keep
the knowing away, the lines seem to come out of nowhere,
they do not descend nor do they rise,
just gleam side by side in the small piece of glance
my two eyes hold in their close-up
vision. There is a flood. There are these two lines.
Then the sun moves up a notch, though still in the in-
visible, and I see, I see it is the 12-ounce glass, its body
illumined twice, white strokes where the very first
light has entered, here, I look again, it seems to gleam, it
gleams, it is the empty glass.

Marie Howe
(1950–)

MARIE HOWE WAS BORN THE oldest child of nine in Rochester, New York. She
attended Sacred Heart Convent School and the University of Windsor, and received an
M.F.A. from Columbia University. Her first collection, *The Good Thief* (1988), was
chosen for the National Poetry Series and received the Lavan Younger Poets Prize
from the Academy of American Poets. Later works include *What the Living Do* (1997),
an elegiac response to her brother John's death from an AIDS-related illness, and *The
Kingdom of Ordinary Time* (2008). She co-edited (with Michael Klein) the essay anthol-
ogy *In the Company of My Solitude: American Writing from the AIDS Pandemic* (1994).
Howe has taught at Sarah Lawrence College, Columbia, and New York University.

Prayer

Every day I want to speak with you. And every day something more important
calls for my attention—the drugstore, the beauty products, the luggage

I need to buy for the trip.
Even now I can hardly sit here

among the falling piles of paper and clothing, the garbage trucks outside
already screeching and banging.

The mystics say you are as close as my own breath.
Why do I flee from you?

My days and nights pour through me like complaints
and become a story I forgot to tell.

Help me. Even as I write these words I am planning
to rise from the chair as soon as I finish this sentence.

James Galvin
(1951–)

BORN IN CHICAGO, ILLINOIS, James Galvin is the author of seven collections of poetry, including *As Is* (2009) and *X* (2003). He has also published a novel, *Fencing the Sky* (2000), and a book of nonfiction, *The Meadow* (1993). He is the recipient of awards from the Lannan Foundation, the Lila Wallace–Reader's Digest Foundation, and the Guggenheim Foundation. He teaches at the University of Iowa Writers' Workshop.

Prayer

O, beginning, daughters of the earth await the sons of heaven, and
vice versa.
                    They all practice trigger-happiness and chicken scratch.

They practice duration and meltdown.
                                        They primp in your glass.

You think that's funny?
                    Never mind.
                                        It's getting really cold in here.
        Who makes the introductions if not you?
                                                Who initiates the
bliss, I ask?
                    Have I not left footprints in hell?
                                                        Mind-out-of-time, I
remain a false apology.
                    There.

All better now?
You gave me a
body so I could learn to live without it, right?
This poem is just a
way of minding my own business.
It flourishes in your darkness.

This poem is not what you think.
It's what thinks you.
It thinks the
only hope we have, bombarding us with zeros, sending us our mail-order teeth.
Initiate the bliss, O, ending.
Take whatever you
want, and don't forget to close the door.

Mark Jarman
(1952–)

MARK JARMAN WAS BORN IN Mount Sterling, Kentucky. His childhood was divided between Scotland and Southern California, where his father served in churches. He earned a B.A. from the University of California, Santa Cruz, in 1974 and an M.F.A. from the University of Iowa in 1976. He is the author of numerous collections of poetry, including *Bone Fires: New and Selected Poems* (2011), *Unholy Sonnets* (2000), and *Questions for Ecclesiastes* (1997), which won the 1998 Lenore Marshall Poetry Prize from the Academy of American Poets. He has also published two books of essays, *The Secret of Poetry* (2001) and *Body and Soul* (2002). He is Centennial Professor of English at Vanderbilt University.

from *Questions for Ecclesiastes*

Dear God, Our Heavenly Father, Gracious Lord,
Mother Love and Maker, Light Divine,
Atomic Fingertip, Cosmic Design,
First Letter of the Alphabet, Last Word,
Mutual Satisfaction, Cash Award,

Auditor Who Approves Our Bottom Line,
Examiner Who Says That We Are Fine,
Oasis That All Sands Are Running Toward.

I can say almost anything about you,
O Big Idea, and with each epithet,
Create new reasons to believe or doubt you,
Black Hole, White Hole, Presidential Jet.
But what's the anything I must leave out? You
Solve nothing but the problems that I set.

from *Unholy Sonnets*

Please be the driver bearing down behind,
Or swerve in front and slow down to a crawl,
Or leave a space to lure me in, then pull
Ahead, cutting me off, and blast your horn.
Please climb the mountain with me, tailgating
And trying to overtake on straightaways.
Let nightfall make us both pick up the pace,
Trading positions with our high beams glaring.
And when we have exhausted sanity
And fuel, and smoked our engines, then, please stop,
Lurching onto the shoulder of the road,
And get out, raging, and walk up to me,
Giving me time to feel my stomach drop,
And see you face to face, and say, "My Lord!"

Alan Shapiro
(1952–)

ALAN SHAPIRO GREW UP IN Brookline, Massachusetts, and attended Brandeis University. Now William R. Kenan, Jr. Distinguished Professor of English and Creative Writing at the University of North Carolina at Chapel Hill, and a member of the American Academy of Arts and Sciences, Shapiro has published eleven books of poetry, one novel, two memoirs, a book of critical essays, and translations of *The Oresteia* by Aeschylus and *The Trojan Women* by Euripides. His honors include the Kingsley Tufts Award, a Guggenheim Fellowship, and an award in literature from the American Academy of Arts and Letters.

Prayer on the Temple Steps

Devious guide, strange parent,
what are you
but the movable ways
I lose you by?
Opulent honeycomb
of nowhere
where the bee-ghosts cluster,
hymning your each cell
with all the sweetness that you hold
from me,
      so I might know
instead the fitful aspic
of this readiness—
           what is it
you bring out of the veils
of air but this, these words—
gate opening on to you
and burning sword
above it turning
every way I turn.

Gjertrud Schnackenberg
(1953–)

BORN IN TACOMA, WASHINGTON, Schnackenberg graduated from Mount Holyoke College. She is the author of six collections of poetry, including *Heavenly Questions* (2010), which won the Griffin Prize in 2011. Other books include *The Throne of Labdacus* (2005), *A Gilded Lapse of Time* (1992), and *The Lamplit Answer* (1985). She was awarded the Rome Prize in Literature from the American Academy in Rome and the Berlin Prize from the American Academy in Berlin. She has been awarded fellowships from the National Endowment for the Arts and the Guggenheim Foundation, and received the Amy Lowell Poetry Travelling Scholarship in 1984. Schnackenberg was married to the American philosopher Robert Nozick until his death in 2002.

Supernatural Love

My father at the dictionary stand
Touches the page to fully understand
The lamplit answer, tilting in his hand

His slowly scanning magnifying lens,
A blurry, glistening circle he suspends
Above the word "Carnation." Then he bends

So near his eyes are magnified and blurred,
One finger on the miniature word,
As if he touched a single key and heard

A distant, plucked, infinitesimal string,
"The obligation due to every thing
That's smaller than the universe." I bring

My sewing needle close enough that I
Can watch my father through the needle's eye,
As through a lens ground for a butterfly

Who peers down flower-hallways toward a room
Shadowed and fathomed as this study's gloom
Where, as a scholar bends above a tomb

To read what's buried there, he bends to pore
Over the Latin blossom. I am four,
I spill my pins and needles on the floor

Trying to stitch "Beloved" X by X.
My dangerous, bright needle's point connects
Myself illiterate to this perfect text

I cannot read. My father puzzles why
It is my habit to identify
Carnations as "Christ's flowers," knowing I

Can give no explanation but "Because."
Word-roots blossom in speechless messages
The way the thread behind my sampler does

Where following each X, I awkward move
My needle through the word whose root is love.
He reads, "A pink variety of Clove,

Carnatio, the Latin, meaning flesh."
As if the bud's essential oils brush
Christ's fragrance through the room, the iron-fresh

Odor carnations have floats up to me,
A drifted, secret, bitter ecstasy,
The stems squeak in my scissors, *Child, it's me,*

He turns the page to "Clove" and reads aloud:
"The clove, a spice, dried from a flower-bud."
Then twice, as if he hasn't understood,

He reads, "From French, for *clou,* meaning a nail."
He gazes, motionless, "Meaning a nail."
The incarnation blossoms, flesh and nail,

I twist my threads like stems into a knot
And smooth "Beloved," but my needle caught
Within the threads, *Thy blood so dearly bought,*

The needle strikes my finger to the bone.
I lift my hand, it is myself I've sewn,
The flesh laid bare, the threads of blood my own,

I lift my hand in startled agony
And call upon his name, "Daddy Daddy"—
My father's hand touches the injury

As lightly as he touched the page before,
Where incarnation bloomed from roots that bore
The flowers I called Christ's when I was four.

Scott Cairns
(1954–)

BORN IN TACOMA, WASHINGTON, Scott Cairns teaches at University of Missouri. His poems and essays have been anthologized in multiple editions of *Best American Spiritual Writing*. His books include *Compass of Affection: Poems New and Selected* (2007), the memoir *Short Trip to the Edge* (2006), *Love's Immensity* (translations and adaptations of Christian mystics, 2007), and a book-length essay, *The End of Suffering* (2009). He received a Guggenheim Fellowship in 2006. A convert to Eastern Orthodox Christianity, Cairns wrote a spiritual memoir, *Slow Pilgrim,* that is being translated for a Greek edition.

The Spiteful Jesus

Not the one whose courtesy
and kiss unsought are nonetheless
bestowed. Instead, the largely
more familiar blasphemy
borne to us in the little boat
that first cracked rock at Plymouth
—petty, plainly man-inflected
demi-god established as a club
with which our paling generations
might be beaten to a bland consistency.

He is angry. He is just. And while
he may have died for us,
it was not gladly. The way
his prophets talk, you'd think
the whole affair had left him
queerly out of sorts, unspeakably
indignant, more than a little
needy, and quick to dish out
just deserts. I saw him when,
as a boy in church, I first
met souls in hell. I made him

for a corrupt, corrupting fiction when
my own father (mortal that he was)
forgave me everything, unasked.

Nicholas Samaras
(1954–)

NICHOLAS SAMARAS IS OF Greek origin. He was born in Foxton, Cambridgeshire, England, and brought back to his parental home on the Greek island of Patmos. He was raised and educated in Greece, England, Wales, Switzerland, Italy, Austria, Germany, Yugoslavia, and Jerusalem. He has since lived in thirteen states in America, and he writes from a place of permanent exile. His father is a Greek Orthodox priest and he follows that denomination. His first book, *Hands of the Saddlemaker* (1992), earned the Yale Series of Younger Poets Award. His next book, *American Psalm, World Psalm*, will appear in 2014.

Benediction

For what we are given.
For being mindful of what we are given.

For those who grieve and those who celebrate.
For those who remain grateful in the face of everything.

For the assembly of words that links us together.
For individual speech that becomes speech shared.

For the transformations a written page may effect in us.
For those who pay attention.

For the teachers who gave us the chrysalis of language.
For the comrades of the heart who left us signposts.

For the parent who gave us the one ethic of discipline.
For ourselves who may take discipline to heart, and not resent it.

For the second chance that is the writing down.
For those who know that half of poetry is silence.

For the language of breath, and the breath that is prayer.
For those who wake to light, and know the depths of sacrament.

For this common meal, and us who bow our heads and partake.
For those who remember that "So be it" is also written

Amen.

Lucie Brock-Broido
(1956–)

BORN IN PITTSBURGH, Pennsylvania, Lucie Brock-Broido is the author of the poetry collections *A Hunger* (1988), *The Master Letters* (1994), *Trouble in Mind* (2004), and *Stay Illusion* (2013). She served as editor of the posthumously collected poems of Thomas James, *Letters to a Stranger* (2008). She has been the recipient of awards from the Guggenheim Foundation, the National Endowment for the Arts, and the American Academy of Arts and Letters. She is a professor in the School of the Arts at Columbia University, where she directs the graduate program in poetry. She lives in New York City and in Cambridge, Massachusetts.

The One Theme of Which Everything Else Is a Variation

    Innocence is a catarrh of the mind, distressed,
As finite as the grade school teacher in Sierra Leone

    Whose arms were axed off only at the hand, first left
And then the right, and then his mouth as he was making noise

    And should be shut. A man can learn to speak again,
But never pray.
              Wisdom is experience bundled, with prosthetic wrists.

    I cannot master anymore the surgical or magical,
I do not know how the specific punishments or amputations are so

    Meted out. When you delete a wing or limb
From a creature's form, it will inevitably cry out against this

Taking, but in the end it will become grievously docile,
Shut; far gone old god, you have been plain.

Let me list here the things I wish to bring with me,
For the life after this or that. I will not go back the way I came,

Carrying my clay Picasso and my tin of ginger,
Flying toward home on my way away from home.

If I am lucky in this life, here, I will go on
Being whole, and speak again old god, I will be plain.

Amy Gerstler
(1956–)

AMY GERSTLER WAS BORN IN San Diego, California. Her most recent books of poetry include *Dearest Creature* (2009), *Ghost Girl* (2004), and *Medicine* (2000). Her collection *Bitter Angel* received a National Book Critics Circle Award in 1991. Her work has appeared in several volumes of *Best American Poetry* and in *The Norton Anthology of Postmodern American Poetry*. Of her spiritual background Gerstler has said, "I feel sympathetic connections to Buddhism, Sufism, animism, the Druse religion, Hinduism, Judaism, Catholicism, and many other ancient and contemporary world religions, especially those involving some form of reincarnation."

A Non-Christian on Sunday

Now we heathens have the town to ourselves.
We lie around, munching award-winning pickles
and hunks of coarse, seeded bread smeared
with soft, sweet cheese. The streets seem
deserted, as if Godzilla had been sighted
on the horizon, kicking down skyscrapers
and flattening cabs. Only two people
are lined up to see a popular movie
in which the good guy and the bad guy trade
faces. Churches burst into song. Trees wish
for a big wind. Burnt bacon and domestic tension

scent the air. So do whiffs of lawn mower exhaust
mixed with the colorless blood of clipped hedges.
For whatever's about to come crashing down
on our heads, be it bliss-filled or heinous,
make us grateful, OK? Hints of the savior's
flavor buzz on our tongues, like crumbs
of a sleeping pill shaped like a snowflake.

Jacqueline Osherow
(1956–)

JEWISH POET JACQUELINE Osherow was born in Philadelphia, Pennsylvania. Educated at Harvard-Radcliffe and Princeton, she has published six collections of poetry, including *Dead Men's Praise* (1999), *The Hoopoe's Crown* (2005), and *Whitethorn* (2011). Recipient of grants from the Guggenheim Foundation, the Ingram Merrill Foundation, and the National Endowment for the Arts, she also received the Witter Bynner Prize. Osherow is Distinguished Professor of English at the University of Utah.

from Scattered Psalms
I (HANDIWORK/GLORY)

To the Conductor: A song of David.
The heavens declare the glory of God,
the firmament tells His handiwork.
Day on day utters speech,
night on night announces knowledge.
There is no speech and there are no words
without hearing their voice.

(PSALM 19:1–4)

Dare I begin: a song of Jacqueline?
But what, from my hearts of hearts, do I say?
Not that it matters, since every line
Will murmur with the heavens, sotto voce,

The knowledgeable night, the chatty day,
Their information constant, simultaneous:
The glory of God and then His handiwork.
Indulge them: theirs is the undiluted lyric
And we can't utter speech without its voice . . .

So how hard could it be to write a Psalm?
Think of David's fairly modest territory,
There are other trees than cedar, willow, palm
(The handiwork of God and then His glory),
So many kinds of praise he couldn't know:
The ferns on their unfinished violins,
The jonquils on their giddy, rail trombones,
The aspens shaking silver tambourines,
Then yellow-gold ones, then letting go.

What did David know about such changes?
The top arc of the spectrum gone berserk?
That when some skyward barricade unhinges
Without even a breath, a noise, a spark
(The glory of God and His handiwork),
No single earthly thing stays as it was,
Except insofar as it still sings.
Hand me an instrument of ten strings;
Everything was put on earth to praise.

The crocodile. The cheetah. Hallelujah.
The nightingale. The lynx. The albatross.
The pine tree. Fir tree. Glacier. Hallelujah.
The hornet's diligence. The gibbon's voice.
The pale reprieve of snow. Hallelujah.
The volcano's unrestricted exultation.
The forest's lazy ease. The desert's fury.
Our own extraneous efforts at creation.
(The handiwork of God and then His glory.)

13 (SPACE PSALM)

Let stars reverse their courses—hallelujah—
Let planets flaunt their necklaces of ice—
Let suns confound eclipses—hallelujah—
Let moons' scavenged radiance rejoice—

Let galaxies recluster—hallelujah—
Let nebulae uncloud and celebrate—
Let meteors spread banners—hallelujah—
Let black holes unleash astonished light—

Let comets jump their orbits—hallelujah—
To jangle inadvertent atmospheres
With rumors of the distance—hallelujah—
Anecdotes—songs—suspicions—prayers

Bruce Beasley
(1958–)

BRUCE BEASLEY WAS BORN IN Thomaston, Georgia, and raised in Macon, Georgia. He studied at Oberlin College, Columbia University, and the University of Virginia, and converted to Catholicism in 1983. He is the author of seven collections of poems, including *Summer Mystagogia* (winner of the 1996 Colorado Prize), *Lord Brain* (2005), *The Corpse Flower: New and Selected Poems* (2007), and, most recently, *Theophobia* (2012). He is a professor of English at Western Washington University.

Having Read the Holy Spirit's Wikipedia
I.

Glossolalic and disincarnate, interfere
in me, interleave me
and leave me through my breathing: like some third

person conjugation I've rewhispered
in a language I keep trying to learn, a tongue
made only of verbs, and all its verbs irregular.

2.

I've been Googling You lately, for some slipped-
loose theoinwardness You've come
to mean, some comfort of Third Person

held as breath, but I can't keep
straight sometimes which one of You
is You:

there's One who fractures off from light
as light, I know, and One
(is that One You?) *eternally begotten,* so never not at just that instant being born.

3.

Being-Without-a-Body, get
to me
and shiver along the nerves

like the *Toxoplasma gondii* parasite
that works its way deep up a rat's brain
and lays its cysts all through the amygdala,

unsnips the dendrites from networks
of instinctive fear that repel
the rat from cat pheromones, and reconnects

the wiring so the rat's testes swell
with attraction at the smell
of cat-piss and so urge the rat straight toward

the predator's mouth, since a cat-gut's
the only place where toxoplasma can breed, and the parasite leaves
the cat's body in the feces another rat will eat

and that rat's brain will also be restrung
from dread to lust for what consumes it: Spirit
of Holy Fear, who's afraid?

4.

If You're in me I don't feel it.
Say Your verb, Your *let-there-be*
deep in *my* amygdala's fear-circuits, speak in me

through the X of Lexapro, its
self-cancellable crux:
tell me about light-from-light, serotonin-

from-synaptic-cleft, tell something about a long
half-life and Your charged
indwelling in the cells.

Here comes Pentecost, that
anti-Easter (one of You up-
vanished, and One come

down, in flame-
from-lingual-flame, that sacral
lick of redescent).

Say me Your babelwords then,
self-tripled One, under
the mind's reruined ziggurat.

5.

Because doves have no gall bladder
they have come
to stand for mildness. They stand

for You, warble, blue
underwing-flash and quaver, con-
and in-substantial

Squab of the Holy Ghost.
Some Ark's scraping some
mud-ridged, just-dried Ararat now

inside me, some dove's
dropped an olive sprig on its bow, meant to stand
once more for the passing of the gall.

6.

Blood-dad,
my son's friend asked me, are you
his blood-dad?

You're no blood-dad, not Yahweh's
hail-curse or locust-flock or Sodom-
smolder, nor Christ-

of-Blisters with His gall-cup
and Shroud-stare, Holy Foreskin
over whose ring of blood You dove-

coo and brood,
not the Father from whom You merely,
mystically, continuously, proceed—

I'm no blood-dad, either, I'm adoptive, Joseph's
not Jesus' birth-dad, my son told me
when I read him the Nativity

"for that which is conceived in her
is of the Holy Ghost":
so Jesus' dad was just like you . . .

7.

Through "spiration" and not "generation" You are said
to *proceed*, but the question of Who ex-pires You—
Father or Son, or both—has led to a thousand years of anathema and schism.

The Wikipedia on just that question goes twenty pages.
Ungenerative, ungenerated, You're like me: recessive and proceeding nonetheless,
      like the wick's
wax-wet and sizzle as it hardens into self-douse.

8.

Explorer has encountered
an unexpected error
and needs to close.

9.

Fricative, constrictive, like a gush
of burnt scrapwood smoke from a neighbor's yard,
its wintercleared thornbushes and rattlesticks in firepit,

greencrackle and sap-hiss, late March Lent-smoke,
ash-smack in back of tongue and eyes, forehead-and-cheek streak of char.
Numinous, pneumatic, Who

bloweth where You listeth, Whom
the world will never know, list to blow
down me.

Michael Chitwood
(1958–)

BORN IN ROCKY MOUNT, Virginia, Michael Chitwood is a freelance writer. He
teaches at the University of North Carolina at Chapel Hill and is the author of a num-
ber of books of poetry, short stories, and essays, including *Salt Works* (1992), *The
Weave Room* (1998), *Finishing Touches* (2006), and *Poor-Mouth Jubilee* (2010). *Gospel
Road Going*, a collection of poems about his native Appalachia, was published in 2002.
His collection of essays, *Hitting Below the Bible Belt*, appeared in 1998.

Here I Am, Lord

The ribbed black of the umbrella
is an argument for the existence of God,

that little shelter
we carry with us

and may forget
beside a chair

in a committee meeting
we did not especially want to attend.

What a beautiful word, umbrella.
A shade to be opened.

Like a bat's wing, scalloped.
It shivers.

A drum head
beaten by the silver sticks

of rain
and I do not have mine

and so the rain showers me.

Jane Mead
(1958–)

JANE MEAD WAS BORN IN Baltimore, Maryland, and attended Vassar College, Syr-
acuse University, and the University of Iowa. Although she comes from generations
of prominent scientists, men and women, she was raised with a worldview in which the
wonders of science and the mysteries of religion were mutually confirming. Christened
and brought up in the Unitarian Church, she still attends occasionally, and is spiritual
and somewhat reclusive by nature. She is the author of four collections of poetry and
the recipient of grants and awards from the Guggenheim, Lannan, and Whiting foun-
dations. For many years Poet-in-Residence at Wake Forest University, Mead farms in
northern California and teaches in the low-residency M.F.A. program at Drew Uni-
versity in New Jersey.

Concerning That Prayer I Cannot Make

Jesus, I am cruelly lonely
and I do not know what I have done
nor do I suspect that you will answer me.

And, what is more, I have spent
these bare months bargaining
with my soul as if I could make her

promise to love me when now it seems
that what I meant when I said "soul"
was that the river reflects
the railway bridge just as the sky
says it should—it speaks *that* language.

I do not know who you are.

I come here every day
to be beneath this bridge,
to sit beside this river,
so I *must* have seen the way
the clouds just slide
under the rusty arch—
without snagging on the bolts,
how they are borne along on the dark water—
I must have noticed their fluent speed
and also how that tattered blue T-shirt
remains snagged on the crown
of the mostly sunk dead tree
despite the current's constant pulling.
Yes, somewhere in my mind there must
be the image of a sky blue T-shirt, caught,
and the white islands of ice flying by
and the light clouds flying slowly
under the bridge, though today the river's
fully melted. I must have seen.

But I did not see.

I am not equal to my longing.
Somewhere there should be a place
the exact shape of my emptiness—
there should be a place
responsible for taking one back.
The river, of course, has no mercy—
it just lifts the dead fish
toward the sea.

Of course, of course.

What I *meant* when I said "soul"
was that there should be a place.

On the far bank the warehouse lights
blink red, then green, and all the yellow
machines with their rusted scoops and lifts
sit under a thin layer of sunny frost.

And look—
my own palm—
there, slowly rocking.
It is *my* pale palm—
palm where a black pebble
is turning and turning.

       Listen—
       all you bare trees
       burrs
       brambles
       pile of twigs
       red and green lights flashing
       muddy bottle shards
       shoe half buried—listen

       listen, I am holy.

Carl Phillips
(1959–)

CARL PHILLIPS WAS BORN IN Everett, Washington. Raised for much of his child-hood on Air Force bases, he eventually settled in Massachusetts, attending Harvard and the University of Massachusetts, and teaching high school Latin for eight years. After the publication of his first book, *In the Blood*, in 1992, Phillips attended Boston University's writing program, then left for Washington University in St. Louis, where he has taught since 1993. He is the author of twelve books of poetry, including the Kingsley Tufts Award–winning *The Tether* (2001), *Double Shadow* (2011), and *Silverchest* (2013). He has also translated Sophocles' *Philoctetes* (2003), and written a book of prose, *Coin of the Realm: Essays on the Life and Art of Poetry* (2004).

from The Blue Castrato

1 TO HIS SAVIOR IN CHRIST

If I did not, as I do, know well
to love you first, I'd love my voice
instead, cause you to yield the throne
whose impossibly precious batting I
could sing all day and never start
to know—it is blasphemy or worse
even to think it (*Domine, me—*
ut placet—me retine).[21] I'd love
my voice that is all I need to know
of a clean, a clear, that I am promised
will never leave me, even should
I want it. Who could want it? Even
in this your difficult field, your vale,
I sing—and see? The grasses open.

5 TO HIS SAVIOR IN CHRIST

Haven't I hymned your praise enough?
What I would not, given the choice, have given,
I gave: my voice is token. For you—
for years, what made for a life—I sang,
I have caused entire crowds to cry
out to you *Uncle;* as pigeons to home,
they sought and came to a kind of resting
upon your deep/your fair/your not-
to-be-understood-in-this-life-
time breast. Forgive me if I say
I'm sometimes sorry. I've licked the broad
tracks that your grace leaves after; sweet?
If I say I've found, known sometimes sweeter,
I'm no less yours. In need, Your Servant.

---

21. Latin: *Lord, to make atonement, preserve me.*

HYMN

Less the shadow
than you a stag, sudden, through it.
Less the stag breaking cover than

the antlers, with which
crowned.
Less the antlers as trees leafless,

to either side of the stag's head, than—
between them—the vision that must
mean, surely, rescue.

Less the rescue.
More, always, the ache
toward it.

When I think of death, the gleam of
the world darkening, dark, gathering me
now in, it is lately

as one more of many other nights
figured with the inevitably
black car, again the stranger's

strange room entered not for prayer
but for striking
prayer's attitude, the body

kneeling, bending, until it finds
the muscled patterns that
predictably, given strain and

release, flesh assumes.
When I think of desire,
it is in the same way that I do

God: as parable, any steep
and blue water, things that are always
there, they only wait

to be sounded.
And I a stone that, a little bit, perhaps
should ask pardon.

My fears—when I have fears—
are of how long I shall be, falling,
and in my at last resting how

indistinguishable, inasmuch as they
are countless, sire,
all the unglittering other dropped stones.

Carl Phillips   375

8

The Twenty-First-Century
Devotional Lyric

THE DEVOTIONAL LYRIC IS proving to be as relevant to early twenty-first-century poets as it was to their forebears. This is due in no small part to the fact that the devotional object, restored to its pre-Modern stability by the post-Modernists, remains firmly and dependably where the post-Modernists placed it: in a familiar, quasi-human sphere far enough removed from Augustine's region of unlikeness to be approachable, yet near enough the unknowable to make the devotional gesture urgent as an action of discovery. And if twenty-first-century poets have accepted thus far the devotional object largely as it was given to them by their immediate predecessors, so too have they inherited from those poets many of the techniques and strategies they used to approach that object. Fragmentation, irreverence, and formal and tonal subversion are as present in early twenty-first-century lyrics—devotional or otherwise—as they are in poems written almost half a century earlier.

It is irony, though, perhaps more than any other tool inherited from the post-Modernists, that has come to characterize the early twenty-first-century lyric. Indeed, in much of the poetry written since 2000, irony has become *the* poetic technique, the primary mode of engagement, as opposed to *a* poetic technique, one of many to be deployed or not as the individual poem requires. The reliance on this single technique, as a number of contemporary critics have noted, is in some cases resulting in a narrowing of the tonal range and a constricting of poetic possibility.

However, such a narrowing is largely absent from the devotional lyrics of the period. The devotional lyric in the early twenty-first century seems to be providing contemporary poets with a mode by which they can investigate sincerity without being accused of sentimentality; it is allowing them to find ways to be skeptical without being detached, authentic without being mawkish or maudlin. The speakers of twenty-first-century devotional lyrics are present and accountable in the lyric moment, serious about the ethical questions they engage. And while their devotional postures reflect the same humor, the same parody and inversion that characterize secular poems of the age, these poems demonstrate a commitment to a sustained and genuine interaction with the mysterious, the unknowable.

FURTHER READING

Greenberg, Arielle. "Revelatory and Complex: 'Plain, Free-Flowing' Spirituality." *American Poetry Review*, 41, no. 3 (May–June 2012): 39–42.

Kaminsky, Ilya, and Katherine Towler, eds. *A God in the House: Poets Talk About Faith*. North Adams, Mass.: Tupelo, 2012.

Levin, Dana. "The Heroics of Style, Part Three: Make It New! Originality and the Younger Poet." *American Poetry Review* 35, no. 2 (March–April 2006): 45–47.

Rubik, Margarete and Eva Müller-Zettelmann, eds. *Theory into Poetry: New Approaches to the Lyric*. Amsterdam: Rodopi, 2005.

Peter Sirr
(1960–)

PETER SIRR WAS BORN IN Waterford, Ireland, and lives in Dublin, where he works as a freelance writer and translator. His awards include the 1998 O'Shaughnessy Award for Poetry and the 2011 Michael Hartnett Award for his collection *The Thing Is* (2009), which was also shortlisted for the *Irish Times* Award. His other collections include *Marginal Zones* (1984), *Ways of Falling* (1991), *Selected Poems,* and *Nonetheless* (both 2004). His novel for children was published in 2013. He is a member of Ireland's Academy of Artists, Aosdána. He is married to the poet and children's writer Enda Wyley, and they have a daughter, Freya.

A Few Helpful Hints

Tell them what you like. Tell them
the world is flat and when you get to the edge you fall
into the usual darkness, hell if you like
but anywhere will do, any storied space
mythical returners have whined of, salty
and smelling of loss. Tell them the rain falls
and steals slyly up and falls, and falls—
tell them everything twice for emphasis
and then again the next day for revision.

Set them tests on the same thing time and time again.
Tell them most of life is repetitive
and this will stand them in good stead.
Tell them about gravity and love,
drop the whole world on their heads
if you have to, the broad curriculum
of hatred and desire and the need for money
and love, tell them some things are permissible
and some less so, though ideally we'd prefer it
if you left that to us. Above all
don't be heavyhanded, keep a light tone,
encourage them to laugh, encourage them to believe
they are getting away with something when they do.
Encourage them to see you as a fragile
merely human being. Forget things, mix up names
and be occasionally unfair in the allotment of marks.
Tell them about yourself if it helps. Allow your emotions
to enter the syllabus, when reading a poem, or telling them
things that have happened. Break down if you have to,
rail against the world and its mindless cruelties.
Tell them we could all be blown out of it
or the sun might go out or too much of it get through.
Tell them not to use aerosols, organize a project
on it. Projects are good. We like to stress
the need to work together. Harmony
is the oil in the machinery, or something
like that. Tell them about the men who came to save us
with beautiful voices and a poetry
we would like to have found time for, we may yet
retire to. Tell them about those
who have still to come, shuffling in awkwardness and anger
from the cardboard slums that tremble even now
on the outskirts, whose poems
may already be struggling in our blood
or hurtling through the dark cathedral spaces
achieved and pure, unsettling the stars.

Leslie Harrison
(1962–)

LESLIE HARRISON WAS BORN in a small town in the former West Germany, and holds graduate degrees from the Johns Hopkins University and the University of California, Irvine. Her first book, *Displacement* (2009), won the Bakeless Prize in Poetry. She was the Roth Resident in Poetry at Bucknell University in 2010, and received a 2011 literature fellowship from the National Endowment for the Arts. She lives in Baltimore, where she teaches at Towson University.

[dear god I ask]

nothing for myself as much of what I love is changed

to salt and stone and ocean only the meadows the deer

the flicker of trees in timelapse light flicker of trains

these endless metal departures dear lord I ask only this

for myself that the stars come evenings out of the black

dark sky the snow fall enough to muffle the ping of pipes

freezing in the walls that the barn dear lord I ask that

there always be a barn built of the carved up bones

the sky one leant so heavily upon the wood weathered

into silver into slivers and whorls be indifferent to us

dear lord be gentle with your angels for they know only

how to fail sing lullabies to the broken the sleep

deprived the flailing failing the falling and the galloping

along sing lullabies to the next storm climbing each horizon

neither bind by bridle nor tame our beloved Leviathan

nor any one of your creatures let us run if that be

our desire let us run into grass and gale and sharp wire

fences into long crumbling afternoons let us run even

back into what we thought was home into the barn

even when even though sometimes as now the barn

be made only entirely of fire

Olena Kalytiak Davis
(1963–)

OLENA KALYTIAK DAVIS WAS born in Detroit to Ukrainian Catholic immigrants who steeped her upbringing in that culture and religion. After attending the University of Michigan Law School, Davis relocated, first to California and then abroad, returning to pursue her literary vocation. She has lived in Alaska for most of the past twenty years. She is the recipient of a Rona Jaffe Award and a Guggenheim Foundation Fellowship, among other honors. Davis's collections include *And Her Soul Out of Nothing* (1997), *shattered sonnets love cards and other off and back handed importunities* (2003), and *The Poem She Didn't Write and Other Poems* (2014). She remains a meditating agnostic.

six apologies, lord

I Have Loved My Horrible Self, Lord.
I Rose, Lord, And I Rose, Lord, And I,
Dropt. Your Requirements, Lord. 'Spite Your Requirements, Lord,
I Have Loved The Low Voltage Of The Moon, Lord,
Until There Was No Moon Intensity Left, Lord, No Moon Intensity Left
For You, Lord. I Have Loved The Frivolous, The Fleeting, The Frightful
Clouds. Lord, I Have Loved Clouds! Do Not Forgive Me, Do Not
Forgive Me LordandLover, HarborandMaster, GuardianandBread, Do Not.
Hold Me, Lord, O, Hold Me

Accountable, Lord. I Am
Accountable. Lord.

Lord It Over Me,
Lord It Over Me, Lord. Feed Me

Hope, Lord. Feed Me
Hope, Lord, Or Break My Teeth.

Break My Teeth, Sir,

In This My Mouth.

D. A. Powell
(1963–)

AMERICAN POET D. A. POWELL was born in Georgia and now lives in California.
Much of Powell's childhood was spent in the Bible Belt of the United States, and the
King James Bible echoes throughout his work. His books include *Chronic* (2009, win-
ner of the Kingsley Tufts Poetry Award) and *Cocktails* (2004), both finalists for the
National Book Critics Circle Award in Poetry.

plague year: comet: arc

down came the irresistible, ghastly HE: beclouded cheval glass
the ugly visitation when the hearse pulls up to the curb
unmaking the night. bugs. the disarray of astonished bodies
hurling through the streets, between buildings broken
into myriad electrons, stitch of illuminated roofs the everlasting

HE: my bedfellow, my taint, the angel as expected
                              forsaking as expected, the apprehended angel
                                        the funerary
angel, the way HE fucks
                    like a bodybag, already empty,
already depositing
                    its contents atop the toxic landfill, giving up the corpus

giving up the skin and the assembly, giving up as expected
leaf and tree and blade, the verdure taken up

stone and monument stone, instead, the concrete
and the crude pigiron hammered into steel

lightless HE. unmerciful HE. sad lamb HE: under the streetlamp
proffering his expendable sex to expendable passers-by
forgive us this flesh, the way it
presses to be admitted
forgive this disheveled drapery of night: pull
back, pull back

End of Days

I have seen a hawk owl's shadow across the street.

That doesn't mean that I have seen a hawk owl.

He could join with me in the perfect guise of a bird.

Wild forms are with us always, though fleeting.

There are no particular things to make me love anyone,
least of all, not you.

On the wings of that great speckled bird.

A. E. Stallings
(1968–)

A. E. STALLINGS GREW UP IN Decatur, Georgia. She attended the University of
Georgia and Oxford University, and has lived since 1999 in Athens, Greece. She has
published three collections of poetry, *Archaic Smile* (1999), *Hapax* (2006), and *Olives*
(2012). She has also published a verse translation of Lucretius for Penguin Classics,
The Nature of Things (2007). She is the recipient of a translation grant from the Na-
tional Endowment for the Arts, and of fellowships from the Guggenheim, USA Artists,
and MacArthur foundations. Stallings describes herself as the result of a mixed mar-
riage (Southern Baptist and Episcopalian), was brought up Episcopalian, baptized her
children Greek Orthodox, and harbors Epicurean sympathies.

Amateur Iconography: Resurrection
AFTER C. P. CAVAFY

The Harrowing of Hell[1]

Jesus is back—he's harvesting the dead.
He's pulling them up out of the dirt like leeks—
By the scruff of the neck, by the wispy hair on the head,
Like bulbs in darkness sallowly starting to grow

From deep down in the earth where the lost things go—
Keys and locks, small change, old hinges, nails.
(That's why the living beseech the dead, who know
Where missing objects lie.) Jesus has a grip

On Adam by the left wrist—he will not slip—
And Eve, by her right. They're groggy and don't understand,
They died so long ago. With trembling lip,
Adam surveys the crowds of new people. And Eve

Looks up the emptiness of her limp left sleeve
For the hand that was unforgiven and is no more,
Ages since withered to dust, and starts to grieve
The sinister loss, recalling the heft in that hand

Of the flesh of the fruit, and the lightness at the core.

G. C. Waldrep
(1968–)

G. C. WALDREP WAS BORN IN South Boston, Virginia, and earned degrees in American history from Harvard and Duke universities before pursuing poetry. His collections include *Goldbeater's Skin* (2003), winner of the Colorado Prize; *Archicembalo* (2009), winner of the Dorset Prize; and *Your Father on the Train of Ghosts* (2011), a collaboration with John Gallaher. He co-edited *Homage to Paul Celan* (2011) with Ilya

---

1. Refers to the belief that following his crucifixion but before his ascension, Christ descended into the realm of the dead to preach. See 1 Peter 3.18–20.

Kaminsky and *The Arcadia Project: North American Postmodern Pastoral* (2012) with Joshua Corey. Since 2007 he has taught at Bucknell University, where he also directs the Bucknell Seminar for Younger Poets, edits the journal *West Branch*, and serves as editor-at-large for *The Kenyon Review*. He is a member of the Lancaster district of the Old Order River Brethren, a conservative Anabaptist communion.

Against the Madness of Crowds
IN MEMORIAM PIERRE MARTORY

Reckon the haste of one wall burning.
There is no thickness there is no terror there is
a transparency like oxygen like fire over this bright space.
And will the ashes that rise meet the ashes that fall.
On a light breeze. In this ruined garden.
Is this not physics is this not too much to ask.
This simple question.
For there is a language of flowers as Smart wrote.
There is a language of clouds, and of their wispy orthography
but it is not comforting.
A prayer for a new image, yes:
have we not studied, have we not pasted our rations
in their strict enrollments their proper homologies.
And here, the arrangement of humors.
What I feel in my ribs now is only an echo.
I stand at one distance, I open my wallet
press flesh against cured hide
and I am ready. The blue of the gentian is nothing to me.
The calla, the violet of the iris are nothing
compared to the sky you bring
with your coming when you come with your singing and your sighing
with your counting backward from one hundred
when you come. Is this not too much to ask,
the venation and the marrow
the clandestine order and meaning of all signs.
So while the ashes that rise meet the ashes that fall
I will be the world, for a little while. As such waiting.
The rose of each lung blooms inside.

Kevin Prufer
(1969–)

KEVIN PRUFER WAS BORN IN Cleveland, Ohio, and educated at Wesleyan University, Hollins University, and Washington University. He is the author of five books of poetry, including *Fallen from a Chariot* (2005), *National Anthem* (2008), and *In a Beautiful Country* (2011). His book *Churches* will appear in 2014. After teaching and editing for many years in west-central Missouri, he is now professor of English in the Creative Writing Program at the University of Houston.

Prayer

What shall I do if I never can reach him?
The bed is a harlot, all laughter and lace.
My teeth like a riot of bridges and gold
so how can he hear me? And what should I say?

The asters and poppies just die in the window,
the rose on its stem is bald where it aches.
The blood fruit rolled from the tale then burst,
so how can I kneel, and whom should I face?

The Lord must be sleeping. The bones in my tongue
are rib-like and caught, my mouth is amazed—
but how should I sing and what shall I call him?
He hasn't a name. I don't know his grace.

Apocalyptic Prayer

Please, with your hands, for the warmth
and Please, on the backs of my ears
                              where they froze.
But the city was a ruin and a mystery,
the cafés closed long ago, their yellow eyes
gone black and still,
                    the bricks caved in.

And a fire, will you start it? Please, with a match
or a lighter. With a flint, which you might
strike on a brick.

                     But the cars were dead on their empty tires,
their needles on zero and still. The bridge folded
and the grass grown wild—
                     Won't you build the city up
with clay or with sticks? Put a fire in the lampposts
so we can see?
                     Only silence from the church
where the steeple was. And silence from the vaults
where the old coins glowed.

C. Dale Young
(1969–)

C. DALE YOUNG GREW UP IN south Florida. Raised in the Roman Catholic faith, he attended Catholic schools for most of his education. The author of three books of poetry—*Torn* (2011), *The Second Person* (2007), and *The Day Underneath the Day* (2001)—he practices medicine full-time, edits poetry for the *New England Review,* and teaches in the Warren Wilson M.F.A. Program for Writers. A recipient of fellowships from the National Endowment for the Arts, the Guggenheim Foundation, and the Rockefeller Foundation, he lives in San Francisco with his spouse, the classical music composer Jacob Bertrand.

Paying Attention

I know everything about my God.
Can you tell me about your own?

Outside the window, rain. Well, the sound
of rain. Why would I start this way?
Because my God prefers a preamble—
Spool of lightning, Fist of night-blooming jasmine.

My God can slice me clean open from head
to the arches of my feet, does so easily
with a swipe of His index fingernail, a clean
slice to show you the back half of me

seen from the front. He sometimes puts me
back together again. But with my front half
gone, He licks the back wall of my throat,
His tongue like sweetened gasoline.

The sound of rain against my window
is louder than expected, is my God
reminding me to pay attention. And my God
despises inattention and punishes me often

for it. He strips me of my clothes and lashes
my back with his cat-o-nine-tails. I am
quick to cry, so quick to promise humility. I am
a liar. I am weak and a liar. And I am punished.

What more can I tell you? What can I say
to explain my God? He has little tolerance
for hatred. He expects undying love
and affection. He leaves the large red

imprints of his fist against my back,
sometimes flowering on my face. He showers
me with expectations. He lifts me up
to remind me of my foolish fear of heights.

Or Something Like That

In the yard today, the pine needles began snowing
down. The way they caught the light was curious.
And the maple's leaves, all red and ochre, were

already littering the walkway. I, well I sat
thinking the same dark thoughts I have had
since childhood. You know the ones. I need

not explain them to You, of all people.
But it is so easy to call things dark thoughts,
a kind of lazy shorthand. Too easy to forget

the maxim that everyone is good in Your eyes.
We both know this is not true, is a lie. I mean,
the high school counselor they put away for life . . .

How can he be good in Your eyes? Sometimes,
I am convinced no one is good in Your eyes.
Dark thoughts, yes. I am doubting again.

I doubt the pine needles, the maple leaves,
the robin carrying on its stupid song,
my own voice mumbling on a slate blue terrace.

Easy to doubt. Always easy. And the old Jesuit
who lectured me on this? Well, he doubted, too.
But I am not quite ready to be broken just yet.

I have a few things left in me, a few surprises.
No magic is as good as Your magic, but I have
hidden cards up my sleeve, twisted the handkerchief,

slipped the coin behind my watch. I still have
a few tricks left to play. And the light shifting
on the terrace, the pine needles coming down,

I know what they mean. I get what You are trying
to get at. I am here, God, I am here. I am waiting
for You to blind me with a sunstorm of stars.

Morri Creech

(1970–)

MORRI CREECH WAS BORN IN Moncks Corner, South Carolina. He is the author of three collections of poetry, *Paper Cathedrals* (2001), *Field Knowledge* (2006), and *The Sleep of Reason* (2013). A recipient of National Endowment for the Arts and Ruth Lilly Fellowships, as well as grants from the North Carolina and Louisiana Arts councils, he is the Writer in Residence at Queens University of Charlotte, in North Carolina, where he lives with his wife and two children.

Triptych: Christ's Sermon to God from the Wilderness[2]

1

To what, Father, shall I compare
the kingdom of man?
Shall I say it is like the son
who forsakes his father
for a landscape emptied
and shimmering as heaven,
where the light forgives
nothing, and the wind
strips the threadbare stalks
of thistle? No metaphor
suffices, when to be human
is merely to live
in the blaze of your silence.
Yet for weeks now
I've spoken to you
of lilies and bridegrooms,
appealed to your logic
in sermons and parables—
and, at last, resorted
to the eloquence of hunger.

2

You who made me
neither lamb nor shepherd
but a keeper of bees
who must approach the hive
slowly, and must feel
each unregenerate sting
blister his hand
to extract the comb you cherish—

tell me, Lord,
has the flesh not made
the honey you feed upon?

---

2. See Luke 4.1–13.

And shall I call forth
the smoke of the spirit
to calm and confuse them,
now I have felt
the swarm that rages
in the chambers of the heart?

3

All morning I have held
this scorpion, and considered
how the spine curves
toward the raised barb of its malice,
and have watched it
stand poised there
in the shadow of my will.

Father, how to explain
why I wept
for its fierce perfection?
When it struck my palm
why did I not let go
and curse its name,
grind it
in the dust beneath my feet?

Yet this is what
I would have you understand,
having starved myself
so long, neither god nor man,
that I might pass
through the narrow gates
of both kingdoms: for the son
so loveth the Father
that he shall turn away
from His example
to teach Him the discipline
of mercy, the venom
that scalds the essential blood.

Maurice Manning

(1970–)

MAURICE MANNING WAS BORN in Kentucky. His first book, *Lawrence Booth's Book of Visions* (2001), was selected by W. S. Merwin for the Yale Series of Younger Poets. His fourth book, *The Common Man* (2010), was a finalist for the Pulitzer Prize. His most recent collection is *The Gone and the Going Away* (2013). Manning teaches in the M.F.A. Program for Writers at Warren Wilson College and at Transylvania University in Lexington. Manning received a Guggenheim Fellowship in 2011. He lives on a small farm in Washington County, Kentucky.

from *Bucolics*

XI

I told that old dog he
could hush Boss I said
there now you're just having
a shaky little dream dream
a dream dream Boss how
about that talking to a dog
that way there there it's just
a little dream dream you
don't have to whimper that's
what I can't stand Boss
to see an old dog whimper
what's in an old dog's dream
dream anyway some rabbits Boss
or barking up a tree say do
you ever have a dream dream
Boss are you running after or
away from me tell me sometime
if your big feet ever twitch

XXII

yes I've tried to hide my face
behind a tree I have been glad
to see the river run with mud
so fast it will not hold my look
but believe me Boss I can not hide
I can not muddy you I can
not chop you from my stony field
you're like a weed you've got yourself
a common name but a name I can't
forget a name like honey Boss
you pour it in my ear you pour
it in my mouth you make me say
it Boss your name it's like a bird
that's come to roost upon my lips
no matter what it will not stir
it sings a single note sometimes
it's just a whisper others it's
a shout it doesn't matter how
I feel about it what I want
from you is nothing Boss compared
to what you want from me you want
it all to always go your way
though I could give you daisies you
would just as soon have weeds if it
were in your favor Boss I guess
you'd prize a briar for its thorns

XXVIII

the two of us we're cut
from the same cloth Boss
though I'm just a thread
compared to you O you
can do it all you raise
the wool up on the sheep
you put the cotton in
the patch I'm just a string
on the spindle Boss that's all

I'll ever be when I
see water running from
a rock I think you must
be down there in the ground
you're a workhorse Boss like me
you work the pump I work
the bucket fair enough
we're tough as leather Boss
tough as nails we go
together don't we the way
nip goes with tuck we grin
we bear it Boss O does
that ever cross your mind

X X X V

is that you Boss is that
you hooting in the hollow
are you a night bird Boss
is that your face behind
the moon is that your hand
cupped to the cricket's ear
do you tell the cricket how
to sing to you say that's it
now softer softer now
you little bug do you
pour moonlight on the river
do you say river let
this silver ride on you
you're up to something Boss
you're like a treetop there
against the sky a wave
you're like a neighbor Boss
is your favorite game a game
of peep-eye Boss are you
as sweet as you can be
you cutie-pie I can't
keep track of you Boss you're just
too many things at once

you're like a lullaby
that never ends a breath
that makes the moment last
again again again

XLIII

if I say I've sprung the spring in my step
does it matter Boss does it matter much
to you when I can't even spit
without it feeling bad when I
can't look the old horse in the face
without a tear on mine because
I know where all days go when they
are done they don't come back they won't
wake up the sun won't show its face
again which means there isn't much
to look at Boss not much to look
at in the dark not even you
you keep a lot of secrets Boss
but now I know a secret too
although the tallest tree may reach
your chin I know one day you'll bend
it over Boss without a speck
of pity not a moment's pause
you'll drag it to the darkest ground
all days go one direction down

LVIII

guess what Boss I'm not even
tired not even blinking hardly
even after all the sunup-to-sundown
sweat on my brow save the end
of daylight I could keep on working
Boss there's nothing now to do
but let the dewdrops drop the way
they do when the day is done what a life
Boss one day to me must be nothing

but a speck to you older than dirt
I guess is it okay if I pretend
I see your fingers bent around the moon
as if your hand is right behind it
something like that Boss that's what
I do when I can't sleep a wink I think
about you Boss I wonder all those yellow
fireflies even though they never make
a peep do they still call you Boss

Paisley Rekdal
(1970–)

PAISLEY REKDAL IS THE AUTHOR of a book of essays, *The Night My Mother Met Bruce Lee* (2002); the hybrid photo-text memoir *Intimate* (2012); and four books of poetry, including *The Invention of the Kaleidoscope* (2007) and *Animal Eye* (2012). Her honors include the Amy Lowell Poetry Travelling Scholarship, a National Endowment for the Arts Fellowship, a Pushcart Prize, a Fulbright Fellowship, and inclusion in the *Best American Poetry* series.

Dear Lacuna, Dear Lard:

I'm here, one fat cherry
     blossom blooming like a clod,

one sad groat glazing, a needle puling thread,
     so what, so sue me. These days what else to do but leer

at any boy with just the right hairline. *Hey!* I say.
     That's one tasty piece of nature. Tart Darkling,

if I could I'd gin, I'd bargain, I'd take a little troll
     this moolit night, let you radish me awhile,

let you gag and confound me. How much I've struggled
     with despicing you, always; your false poppets, relentless

distances. Yet plea-bargaining and lack of conversation
  continue to make me

your faithful indefile. I'm lonely. I've turned
  all rage to rag, all pratfalls fast to fatfalls for you,

My Farmer in the Dwell. So struggle, strife,
  so strew me, to bell with these clucking mediocrities,

these anxieties over such beings thirty, still smitten
  with this heaven never meant for, never heard from.

You've said we're each pockmarked like a golf course
  with what can't be said of us, bred in us,

isn't our tasty piece of nature. But I tell you
  I've stars, I've true blue depths, have learned to use

the loo, the crew, the whole slough of pill-popping
  devices without you, your intelligent and pitiless graze.

Everyone knows *love* is just a euphemism
  for *you've failed me* anyway. So screw me.

Bartering Yam, regardless of want I'm nothing
  without scope, hope, nothing

without your possibility. So let's laugh
  like the thieves we are together, the sieves:

you, my janus gate, my Sigmund Fraud,
  my crawling, crack-crazed street sprawled out,

revisible, spell-bound.
  Hello, joy. I'm thirsty. I'm Pasty Rectum.

In your absence I've learned to fill myself
  with starts. Here's my paters.[3] Here's my blue.

I just wanted to write again and say
  how much I've failed you.

---

3. That is, *pater nosters,* the Latin name for the Lord's Prayer, from its first two words: "Our Father" (see Matthew 6.9–13).

Mary Szybist
(1970–)

MARY SZYBIST WAS BORN AND grew up in Williamsport, Pennsylvania, where she attended mass at the Church of the Annunciation, which had Tiffany stained glass in her favorite window. She is the author of *Granted* (2003), which was a finalist for the National Book Critics Circle Award, and *Incarnadine* (2013). Since 2004 she has taught at Lewis & Clark College in Portland, Oregon.

Hail

Mary who mattered to me, gone or asleep
among fruits, spilled

in ash, in dust, I did not

leave you. Even now I can't keep from
composing you, limbs & blue cloak

& soft hands. I sleep to the sound

of your name, I say there is no Mary
except the word Mary, no trace

on the dust of my pillowslip. I only

dream of your ankles brushed by dark violets,
of honeybees above you

murmuring into a crown. Antique queen,

the night dreams on: here are the pears
I have washed for you, here the heavy-winged doves,

asleep by the hyacinths. Here I am,

having bathed carefully in the syllables
of your name, in the air and the sea of them, the sharp scent

of their sea foam. What is the matter with me?

Mary, what word, what dust
can I look behind? I carried you a long way

into my mirror, believing you would carry me

back out. Mary, I am still
for you, I am still a numbness for you.

Kazim Ali

(1971–)

KAZIM ALI WAS BORN IN THE United Kingdom to Muslim parents of South Asian and Middle Eastern descent. His books of poetry include *The Far Mosque* (2005), *The Fortieth Day* (2008), *Bright Felon: Autobiography and Cities* (2012), and *Sky Ward* (2013). He has also published novels, translations, and two collections of essays, *Orange Alert: Essays on Poetry, Art and the Architecture of Silence* (2010) and *Fasting for Ramadan: Notes from a Spiritual Practice* (2011). Founding editor of Nightboat Books, he teaches at Oberlin College and in the Stonecoast M.F.A. program, and is a certified Jivamukti yoga instructor.

Lostness

dear God of blankness I pray to dear unerasable

how could I live without You if I were ever given answers

the summer thickens with lostness

lovers who will not touch each other but look out into space

thinking I do not belong in the world

news always travels inland but how can this storm

be undone or the treacherous rain unravel or the train

arriving one street over and all night long

on an island at the end of islands a foresworn vow

a river blasted through and another river filled in

dear afternoon God dear evening God my lonely world

the circles of water and wanton violence

dear utterly unmistakable ether

dear Lostness your careless supplicant drops everything

and rakes over me on his way to an implacable place

Afternoon Prayer

God, a curt question or a curtain,
the call to prayer fading away.

May I request evening or more rain?
Doing laundry, getting new tires—

May I invest smartly, catch a later train?
Snow fills the margins, sunset across the river.

As we rush north, everything is pulled back,
God, a day's work, the echoing tracks—

Dear Lantern, Dear Cup

should You light the way
or should You hold me

dear earthquake in the ground
who is waiting

am I shining into infinite space
or will I be spilled

Josh Bell

(1971–)

JOSH BELL WAS BORN IN Terre Haute, Indiana, and is a graduate of the Iowa Writers' Workshop. He has taught at the University of Wisconsin and in the M.F.A. program at Columbia University. He is currently Briggs-Copeland Lecturer in English at Harvard University. His first book is *No Planets Strike* (2004).

Zombie Sunday (A Short Poetical History of Spring)

Gentle handed holy father, or whomever,
I mentioned daffodils, and the crowd went wild.
I had them, briefly, nibbling from my blistered hand.
Then I called attention to the dandelions,
popping forth like sunny, tethered corks
from the busy lawn, and the crowd went
home. Lucky for me they left. Mine
was a short list of flowers beginning
with "d," and too late, skulking through the park,
did I recall the daisy, the dahlia,
too late did I invent the dog-wort
and the dwarf poppy. Modern ways.
April. Motorcycles have begun thundering
down the wet avenues like armored bees
slick with the shattered, puddle blooms
of fragrant gasoline and oil, and I've noticed,
from a distance, that in early Spring
the trees don't, all at once, jump to life
like you've read about, but gather to them
a smoky cloud of blue, like tall children
puffing on cigarettes, until, late April, they cough up
a few green leaves. That was my mistake.
Chaucer couldn't name his flowers, either,
or he could *name* them, but couldn't tell
them apart, or I missed it if he did. It was
Spring. I was involved, moaning in the hedge

and watching college kids whack golf balls
into the drive-in movie screen, which seems,
at night, across the field, like the forehead
of a giant, worried monk, bent over and tending
to his proliferating, moonlit vegetables.
Speaking of monks, I need to read
more Chaucer. Then T. S. Eliot, about
a hundred years later, wasn't he clever?
Bravo, Tom. I can barely look a lilac
directly in the stamen, a word that never seems right
no matter how I spell it, a word little more
than a word, if that, and I always guessed Eliot
a little mortuary in the sack. That, or
(your theory) he was frightened
of the shadow of his penis, rolling unbidden,
like a scuttled go-cart, across the grooved sheets.
And the hyacinths, oh the hyacinths, a flower
I'd like to take by the pistil and fling, if only I could tell one
from a hydrangea, my second flower
beginning with "h." But about old master Eliot
we both were wrong. How like me he is.
I imagine him now, sucking flowers
into the earth like a cartoon gopher,
he was a petal hoarder. I much rather
would have slept with Williams, though he did
nothing for Spring, at least in the anthologies,
our able doctor, tapping out his poems
while a lithe America undressed in the boxy
examination room across the hall.
Read Williams in a paper gown, you tell me,
and all your dreams will come to pass.
But I forgot Emily Dickinson. We all
wanted to sleep with her. She was right
about Spring, if she wrote about it, and she
had those tendencies. My new neighbor,
homeless Jack, greets Spring with a holler.
Emily would have hated him. Me, too,
though she had a thing for abomination.
But what's Emily Dickinson got to do
with the price of methedrine, Jack might

ask. Bravo, Jack. And Rilke, Jack, Rilke was an autumn.
The tree-line overtaking the movie screen
warbles. The aforementioned flowers,
all varieties, rise like European soccer fans,
and charge the field. Spring, you sent the rain
down this rented stretch of gutter-pipe
on the wretched corner of Thomas and Lafayette.
The college kids whack arc after arc
into the monk's forehead, into the tree-line,
into the onanistic wave of oncoming
flowers. I wish I could welcome these days
when the blood begins its rolling boil,
and like a chef, in my immaculate white hat,
I could use the blood to cook a meal
That would finally please you. Daylily,
digitalis, delphinium, dianthus.

Zombie Sunday

Gentle handed holy father, or whomever,
we have ways of making you talk,
and I am tired of your illustrious distractions,
the sunlight, the hortatory sex, the Marcel Proust
and all those pulsing vegetables
you've hidden in the garden, and when I hear a certain piece of music,
the kind invented by your better children
to replace the load-bearing voices
we misplaced so long ago—that professional and winged chorus
once strong, now trembling and withdrawn
to a drizzling echo in barrels of sludge
buried behind the supermarket,
the angelic orders individually wrapped
in garbage bags and vibrating out of whack
in watery ditches on the sides of highways—
your sad and higher class of road-kill—
and when I hear that certain piece of music
built to replace them, and, for an instant,
can hear fingers brushing across strings,
slender fingers, or hear that sharp,

vulnerable intake of breath before singing,
the breath which gathers up the shapeless air
and drags it down the throat and back,
different now, beautiful, a clean sound
like a clear piece of tile which perfectly fits
the space the lungs pulled it from,
then fades back into nothing, and the same air
can be breathed over and over
and sung again, different voices or the same,
your dirty wedding song or hateful lullaby,
and when I hear this certain piece of music,
what is the stroke of faltering light
that flashes across the hearer's closing eye?
There's a word for it, just as there's a word
for this tree I crouch behind, waiting
for someone to pass, the white bark like cigarette-paper
and these pallid roots, whose each subtle declension I am studying.
I'm afraid it is you, hiding or seeking,
pulsing in the down-beats, riding with us
through the rests, glowing white
like phosphorescent algae on the singer's tongue,
you gathering up a responsible speed in the human lung
and coming out a scream which combs the moon,
like a knot of hair, bleeding from the trees.
Lastly, I thank you for this morning's latest headache,
which is a good one, as you know,
a piece of work you must be proud of,
this ugly siren toward which all cares
are drawn and annihilated, as once a sudden violin
I heard coming from a basement radio
a million years ago, stood up through the coda
then engulfed it, like a golem waking in a forest
to breakfast on the throbbing trees.
Send me more cudgelings, more suppurations,
the very awful kind that tamed your seething martyrs
into glory, the masterful flourishes
and gristled fret-works which caused the chosen few
to take it, and when they took it, like it.
But this is your kind of speech, now, isn't it,
you with the spirits in moraine about your boat-like feet?

I'm tired of the several wonders, the bland musics,
the universal weeping, the human songs
made of lost words that twitch and ache like phantom limbs.
You should have left me to my own devices,
which are legendary, spider-like, and fashioned
from rusted fence-wire, then thrown mine body unto kites.
How do you it? How should we resist?
Let me never plead to imp my tongue
to the likes of yours, which speaks planets into orbit,
for have I not been afflicted with the Earth, barely spinning as it is?
And won't your words come limping back
from the former void to help us fall apart,
in the arranged directions, piece by piece,
like any good orchestra, some words now,
please, even with their several meanings spattered
by the gone machinery of others I have lost?

Zombie Sunday

Gentle handed holy father, or whomever,
            the stars swing in like buccaneers
                        through the window, and they are
beautiful, and they are yours, of course,
            ditto cherry tree, and wildebeest—
                        how many times must you remind me?—
and I am searching, now, for the French phrase
            for *albino field of wheat. O mon pere* etc
                        doux ouvrier sacre,[4] your white teeth
are learned. They read much of the night,
            they go South in Winter, they ripple loosely
                        along the pale gum-line like those spirits
on the haunted shore, which have elsewhere
            been compared to leaves, but are really
                        more akin to grease, also rippling
loosely. Oh asphodel! that something
            flower. Oh but we should be able
                        to walk said shore and name the genus

---

4. French: *O my father . . . gentle holy laborer.*

and the species. O GHHF, your coffee beans
        meant nothing. They kept me on the phone
            all night. I am a burnt arrow now, loosed
from the Anglo Saxon bow you body.
        You dream like a battleship turns.
            Your two hands blooming folded,
from a black vase, was an image
        I thought up, once, to help get me to sleep.
            Oh but the sleep I lost, considering your sleep.
And I am mostly sure that loss is French
        (*le* terror-dome) and will follow me
            as far as Pittsburg, human sacrifice or no, but I know
for sure that loss transforms the delta, and is also how
        you change your mind. Even now
            the Mississippi bends to your fuzzy will
and carves toward Jerusalem. I am the paraclete of loss
        in the House of Catalepsis. I am bald
            as the wind. Or was it lorikeet, like Matthew said?
Matthew, patron saint of the poult-footed and the rain.
        O GHHF, you should read him, you might
            learn a thing or two about yourself.
Thirty shekels is lot of jack, anyhow.
        And I have failed your comprehensive tests before, oh lord.
            I am searching, now, for the French phrase
for *lorikeet of loss*, scaly breasted and/
        or blue-fronted rainbow, *Trichoglossus chlorolepidotus*
            and *Charmosyna toxopei*, respectively.
I pilot the cuttlefish and tree the seeds.
        I will burn the very Latin from the world.
            I weep for every cheating drink
I have forgotten, that hooligan wine
        in Cerbere, for example, who loved the carpet
            so well, so much more than it loved me,
and I am circling over this your every sentence
        as you drive it, looking for the loophole,
            but you will evade me in the driveway,
you will leave me for the rumored
        carpet, you will ditch me cold forever
            on the airless, sunspot runway where our bodies
made more sense. They called me

the hyacinth girl. The ocean was my stepsister,
pregnant with a style of fish you dreamed
last autumn, but in any language I am Isadora,
zombie queen of the Appalachians.
I knelt beside you yesterday.
I bet you prayed for rain.

Katharine Jager
(1971–)

KATHARINE JAGER WAS BORN in Evanston, Illinois, to a Quaker family. Raised within the Religious Society of Friends, she is a member of Northside Monthly Meeting, Illinois Yearly Meeting. She was educated at Grinnell College, and received an M.F.A. in poetry from New York University and a Ph.D. in English literature and medieval studies from the Graduate Center of the City University of New York. The Center for Book Arts and Red Dragon Fly Press have published her poems as broadsides. Jager regularly co-authors the Chaucer chapter for *The Year's Work in English Studies*. She teaches at the University of Houston–Downtown, and lives in Houston, Texas, with her twin sons.

Vita Brevis, Ars Longa[5]

Praise for the names of songbirds
for the edge of metal
Praise for the finger's whorl of grease
for the traffic rattle.

Praise for fire's raw alchemy
for the bolting lettuce
Praise for the border that invention serves
for the silt of rivers.

---

5. Latin: *Life is short, Art is long,* an aphorism attributed originally to ancient Greek physician Hippocrates (c. 460 B.C.E.–c. 370 B.C.E.).

Praise for the dog retrieving geese
for the lathe-wrought vessel
Praise for the red barn's poetry
for the work and wrestle.

Brett Foster
(1973–)

BRETT FOSTER WAS BORN IN Wichita, Kansas, and grew up in Jefferson City, Missouri. After studying journalism and English at the University of Missouri, he completed graduate degrees in creative writing and English literature at Boston University and Yale University, and held a Wallace Stegner Fellowship at Stanford University. Currently he teaches Renaissance literature and creative writing at Wheaton College, outside of Chicago, and attends All Souls' Anglican Church. His volumes of poetry include *The Garbage Eater* (2011) and *Fall Run Road* (2012).

Longing, Lenten

The walk back, more loss. When I open the door
it's over, so I set to piddling: tidy
end tables, check the mail, draw a bath.
The restless energy finally settles
as I pass the mirror. I peer into it.
My nose touches glass. Not much left,
already effaced, not even a cross
to speak of. A smudge. A few black soot stains
like pin points on the forehead. The rest
of the blessed ash has vanished to a grey
amorphousness, to symbolize . . . not much.
Except a wish for those hallowed moments
to be followed by sustaining confidence.
Except spirit, which means to shun its listless
weight for yearning, awkward if not more earnest
prayer and fasting in the clear face of dust.

Matthea Harvey
(1973–)

MATTHEA HARVEY WAS BORN in Germany. She is the author of four books of poetry—an illustrated erasure entitled *Of Lamb*, with images by Amy Jean Porter (2011), *Modern Life* (2007), *Sad Little Breathing Machine* (2004), and *Pity the Bathtub Its Forced Embrace of the Human Form* (2000). She is also the author of two books for children. She teaches poetry at Sarah Lawrence College.

from Ceiling Unlimited Series
(CEILING UNLIMITED)

God of seedpods, we are wallowing in it.
The hay has been gathered into gold rolls
in the field. Why the calves in concentric circles?
Why every other picket in the fence pulled out
to be sold at the store? Yes the papery poppies
are a bit like the dry side of a foot & hence
the unnecessary massacre, but that's no reason
to condemn the pelicans or throw out the wedding cakes
when they turn grey. You said when a semi spills
its cargo of oranges the driver has a choice:
flamingo on the salt flats or canary in the mines.
I want the former. I've waited years for the xerox flash
& still no inkling. Lately I've been thinking you
love the groves & don't know how to tell us.
I think you made the steps slick for a reason.

(SILVER PRINT)

The lock sticks again. I can make a self-
portrait out of anything. My silhouette
in the window is all elbows. Blossom to stem—
the rust roses on the pipes are blooming
backwards. The head pushes its way out,
learns how to waver later. Upside-down

in the spoon, I think I am getting closer—
second-hand skimming time, blue windows
everywhere, sharp smell of keys in the air.
Where are you inevitable slap? I have propped
the storm windows against the side of the house
for you: twenty paintings of the sky & five grills
heaped with charcoal so the air above them
shimmers, shatters. Tell me I'm not just forging
a copy, tell me you're more than the moon.

(HORROR VACUI)[6]

I would have liked an answer.
In the abandoned orangery, caterpillars
have chewed constellations from the leaves.
In the picture I look like part of the gate.
The crows with their nib-like beaks stay
outside like all lacunae, watching dust
sift slowly onto the river. Each time I step
forward the starlings scatter, despite the gentle
diagonals I choose, my indifferent mouth.
The experiment with sand & violin
failed, no music emerged, no voice was
conjured up. I've been dreaming in duplicate
but we have nothing in common. I know now
how to kneel, that's all. I wasn't just another
worn coin. I would have liked an answer.

---

6. Latin: *fear of empty space*. In science, the idea is communicated in the maxim "Nature abhors a vac-
uum." In visual art, the term is used to describe the filling of every available space with detail.

Melissa Range
(1973–)

MELISSA RANGE'S FIRST BOOK of poems, *Horse and Rider* (2010), won the 2010 Walt McDonald Prize in Poetry. Range is the recipient of the Rona Jaffe Foundation Writers' Award and the "Discovery"/*The Nation* prize. Originally from East Tennessee, she is pursuing her Ph.D. in English at the University of Missouri.

Kermes Red

Called crimson, called vermilion—"little worm"
in both the Persian and the Latin, red
eggs for the carmine dye, the insect's brood
crushed stillborn from her dried body, a-swarm
in a bath of oak ash lye and alum to form
the pigment the Germans called Saint John's Blood—
the saint who picked brittle locusts for food,
whose blood became the germ of a crimson storm.
Christ of the pierced thorax and worm-red cloak,
I read your death was once for all, but it's not true:
your kings and bishops command a book,
a beheading, blood for blood, the perfect hue;
thus I, the worm, the Baptist, and the scarlet oak
see all things on God's earth must die for you.

Gold Leaf
THE GOSPEL-BOOK OF OTTO III, CA. 10TH CENTURY

Shines forth from the vellum this film of sun,
the precious metal pounded thick as air,
then bound to the page with gesso or with glair—
more than one hundred leaves of gold from one
ducat. Otto, on the gold-leaf throne
which he commissioned—servant of Christ, ruler
of the world—surveys his gilded empire,
and the hand of God adjusts his crown.

O Christ, how I have loved you, with my heart shut
like an emperor's fist or a golden door,
a Bible with its pages locked up tight.
In my poverty I sought a poor God to adore,
a love I could buy with my widow's mite.
But this is not a Bible for the poor.

Lampblack

Black as a charred plum-stone, as a plume
from a bone-fire, as a flume of ravens
startled from a battle-tree—this lantern resin
the monk culls from soot to quill the doom
and glory of the Lord won't fade. The grime
of letters traced upon the riven
calf-skin gleams dark as fresh ash on a shriven
penitent, as heaven overawing time.
World's Glim, Grim Cinderer, is it sin
or history or a whimsied hex that burns
all life to tar? We are dust, carbon
spilled out from your Word, a lamp overturned
into the pit of pitch beneath your pen,
the inkhorn filled before the world was born.

Jericho Brown
(1975–)

JERICHO BROWN GREW UP IN Shreveport, Louisiana, and worked as speechwriter
to the mayor of New Orleans before receiving his Ph.D. from the University of Hous-
ton. Recipient of the Whiting Writers' Award and fellowships from the National En-
dowment for the Arts and the Radcliffe Institute at Harvard University, Brown teaches
at Emory University. His first book, *Please* (2008), won the American Book Award.

Prayer of the Backhanded

Not the palm, not the pear tree
Switch, not the broomstick,
Nor the closest extension
Cord, not his braided belt, but God,
Bless the back of my daddy's hand
Which, holding nothing tightly
Against me and not wrapped
In leather, eliminated the air
Between itself and my cheek
Unworthy of its unfisted print
And forgive my forgetting
The love of a hand
Hungry for reflex, a hand that took
No thought of its target
Like hail from a blind sky,
Involuntary, fast, but brutal
In its bruising. Father, I bear the bridge
Of what might have been
A broken nose. I lift to you
What was a busted lip. Bless
The boy who believes
His best beatings lack
Intention, the mark of the beast.
Bring back to life the son
Who glories in the sin
Of immediacy, calling it love.
God, save the man whose arm
Like an angel's invisible wing
May fly backward in fury
Whether or not his son stands near.
Help me hold in place my blazing jaw
As I think to say, *excuse me.*

Malachi Black
(1982–)

MALACHI BLACK WAS BORN in Cambridge, Massachusetts, and raised in Morris County, New Jersey. He is the author of *Storm Toward Morning,* forthcoming from Copper Canyon Press, and two chapbooks: *Quarantine* (2012) and *Echolocation* (2010). He was awarded a Ruth Lilly Fellowship in 2009. Since 1998, he has worked in various editorial capacities for *The New York Quarterly.*

from Quarantine
VESPERS

My Lord, you are the one:
your breath has blown away
      the visionary sun
and now suffocates the skyline
      with a dusk. If only once
I wish that you could shudder
with my pulse,   double over
and convulse   on the stitches
in the skin that I slash wishes in.
      But, Lord, you are the gulf
between the hoped-for
      and the happening:
You've won.   So what is left for me
when what is left for me has come?

Credits

Index